WALLED CULTURE

ALSO BY GLYN MOODY

Rebel Code

Digital Code of Life

WALLED CULTURE

How Big Content Uses Technology and the Law
to Lock Down Culture and Keep Creators Poor

Glyn Moody

BTF Press
Antwerp, Belgium

Walled Culture:
How Big Content Uses Technology and the Law to
Lock Down Culture and Keep Creators Poor

978-946459495-9 (paperback)
978-946459849-0 (eBook)

Published by BTF Press, 2022

publishing@btfpress.org

To my family.

Contents

Foreword

Tragically, the internet is turning from our dreams of a more democratic and open publishing system to one that is increasingly controlled by a shrinking number of international corporations. These corporations, publishers as much as tech companies, are using the connected nature of our technologies to assert new controls that were never possible in the analog era. What is happening? And what can we do to get back on track?

Many of us have spent our careers building toward a decentralized Great Library, where the published works of humankind would be available to those curious enough to want access. Further, this Library would be inclusive of all voices as everyone would have the opportunity to share their works and many would get enough readership to earn a living. New computer and network technologies would help everyone to sort through the vast troves of information. We have made progress, but we have had setbacks.

The internet now connects most people around the world, but countries are starting to block access. Server technology, once very distributed, is becoming more concentrated in a few companies' "cloud services."

But maybe the most alarming is the assertion of unprecedented control by multinational media conglomerates leveraging the connected nature of the internet. Some publishers and technology companies will not sell digital publications, but continue to keep control through long tentacles afforded by a combination of licenses and digital rights management technologies. This could mean that libraries and individuals may never own books and other works in our digital age – making every reading event a permissioned event by some remote and massive corporation.

A future where corporations can say exactly who can read what, when, and for how long, and changing what can be read at any time, can sound like a dystopian science fiction story but it is starting to happen now. This book comes out at an important time — a time where we can still change what happens.

I am so glad this book is being published, and published openly; it will help us build strong institutions to counter the dystopian impulses of some organizations and build an information ecosystem that has many winners, many voices, and much to celebrate.

Brewster Kahle
July 2022
San Francisco

CHAPTER 1

From Analogue to Digital

Big Content's plan to take total control online

The modern world is digital. We meet people online, we pay for things online, we deal with the government on-line. But the digital sphere is not just the latest version of the traditional, analogue world. It is fundamentally different. The transition from an analogue world to a digital one is a step change; in any civilisation's history, it only happens once. This book is about what happens when one aspect of the analogue past—copyright—resists and fights against the digital future, as represented by the Internet.

Copyright was born 300 years ago in a world that was an-alogue but unaware of it. It could take for granted the fact that making copies of material was slow if done by hand, and expensive and complicated if done with a machine such as a printing press. This made policing copyright straight-forward: just arrest the copier and confiscate the equipment.

Copyright for books seemed to work well and so was extend-ed. First, in terms of reach to other forms of material such as music, maps and drawings, and subsequently, as regards its duration. The initial term of modern copyright, drawn up in the British Statute of Anne[1] in 1710, granted state-backed protection to an author for fourteen years, renewable to twenty-eight years. When the young United States of America drew up its own copyright law in 1790, it adopted a similar twenty-eight-year term. In 1831, copyright term in the United States was extended to forty-two years and then in 1909 to fifty-six years. By the time of most recent US copyright act, copyright term had reached life of the author plus seventy years and hence there is typically more than one hundred years of government protection.

At the same time, similar copyright laws were passed around the world and a common framework for them was established in 1886 under the Berne Convention,[2] which was updated over the next century. A key feature of the Berne Convention is that it sets minimum standards for copyright laws for the signatory countries. One of which is that the term of copyright must be at least the duration of the creator's lifetime plus fifty years. Another aspect of the treaty, which is arguably even more far-reaching, is that copyright arises with the creation of a work. Hence it does not require any formalities, such as a registration process. The measures effectively baked copyright into all acts of creativity as soon as they are written down, recorded, or entered into a computer—something that always takes place and cannot be easily turned off.

Removing formalities was an important change for US law: for example, when the United States acceded to the Berne Convention in 1989[3] it was no longer necessary for a copyright notice to be displayed on a work. At the time, that might have seemed a minor change. People who created material professionally doubtless welcomed it. It meant they had no need to ensure proper copyright notices appeared or to go through an additional registration process in order to qualify for copyright protection—it was just automatic. For the public, it was an irrelevance that things such as their handwritten messages or photos of friends and family were now covered by copyright because there was no easy way to make a copy of them anyway.

The rise of digital computers in the latter part of the 20th century changed everything. Yet initially, the important role computers were to play in creativity was not evident. Since digital computers have numbers—specifically, binary numbers—at their heart, it was natural that they were used for complex computations. However, once computers were powerful enough, they were able to manipulate not only numbers but information represented as numbers. For text, that is simple enough, but for other material such as images, sound and video, progressively more data is needed to represent such information faithfully. Moore's law[4] meant that the cost of a computer able to handle increasingly large amounts of data continued to drop precipitously, until home computers in the form of the first microcomputers and then PCs became affordable by millions of people.

At this point, the hitherto aloof world of copyright lawyers realised that computers were about to have a huge impact on their field. A 300-year-old assumption that making near-perfect copies of a work was difficult started to crumble. Although imperfect copies produced by photocopiers had been around for a while, they did not offer anywhere near the original experience, and so represented only a moderate threat. By contrast, digital copies of a file are perfect and indistinguishable from the original, which means that even copies of copies are also perfect and identical to the original.

The first instance of this threat appeared in 1987 in the form of Digital Audio Tape (DAT).[5] Unlike analogue tape that stores sound in the form of smoothly varying magnetic fields, digital tape turns sound information into binary digits that are stored on the tape. Whereas the fuzzy magnetic fields could not be copied with 100% accuracy, and so copies of copies gradually degraded in quality, just as a photocopy of a photocopy does, digital data does not have this problem. Error correction ensures that the copy of a digital tape is identical to the original. This means DAT had the potential to allow any number of perfect copies to be made from an original or even from a copy.

Faced with this new development, the copyright industry responded by lobbying for new legislation designed to deal with it. As a result, in 1992 the Audio Home Recording Act (AHRA)[6] was passed in the United States. In return for the copyright industry abandoning its attempt to kill off DAT, digital device manufacturers agreed to pay a royalty on every system and digital tape sold. The AHRA also required DAT recorders to incorporate technology that allowed first-generation copying of sound recordings but prevented copies being made from copies. Although that stopped people making perfect copies, as the copyright industry demanded, it was also one reason why the DAT format never replaced the traditional analogue cassette tape as a mass medium. The public were not prepared to pay a premium price for a technology whose great advantage—its ability to make perfect copies—was sabotaged in this way. It was a good example of how the copyright industry wanted to ensure that digital technology had the same limitations as analogue systems when it came to making copies.

However, in what would turn out to be a significant move, computer manufacturers managed to obtain an exemption from the AHRA. Computers with their increasingly popular sound cards were not required to implement the serial copy system used with DAT recorders, and computer discs were not subject to the DAT tax. The means to make perfect copies of digital files, just like DAT, but without the restrictions of the DAT copy controls, were now readily available for the first time.

Shortly after the AHRA came into force, another technology started to enter the mainstream, one whose ability to make perfect copies could never be removed, since it lay at the heart of its operation. The Internet, which began its journey into the heart of modern life around the same time, in the early 1990s, functions by making repeated copies of digital information that it sends to users around the world at close to the speed of light. Hence the Internet is constantly full of perfect copies of digital files, which is the ultimate nightmare for the copyright industry. The latter were naturally aware of this threat, and took the usual route of pressing for new legislation to deal with it.

As the country with the most advanced digital technology companies and the biggest media corporations, the United States was the natural place for lobbyists to push for the first laws that would make the 'information superhighway',[7] as it was originally known, into a place where copyright was respected and enforced. In 1993, the White House rebranded the information superhighway as the more serious sounding 'National Information Infrastructure' (NII).[8] It also appointed an Information Infrastructure Task Force (IITF) to formulate government policy in this new area, chaired by commissioner of patents and trademarks Bruce Lehman.[9] In

Digital Copyright,[10] the definitive history of US copyright law during this period, Jessica Litman,[11] John F. Nickoll Professor of Law at the University of Michigan, explains the downsides of his appointment at a time when people were wrestling with the unprecedented transition to an online digital world. Not only had Lehman represented the software industry on copyright issues before he moved to the United States Patent and Trademark Office (USPTO),[12] many of his senior staff were former copyright lobbyists for the computer and music recording industries. This meant that the IITF came to the problem with a mindset shaped by traditional, analogue copyright.

Predictably, such a background produced a disastrous outcome when the Lehman Working Group, set up as part of the IITF, issued a draft Green Paper report on its preliminary analysis of how copyright should work on the NII. Litman describes how the Green Paper had three key aspects, all of which reflected the demands of the copyright industry and all of which were indifferent to the technological possibilities of the new online world.

The first was that it endorsed the legal argument that a copyright work was reproduced every time it was read into a computer's random-access memory (RAM),[13] its short-term store of data. This meant that traditional copyright law would apply to everything that a computer did with materials that were covered by copyright. Next, the Green Paper claimed that transmissions of copyright works across the NII were effectively performances of those works, and thus should be under the control of the copyright holder. Finally, the Working Group said the first-sale doctrine,[14] which allows people to do things like re-sell their legally purchased books or CDs to others, should not apply to transmission across the NII.

This aimed to prevent people from sharing copies of copyright materials even if they had acquired them legally.

The Green Paper did not simply call for transmissions to be excluded from the first-sale doctrine. No doubt pushed by the copyright industry, the Working Group went further and called for the introduction of copyright-protection technology to prevent people sharing copyright materials. Conscious that people would always be able to get around such systems, the Green Paper went so far as to call for a law to prohibit their circumvention and stop the sale of any device or service to help do so. In effect, the Working Group wanted to make unauthorised copying impossible by deploying every legal and technical means available.

The copyright industries were naturally delighted by the control the Green Paper would grant them over every aspect of computers and the online world. However, computer manufacturers, the first online services such as CompuServe[15] and AOL,[16] as well as libraries, were aghast. In addition, nobody really cared what the public thought. In her history of the legislative struggles, Litman suggests that the Lehman Working Group came up with such extreme proposals because it believed that nobody would ever make material available on what became the Internet unless publishers were given powerful new rights to control its use. In fact, there was already a flourishing culture of creation online but it seems that few of the Working Group members had any experience of the reality of the early Internet. They also apparently lacked the imagination to envisage the new possibilities that it provided. The desire of powerful media companies to keep things as they were combined with an inability to see even vaguely what the future might hold, was to prove a recurrent theme over the next three decades.

The final report of the Lehman Working Group, the White Paper, appeared at first glance to be quite different from the Green Paper and yet its substance was almost identical. It achieved this contradiction thanks to a clever ploy: by asserting that most of the extra protection it believed copyright companies would need was already available under current law—if you interpreted it in a particular way. This meant interpreting every ambiguity in the law in favour of the copyright industry and against the users of digital technologies. Even though the White Paper claimed that little needed to be done to bring copyright into the digital age, the practical implications of its approach were astonishing. Litman spells them out in *Digital Copyright*:

> "since any use of a computer to view, read, reread, hear, or otherwise experience a work in digital form would require reproducing that work in a computer's memory, and since the copyright statute gives the copyright holder exclusive control over reproductions, everybody would need to have either a statutory privilege or the copyright holder's permission to view, read, reread, hear, or otherwise experience a digital work, each time she did so. The purchaser of an e-book would need permission each time she read any part of that e-book; the owner of a compact disc would need a license every time she listened to the music on the disc. Someone catching sight of an image posted on the World Wide Web would need the permission of the owner of the copyright in that image (who might not be the person who posted the image) each time it appeared on her computer screen. Not only individuals, but their Internet Service Providers and the proprietors of any computers that assisted in the transfer of files were, and should be, liable for copyright infringement in these cases, regardless of whether they knew someone's in-

tellectual property rights were being invaded, or even what content was moving through their equipment."[17]

Historically, copyright laws were subject to a variety of limitation and exceptions[18] that provided some leeway to those affected. The White Paper's proposals offered none. Indeed, it would give the copyright industry unprecedented control over how people used any kind of digital system that could access material under copyright. This meant that activities such as reading a book, listening to music or watching a film, whenever and however the owner of those items wanted, were replaced with requirements to ask permission from copyright companies once these pursuits became digital activities.

As more people came to realise the implications of what the White Paper proposed, so resistance to it grew. An informal alliance called the Digital Future Coalition[19] was formed from three main groups: law professors, libraries and the Home Recording Rights Coalition.[20] Although the alliance was ostensibly puny compared to the lobbying might of the copyright industry, it possessed a number of key strengths. The law professors were able to point out the flaws in the White Paper's reasoning in a convincing manner, along with the practical problems they would engender. Library groups cared about the practical implications of copyright law and could quickly spread the professors' analyses across the United States. The Home Recording Rights Coalition, which was formed and backed by the consumer electronics industry, already had its own lobbying machine, which aided efforts to spread the word quickly.

In addition, there was another section of society that proved vital in providing resistance. Many of those most opposed to the White Paper were already using the Internet, and understood its power and potential. As a result, they were able to use the burgeoning digital network to warn other online users about the terrible ideas the US government was hoping to turn into law. Among the early Internet adopters were journalists, writers, students, academics and lawyers. Collectively, they had a power and influence that went way beyond their relatively small numbers. The more such pioneers of Internet world became active against—and angry about—the White Paper, the more the mainstream media picked up on the issue, and the more heated the debate became. Consequently, by the summer of 1996 the efforts to enact the NII copyright law were going nowhere. This was in stark contrast to the initial view of the copyright industry that the process would be a mere formality. For the first time in history, the public's concerns about what copyright could and should do became a factor in the legislative process.

It was not just the copyright industry that were overconfident in assuming that the new copyright law would be passed quickly. So was Lehman, and this led him to attempt something even more ambitious. He called for a meeting of the World Intellectual Property Organization (WIPO),[21] which administers international copyright treaties. His plan was to use the fact that the United States was about to update its copyright law for the digital realm to press for a new global copyright treaty that would see all the other WIPO signatories follow suit, basing their own legislation on the US law for the NII. This would allow the US copyright industry, which was already a dominant force worldwide, to control what ordinary people in other countries did with computers and online, just as the White Paper aimed to do in the United States.

The relevant WIPO meeting, formally referred to as a 'Diplomatic Conference', took place in December 1996. Lehman's original plan to use the new NII copyright law as the template for a WIPO treaty was stymied because the United States had failed to agree on what the legislation should say. So Lehman adopted a different strategy. He pushed for a new WIPO treaty based on the ideas found in the NII White Paper. Once the United States signed the WIPO treaty, the nation would be obliged to implement it by passing local legislation that would embody the White Paper's principles. Such 'policy laundering'[22]—using an international forum to force through unpopular national legislation—was a smart stratagem, and one that would be employed over and over again in later years. However, in this instance the plan failed because the other nations at WIPO refused to embrace the evidently extreme proposals in the White Paper. Instead, a diluted version of Lehman's proposals was agreed, forming the WIPO Copyright Treaty,[23] which was signed on 20 December 1996.

Despite the form in which the Copyright Treaty was passed, the US copyright industry hoped to use it to push through the stronger measures advocated in Lehman's White Paper. For example, it wanted to prohibit any circumvention of copyright protection systems for any reason—even if it were for a legal purpose. This meant that if a work's copyright had expired, it would be illegal to access the work if doing so required circumvention of any protection that had been applied. In effect, copyright term would become infinite.

A fierce battle began over whether there should be a fair use[24] exemption to anti-circumvention legislation. Fair use is a concept in US law that allows the limited use of copyright material without needing to acquire permission from the copyright holder beforehand. It acts as a flexible 'safety valve' for copyright, but often requires an expensive lawsuit to establish its exact boundaries. There is a widespread belief that all personal, non-commercial uses are fair use, but this is not true.

The battle is described in what Litman herself calls 'mind-numbing detail'[25] in her history of the birth of digital copyright, in order to give an impression of how the legislation came about. The process is a depressing tale of lobbying and counter-lobbying, proposal and counter-proposal. Finally, a compromise deal was reached, and its flawed concepts haunt copyright around the world to this day.

Eventually, the Digital Millennium Copyright Act (DMCA)[26] was passed on 28 October 1998. It introduced a provision for a so-called Internet service provider 'safe harbour'. Importantly, this laid down the conditions under which online service providers could avoid liability when material that infringed on copyright passed through their systems. Without such considerations, investments in the new NII would have been much harder to obtain, given the potential and costly liability of service providers for copyright infringements carried out by users.

The second aspect of the DMCA was to ban the circumvention of copy-protection technologies. This has effectively made it impossible to take advantage of copyright exceptions for nearly every modern digital work. That's largely true both in the United States under the DMCA, and in the European Union, which implemented the WIPO Copyright Treaty in 2001 with the Information Society Directive.[27]

By the time the DMCA and Information Society Directive had been passed, it was clear that the Internet was the most significant technology advance in decades, and that its impact on society was likely to be huge. The dot-com bubble[28] in the early years of the present millennium had come and gone, but companies such as Google and Amazon were already in existence, laying down the basis for their future success and online dominance.

Where the Internet was clearly a key part of the future, the new laws in the United States and the European Union were backward looking, born of the copyright industries' desire to constrain the digital world to operate as if it dealt with traditional, scarce analogue material. The DMCA and Information Society Directive were designed to stop people making copies of digital material that they owned. The weak technology used to achieve that, when combined with the strong legal remedies against circumvention, meant that the copyright industry gained not just the power to control how digital objects were shared but even outlined how they could be used.

The new laws protecting what came to be known as 'digital rights management' (DRM)[29] technology effectively nullified many of the gains that had been won in the form of fair use and copyright exceptions. As the author and digital rights activist Cory Doctorow[30] puts it in a *Walled Culture* interview, 'Digital rights management is some system where a party other than you gets to give orders to a computer that you own, and when you try to countermand those orders, your computer says, "No". It's like Hal from 2001 saying, "I can't let you do that, Dave."'[31]

The anti-circumvention requirements of the US DMCA and EU's Information Society Directive trumped users' rights, strengthening copyright in unexpected and unreasonable ways that would only become apparent in later years when it was too late to do anything about it. The following chapters explore some of the most egregious examples of the way in which the newly fortified copyright laws would constrain innovation in the digital world, as well as impoverish society and its freedoms by building new legal and technical walls around culture.

CHAPTER 2

Hostage Works and Vanishing Ebooks
Publishers sue Google and the Internet Archive
for sharing knowledge and culture

The constant extensions of copyright term described in the previous chapter and the removal of the copyright formalities[32] previously required took from the public domain[33] without giving anything in return. They also brought with them a new problem that grows in seriousness every day: so-called 'orphan works'.[34]

When there were formalities such as registration and the requirement to display the proper copyright notices, works had an identifiable owner. Without such simple formalities, it was often unclear who could give permission for works to be reused, for example. The situation was made worse by the constant lengthening of copyright well beyond the death of the creator. The absence of any requirement to register or re-register copyright ownership made it hard to establish who owned a work. This in turn meant that it was almost impossible to obtain the necessary permissions for reprinting or other uses such as public display, public performance or putting something online. Without those permissions, it would generally be a copyright infringement to proceed with any kind of reuse. Consequently, people simply avoided using orphan works since they lacked a clear owner.

The use of 'orphan' as a metaphor in the phrase 'orphan works' sounds as if the situation is simply unfortunate. But as Lydia Pallas Loren, Henry J. Casey Professor of Law, Lewis & Clark Law School, points out in her paper 'Abandoning the Orphans: An Open Access Approach to Hostage Works' (2012) a better name for them would be 'hostage works',[35] since they are in fact victims of lengthy copyright term and the lack of formalities. The central problem is how to liberate these hostages.

One of the first major studies of the orphan/hostage work problem was published by the United States Copyright Office[36] in 2006. It suggested that 'any system to deal with orphan works should seek primarily to make it more likely that a user can find the relevant owner in the first instance, and negotiate a voluntary agreement over permission and payment, if appropriate, for the intended use of the work.'[37] Loren had an interesting alternative proposal, with more emphasis on maximising the benefit of liberating such works by creating a new digital copy:

> "If an entity is not negligent in gathering and disclosing information that identifies a work as a 'hostage work' and that entity provides an open access copy of the work together with the hostage freeing information, then that entity should be immune from monetary liability for infringement. Copyright owners should retain the ability to obtain injunctive relief to either correct inaccurate status or owner information, or obtain removal of the digital copy of the work from an open access database. This injunctive power would translate into an enforceable obligation of open access providers to update inaccurate information and remove works in-

> appropriately designated as hostage works. For deriva-
> tive work creators, courts should freely apply equitable
> doctrines to prevent inappropriate injunctive relief and
> limit the ability of later re-surfacing copyright owners
> to sue derivative work creators."[38]

This open access copy would be a kind of halfway house between copyright and those works for which copyright has expired or to which copyright never applied, commonly referred to as the 'public domain'.[39] It could be treated as in the public domain unless the owner reappeared, in which case it would be covered by normal copyright terms. In such a scheme, the presumption is that the hostage work is analogue and would need to be converted to a digital form. But the rise of the Internet—and of social media in particular— has radically changed that situation.

As copyright lawyer Lila Bailey[40] wrote in her article 'Digital Orphans: The Massive Cultural Black Hole On Our Horizon'[41] in 2015, most of today's online material is created by amateurs, much of it anonymously or pseudonymously by young people. The majority have no interest in making sure that posterity knows who they are or what they have done, since their posts, videos and photos are creations of the moment. But copyright will protect that material until seventy years after their death—probably more than a century after it was created.

Despite the magnitude of the problem, legislative efforts so far to address it have been half-hearted at best, and largely useless in practice. The most significant law in this area has been passed by the European Union, in the form of its Orphan Works Directive[42] of 2012. As is so often the case for copyright legislation, its terms of reference are firmly rooted in the past. It applies to 'works published in the form of books, journals, newspapers, magazines or other writing', as well as 'cinematographic or audiovisual works and phonograms'. Similarly, the directive seems unable to imagine that ordinary people might be interested in using material from orphan/hostage works. The directive is only applicable to 'publicly accessible libraries, educational establishments and museums, as well as archives, film or audio heritage institutions and public-service broadcasting organisations.'

Permitted uses are limited to making a work available to the public and reproducing a work for the purposes of digitisation, indexing, cataloguing, preservation and restoration. Moreover, any such use must be in accordance with the public interest mission of the institutions involved. This does not only exclude ordinary citizens, companies are also unable to draw on the riches of orphan works. Businesses are unable to offer them again, possibly in new forms, to the public, or to use them as input data for important new techniques such as machine learning[43] in the field of artificial intelligence.

So it is no wonder that the results have been dismal. Currently, the official EU Orphan Works Database[44] contains just 6,000 entries. In 2012, the British Library estimated that 40% of its copyrighted collections—150 million works in total—are orphan works.[45] The figure now will be even higher—and that is just one institution's collection of carefully selected material. There are probably billions, possibly trillions, of items on social media that are doomed to become hostage works in the future. At least when the UK government came to passing its national orphan works legislation, it recognised that there was an important economic dimension to the problem:

> "The Government's position, following the Hargreaves Review, is that it benefits no-one to have a wealth of

copyright works be entirely unusable under any circumstances because the owner of one or more rights in the work cannot be contacted. This is not simply a cultural issue; it is also a very real economic issue that potentially valuable intangible assets are not being used, and an issue of respect for copyright if they are being used unlawfully. The Government therefore proposed an orphan works scheme that allows for both commercial and cultural uses of orphan works, subject to satisfactory safeguards for the interests of both owners of 'orphan rights' and rights holders who could potentially suffer from unfair competition from an orphan works scheme."[46]

A press release from the UK government in October 2014 claimed that the new UK licensing scheme, brought in to address the orphan works problem, 'could give wider access to at least 91 million culturally valuable creative works—including diaries, photographs, oral history recordings and documentary films.'[47] In 2019, Merisa Martinez[48] of the Swedish School of Library and Information Science and Melissa Terras[49] of the College of Arts, Humanities and Social Sciences University of Edinburgh, looked at how things had gone in the four years since the UK Orphan Works Licensing Scheme had started operation:

"As of October 2018, 144 licenses have been granted of a total of 877 items. That is an average of 18 works per month over the 48 months that the Scheme has been operational, a far cry from the UK IPO press release dated 29 October 2014, entitled 'UK opens access to 91 million Orphan Works' (2014). This perfectly illustrates what the impact assessment commissioned by the UK IPO predicted: that such a bureaucratic system requiring individual licensing and data entry would be 'very little used'."[50]

Yet another in-depth report by the US Copyright Office on the subject of orphan works was released in 2015, entitled 'Orphan Works and Mass Digitization'.[51] One difference from the US report ten years earlier was that it contained a major section concerning a new, separate problem from that of orphan works: mass digitisation.

The shift from analogue to digital meant that millions of books—and billions of cultural artefacts that already existed as physical objects—needed to be converted into a form that could be viewed on computers and sent over the Internet. If not, the cultural riches of the past risked becoming museum pieces that were of little relevance to the modern world and its citizens. One of the first people to realise this and to do something about it was the US author Michael Hart,[52] who started Project Gutenberg to address the problem:

> "The first ebook was available on July 4 1971 as eText #1 of Project Gutenberg, a visionary project launched by Michael Hart to create free electronic versions of literary works and disseminate them worldwide. In the 16th century, Gutenberg allowed anyone to have print books for a small cost. In the 21st century, Project Gutenberg would allow anyone to have a digital library at no cost."[53]

In order to avoid copyright problems, Project Gutenberg concentrates on books that are in the public domain. In spring 2002, Project Gutenberg's holdings represented 25% of all the public domain works freely available on the Web. Today, there are more than 60,000 ebooks, which can be downloaded in a variety of formats. The length of copyright in most countries means that Project Gutenberg mainly digitises classic literature, rather than more modern works. However, 'A few numbers are reserved for 'special' books. For example, eBook #1984 is reserved for George Orwell's classic, published in 1949, and still a long way from falling into public domain.'[54]

Turning books, paintings, drawings, maps and music into digital images is straightforward technically. The problem for works that are not in the public domain is copyright. In legal terms, the conversion process is copying. As a result, the appropriate permission may be needed for every single work that is still in copyright before conversion can take place.

For orphan works, that is impossible by definition. Even for works where the owner is known and contactable, the digitisation process presents huge logistical difficulties. To digitise the holdings of a library, for example, every artefact would need to be examined, its owner established, where possible, and then permission sought. That permission might be given freely or—more likely—subject to yet more negotiations about the terms on which it would be allowed. What was already an unprecedented challenge became impossibly complex. Research by Julia Fallon and Pablo Uceda Gomez from the Europeana Foundation[55] has revealed the dramatic impact of copyright on digitisation projects, leading to the '20th century black hole' in Europeana's[56] collections from more than 3,000 institutions:

> "As cultural heritage institutions across Europe digitize more and more of their collections and make them available online, an alarming pattern is starting to emerge. Collections that consist of works dating from the 20th century or that contain large proportions of works from that period are available online to a much

> lesser degree than collections from the periods before or after the 20th century. This effect has been called 'the 20th century black hole' and can be attributed to the way copyright interacts with the digitization of cultural heritage collections."[57]

Fortunately, in the 1990s, two people were already thinking about the issues involved in digitising both out-of-copyright and recent books on a large scale, as the official history of what became Google Books explains:

> "In 1996, Google co-founders Sergey Brin and Larry Page were graduate computer science students working on a research project supported by the Stanford Digital Library Technologies Project. Their goal was to make digital libraries work, and their big idea was as follows: in a future world in which vast collections of books are digitized, people would use a 'web crawler' to index the books' content and analyze the connections between them, determining any given book's relevance and usefulness by tracking the number and quality of citations from other books."[58]

The web crawler became the core search technology behind Google, which was launched in 1998. Once their company became established, Brin and Page began to explore the idea of scanning books to carry out the indexing and analysis they had discussed earlier. In 2002, a secret 'books' project was launched that explored the practicalities of scanning millions of books. The first 300-page volume took 40 minutes to scan using existing technologies. One of the pioneers of library digitisation, the University of Michigan, estimated that even with a more honed approach, its library's 7 million volumes would take around 1,000 years to scan. According to the official Google history of the project, Page told the university that he believed Google could do it in six years.

In due course, the Google team came up with a non-destructive scanning technique that allowed even curved pages to be scanned at up to 6,000 pages per hour. Optical Character Recognition (OCR)[59] then converted the scans into digital texts.

In 2004, what had originally been called Project Ocean was formally announced as Google Print. By then a number of universities and publishers had joined the project. Later that year, Google announced the Google Print Library Project and its plans to digitise 15 million volumes within a decade. The original aspiration to index and analyse the world's books had expanded: Google now planned to display snippets of the books it scanned, which would not only be older titles in the public domain but also those still in copyright. If they wished, publishers were able to sell ebook versions of their titles that had been digitised by Google.

Despite the option to make money from what became known as the Google Books[60] project, not all authors were pleased. In September 2005, three authors and the Authors Guild of America[61]—the oldest and largest professional organisation of writers in the United States—filed a lawsuit against Google, alleging 'massive copyright infringement'.[62] A month later, the Association of American Publishers (AAP) brought its own legal action against Google,[63] on behalf of the publishers McGraw-Hill, Pearson Education, Penguin Group, Simon & Schuster, and John Wiley & Sons. As journalist James Somers pointed out in a subsequent feature about the Google Books project in *The Atlantic*,[64] the stakes were high. Statutory damages for 'wilful infringement' of copyright in the United States can be $150,000 for each instance. Google's potential liability for scanning tens of millions of books without permission might have been billions of dollars. Google based its defence on the fair use provision of US copyright law, that allowed certain kinds of uses of copyright material without permission.

Somers explains how eventually the two parties came to an agreement that not only allowed Google to move ahead with its plans, but along the way also addressed another major problem with the copyright system: out-of-print books. To reprint a physical book requires a considerable investment that can only be justified for the most successful books. Rather than risk having a warehouse of reprints that no one wanted, publishers preferred to let old titles fall into obscurity. Copyright meant that no one else could reprint them until the copyright term had expired, by which time the title would probably be forgotten or no longer be of interest.

The ill-fated Google Books Search Amended Settlement Agreement[65] foresaw Google paying \$125 million to settle outstanding claims. It allowed authors and publishers to opt out books at any time, and out-of-print books to be displayed and sold as ebooks at prices determined by the owner or algorithmically. Universities could buy access to a special database of all out-of-print books that allowed people to search and read the full collection. The agreement was a novel and imaginative solution given the constraints of US copyright law. It would have made more books more available than ever before, while providing much-needed extra revenue for publishers and authors.

The judge presiding over the case brought against Google put out a call for comments on the proposed settlement. Despite its clever approach, and the way in which everyone seemed to get something from the proposed solution, there were a number of major concerns about what such an agreement would involve when implemented. For example, it was felt to be too US-centric, ignoring the huge body of literature in languages other than English. Siva Vaidhyanathan,[66] at that time Associate Professor of Culture and Communication, New York University, saw it as a danger to the functioning of copyright in the digital world:

> "The Google case is the most potentially disruptive copyright battle since the invention of sound recording technology. It strikes at the very heart of the copyright system and reveals that we tend to rely on the rickety structure of fair use to support too many essential public values. Google's Library Project threatens to unravel everything that is good and stable about the copyright system. It injects more uncertainty and panic into a system that is already in disequilibrium."[67]

Another concern was that while the Library Project would create an incredible resource, it would also be entirely under Google's control. Robert Darnton, then president of the Harvard Library, is quoted in *The Atlantic* as saying: 'Did we want the greatest library that would ever exist to be in the hands of one giant corporation, which could really charge almost anything it wanted for access to it?'[68]

The central problem was that if any other company wanted to sell out-of-print books in the same way as Google, it would need to carry out a similar mass digitisation, get sued in a similar class action and then agree a similar settlement to Google's. That clearly would never happen, leaving Google with its monopoly control. For this and other reasons, the US Department of Justice objected to the deal. Together with the complaints from rival companies, and from some institutions and activists similarly concerned about the great power the arrangement would give to Google, there was sufficient resistance to convince the judge to rule in 2011 that the settlement was not 'fair, adequate, and reasonable'.

In October 2014, the AAP settled with Google.[69] A year before, the judge ruled that Google's use of copyright works was fair use.[70] The Authors Guild of America appealed but the judges of the new court ruled unanimously in Google's favour. In 2016, the US Supreme Court declined to intervene when requested by the Authors Guild to do so, leaving the original ruling in favour of Google.

Yet that was not the end of the fight by the Authors Guild. In September 2011, along with the Australian Society of Authors, the Union Des Écrivaines et des Écrivains Québécois, and eight individual authors, the Authors Guild had filed a lawsuit against the non-profit digital repository for the books digitised by Google, HathiTrust.[71] Founded in 2008,[72] HathiTrust was a consortium of research libraries at US universities that aimed to create a digital repository of their holdings. At inception, HathiTrust held scans of more than 2 million volumes and around 750 million pages. About 16% of the material was in the public domain and available for anyone to read online. Items still covered by copyright were scanned in order to archive and provide academic access to the underlying physical objects, but they were not generally available online.

The problem for the Authors Guild was that HathiTrust had a close working relationship with Google. According to a report in *Publishers Weekly*,[73] the lawsuit alleged that HathiTrust was built with millions of 'unauthorised' scans created by Google. In 2011, the HathiTrust project had digitised more than 9.5 million volumes and the Authors Guild claimed that the universities were engaging in 'one of the largest copyright infringements in history'.[74] The suit sought an injunction banning libraries from carrying out any future digitisation of works still under copyright, for example by providing books to Google, and from carrying out a plan to allow access to orphan works. The suit also asked the court to impound all the scans and hold them in escrow 'pending an appropriate act of Congress'[75] that would regulate how they could be used.

Unlike the Google Books lawsuit, which dragged on for years, the one against HathiTrust was resolved quickly. In October 2012, the presiding judge ruled that the digitisation programme was clear fair use under US copyright law, because scanning books in order to index them was a 'transformative'[76] act. The judge also recognised that copying entire works was necessary in order to provide full-text searching and access by the visually impaired. As the *Publishers Weekly* report on the judgment notes:

> "[The judge] clearly was impressed by the access the project affords to the blind and print disabled (who had intervened in the case via the National Federation for the Blind), citing it often in his opinion and at one point writing that the 'unprecedented ability of print-disabled individuals to have an equal opportunity to compete with their sighted peers' was perhaps the 'most important' transformative use of the scans."[77]

The judge raised a key issue: copyright in general prevents those who are visually impaired from making accessible versions of texts. In 2013, a treaty on copyright known as the Marrakesh Treaty[78] was adopted that allowed countries to bring in copyright exceptions to facilitate the creation of versions of works that could be accessed by the visually impaired. It took so long for what seems to be a simple matter of fairness, inclusivity and equality because the copyright industries lobbied fiercely against doing so.

One of the people who led the campaign for a treaty was James Love,[79] Director of Knowledge Ecology International,[80] an NGO working on knowledge governance. In a *Walled Culture* interview, he said: 'the initial opposition was from the publishers, and the publishers did everything you can imagine to derail this.'[81] An in-depth report on the Marrakesh Treaty from the corporate lobby watchdog Corporate European Observatory explains:

> "Industry's lobby efforts have attempted to re-frame the Marrakesh Treaty away from being a matter of human rights, education, and social justice, towards a copyright agenda by portraying it as a threat to business' interests. But contrary to the obvious benefits of the ratification and implementation of the Marrakesh Treaty for the 30 million blind or visually-impaired people in Europe (and 285 million worldwide), several EU member state governments have instead bought the business line that these issues should be viewed through the lens of copyright."[82]

Partly as a result of this lobby, it was not until 2016 that the treaty was effective, following its ratification by twenty nations. That the visually impaired had to wait so long until there was a global framework that made it possible for them to take advantage of digital technology to create accessible versions of works is a good example of how copyright has acted as a barrier to progress—and, in this case, social justice.

Although both Google and HathiTrust won their respective legal battles against the Authors Guild, the two projects have developed quite differently. As an article from 2017 in *Wired* reviewing the status of the Google Books project put it, after the heady early days when it seemed possible to create a database holding digitised versions of every book in the world, 'Google Books has settled into a quiet middle age of sourcing quotes and serving up snippets of text from the 25 million-plus tomes in its database.'[83] That is still a valuable endeavour, especially for public domain books, but it is a far cry from what Google Books could have been had the original vision been realised.

Google Books chugs along, which has led to HathiTrust continuing to grow. By 2016, it had nearly 15 million scanned volumes[84]—with 1 million entering the collection in 2016 alone—from the library collections of thirty-nine organisations. Around 38% of the collection is available to general users, some 5.7 million volumes. In 2016, the collections received more than 6 million visitors who conducted 11 million sessions. In 2022, there were more than 17 million scanned items.

HathiTrust is not the only consortium working to digitise existing materials on a large scale, which is now widely recognised as a key task for global culture. For example, the Europeana project, funded by the EU, draws on digitisation carried out by galleries, libraries, archives and museums to provide online access to European cultural heritage material.[85] In 2022, there were around 30 million images, 22 million documents, 750,000 sound recordings, and 500,000 videos available. In the United States, the Digital Public Library of America[86] carries out a similar function. In 2022, it held 45 million images, texts, videos and sounds from across the nation.

The efforts of both of these entities are dwarfed by that of the Internet Archive.[87] In 2005, the Internet Archive announced the Open Content Alliance,[88] which coordinated hundreds of libraries to digitise millions of books. The Open Library[89] project has created a catalogue of books that helps people find scanned books on archive.org[90] as well as in other projects. This was an open alternative to the Google project, and has continued to digitise over 1 million books per year.

As well as the Internet Archive's unique archive of the Internet over the last twenty-five years, which amounts to nearly 600 billion Web pages, there are also scans of 28 million books and texts; 14 million audio recordings (including 220,000 live concerts); 6 million videos (including 2 million TV news programmes); 3.5 million images; and 580,000 software programs. The founder of the Internet Archive, Brewster Kahle, explained the background to this immense project:

> "The idea for me, at least for the Internet, was to try to build the Great Library. The idea of building the library comes with every new publishing medium. So we just do what libraries have always done: we purchase materials, or if they're available for free, we collect them, we preserve them, and we lend them. So we're not republishing materials. For the World Wide Web, we crawl Web pages and archive them and make them available to people with a banner saying that it's not the original website, it's from this particular time.
>
> It's too bad this is required. But the Web technology is so simple, that they didn't build in any way that publishing has always worked, which is usually a publisher puts something out, and it goes into a bunch of different libraries such that if any of those go down, then you have the other copies. That's not how the World Wide Web works. There's only one copy and it's on one serv-

er. And if that goes and changes, or goes down, then it's not available at all."[91]

In 2020, the Covid-19 pandemic added an extra relevance to mass digitisation projects. During times when physical access to libraries and museums was difficult or impossible, the digital versions offered a way for people anywhere to access materials. In early March 2020,[92] HathiTrust began to work on what it came to call the 'Emergency Temporary Access Service' (ETAS),[93] which was formally launched on 30 March that year. The service aims to make 'it possible for member library patrons to obtain lawful access to specific digital materials in HathiTrust that correspond to physical books held by their own library.'

ETAS is an example of Controlled Digital Lending (CDL)[94] by libraries. A site of the same name defines this as 'the digital equivalent of traditional library lending. A library can digitize a book it owns and lend out a secured digital version to one user at a time, in place of the physical item.'[95] On the thorny issue of whether CDL requires the permission of the copyright owners, the site FAQ says: 'CDL proponents believe that the conversion from one format to another, for a use consistent with a library's mission, and where the copyright owner has already been compensated for a legitimately acquired item, is fair use.'[96]

In 2016, Kahle laid out his vision for the Internet Archive Open Libraries[97] project, launched in 2010,[98] based on the idea behind CDL:

> "Today, people get their information online—often filtered through for-profit platforms. If a book isn't online, it's as if it doesn't exist. Yet much of modern knowledge still exists only on the printed page, stored in libraries. Libraries haven't met this digital demand,

> stymied by costs, e-book restrictions, policy risks, and missing infrastructure. We now have the technology and legal frameworks to transform our library system by 2020. The Internet Archive, working with library partners, proposes bringing millions of books online, through purchase or digitization, starting with the books most widely held and used in libraries and classrooms. Our vision includes at-scale circulation of these e-books, enabling libraries owning the physical works to substitute them with lendable digital copies. By 2020, we can spark a new 'Carnegie moment' in which thousands of libraries unlock their analog collections for a new generation of learners, enabling free, long-term, public access to knowledge."[99]

By 2022, the Open Libraries project had digitised 2.7 million books, and the Internet Archive had been operating its digital lending library for a decade. However, for 12 weeks during the spring of 2020, the Internet Archive's system worked a little differently. The global Covid-19 pandemic forced libraries around the world to close their physical locations, and library patrons could not access the millions of books that libraries had bought from publishers. Libraries and schools across the globe reached out to the Internet Archive for help. Under those unprecedented circumstances, the Internet Archive lifted its one-to-one owned-to-loaned ratio (while retaining other controls, such as a two-week loan period and DRM to prevent copying and redistribution) and launched, along with over 100 library endorsements,[100] the 'National Emergency Library' (NEL). Authors could opt out if they felt strongly that they did not want their works shared in this way. As the headline on Jill Lepore's article in *The New Yorker* read: 'The National Emergency Library Is a Gift to Readers Everywhere.'[101]

Despite all these precautions, and the extreme circumstances of that moment in time, the Authors Guild said it was 'appalled'[102] by the announcement of the National Emergency Library. Similarly, the Association of American Publishers (AAP) claimed to be 'stunned'[103] by the news. On 1 June 2021, four publishers—the Hachette Book Group, Harper-Collins Publishers, John Wiley & Sons and Penguin Random House—in coordination with the AAP filed a lawsuit against the Internet Archive[104] alleging copyright infringement, and seeking damages and lawyers' fees. According to the legal complaint, the lawsuit was regarding the Internet Archive's 'purposeful collection of truckloads of in-copyright books to scan, reproduce, and then distribute digital bootleg versions online.'[105] The hyperbolic term 'bootleg' was used no less than five times in the document. As a result of the lawsuit, the Internet Archive announced that it was closing the National Emergency Library two weeks early,[106] on 16 June 2021. Kahle explained:

> "[It] was to run for fourteen weeks, and the publishers sued. And they sued really not so much based on the National Emergency Library—it's just a lending library, after all. They sued about 127 books. What their demand is, is because of these 127 books, they want us to destroy 1.3 million digital books. So it's outrageous. The lawsuit continues, and it'll continue for years and cost millions and millions of dollars."[107]

At the time of writing, the matter is still pending in court.

The president of the Authors Guild, Douglas Preston, said: 'The Internet Archive hopes to fool the public by calling its piracy website a "library," but there's a more accurate term for taking what you don't own: it's called "stealing".'[108] Once more, there was an attempt to frame the digital world of abundance in terms of analogue scarcity and to negate the key advantage of the digital format. But the Internet Archive owned the books, which it lent out just like any other library.[109]

Preston also said that free ebooks were available through libraries if people wanted them. But every library in the US (and elsewhere) was closed; and the ebooks were not available, as the National Emergency Library's FAQ explained: '[We] have focused on acquiring and digitizing books from the 1920s–1990s that don't have an ebook available except for our scanned copy.'[110] The Internet Archive's National Emergency Library was not only fulfilling a pressing need for access to key works for students, it also revealed a major failure by the traditional publishing industry to meet this demand by embracing digital technology fully.

This scenario illustrates a problem that has been getting worse, not better, over time. In 2013,[111] all the 'Big Five' publishers—Hachette, HarperCollins, Macmillan, Penguin Random House and Simon & Schuster—had at least some of their catalogues available to libraries as ebooks. Yet just five years later, Macmillan started to get cold feet, announcing that newly released ebooks from its Tor Books division would not be available to libraries for lending until four months after their retail on-sale date. According to a report in *Publishers Weekly*, Macmillan said this was because 'current analysis on eLending indicates that it is having a direct and adverse impact on retail eBook sales.'[112]

Around this time, other publishers started hobbling their own ebooks in various ways.[113] For example, Hachette began licensing ebooks to libraries for two-year terms instead of forever. Penguin Random House introduced a 'metered' approach that counted how many times an ebook was lent out. HarperCollins met outrage when it first offered a metered option in 2011,[114] but undeterred went on to introduce a 'cost per circulation' option, whereby a fee is charged to a library whenever an ebook is loaned out.

In July 2019, Macmillan announced an eight-week embargo[115] for all its ebooks. Libraries could buy just one 'perpetual access' ebook during the first eight weeks of publication—but only then—for $30, no matter the size of the library; additional copies could be bought after the embargo, when they would generally cost $60. However, the ebook licence was metered for two years or fifty-two loans, whichever came first. The general embargo provoked widespread criticism. The American Library Association 'denounced' the move; its president, Wanda Brown, said: 'Macmillan Publishers' new model for library ebook lending will make it difficult for libraries to fulfill our central mission: ensuring access to information for all.'[116] The association urged library customers of Macmillan to voice their objections.

Less than a year later, in March 2020, Macmillan announced that it was abandoning the ebook embargo. Perhaps it was because of the backlash, or because Macmillan recognised that the public had a pressing need to access ebooks as a result of the Covid-19 pandemic. In a brief note addressed to 'Librarians, Authors, Illustrators and Agents', the company's then-CEO John Sargent wrote: 'There are times in life when differences should be put aside.'[117]

Maybe Macmillan also recognised that the ebook market for libraries was booming, and to put obstacles in the way of its titles was foolish—especially since the data showed ebook sales to the public were thriving. Figures published by digital content distributor OverDrive[118]—which is considered a worldwide leader for library and school digital books—indicated that daily averages for ebook loans had increased 51%[119] after the Covid-19 national emergency declaration in March 2020. In December 2020, the AAP announced that 'eBook revenues were up 20.4% for the month [of October 2020] as compared to October of 2019 for a total of $96.9 million. On a year-to-date basis, eBooks were up 16.5%, coming in at $956.3 million for the first ten months of 2020.'[120]

As ebooks became more central to the role of public libraries, it was increasingly evident that the terms under which they could be acquired, and which had evolved in an *ad hoc* way over the previous decade, were unsatisfactory and unfair. In the United States, this has led to proposals for new laws requiring publishers to license ebooks to libraries on 'reasonable terms', without specifying what exactly that meant. A post on the Authors Alliance Web site explains:

> "The legislation responds in part to publishers' trend in recent years of charging libraries higher prices for e-book licenses than they do consumers: in some cases, libraries must pay up to five times as much as an individual consumer for an e-book license. Moreover, these licenses often come with restrictive terms, such as limits on the number of times an e-book can be checked out before the license is terminated. The issue gained particular salience during the COVID-19 pandemic, as libraries across the country shuttered in-person operations, and patrons were forced to turn to e-books and other digital services in order to access library resources."[121]

In March 2021, the Maryland state legislature[122] unanimously passed one example of this law. It requires 'a publisher who offers to license an electronic literary product to the public to also offer to license the product to public libraries in the State on reasonable terms that would enable public libraries to provide library users with access to the electronic literary product.' This hardly seems onerous but it was too much for the AAP, which once again filed a lawsuit to halt a move that would have brought some minor benefits to the public. In its complaint, the AAP claimed that 'the vitality of the publishing industry' required giving publishers the ability to 'make decisions about the timing, pricing, and formats of their books'.[123]

The United States is not the only country where ebook pricing for libraries is problematic. As the UK academic librarian Yohanna Anderson wrote in her guest post on the *Walled Culture* blog:

> "In the early weeks of campus lockdown, the big publishing houses announced, with much congratulatory fanfare from their press officers, that they had opened their ebook collections to universities for free. This was welcomed by universities. However, access to these books was quietly withdrawn as early as June 2020, when the pandemic was still raging. In their place, universities were offered exorbitantly priced subscription-based bundled packages of the ebooks or individual ebook licenses priced at as much as 500% more than the hardcopy. The cynical among us could be forgiven for concluding that the initial generous offer was nothing more than a ploy to manipulate the market by forcing libraries, desperately trying to support students studying remotely, into signing up to expensive and unsustainable subscription ebook models."[124]

To highlight and address this problem, in September 2020,[125] Anderson formed the campaign group #ebooksos[126] along with two other librarians, Caroline Ball and Rachel Bickley. To date, nearly 5,000 librarians, students, researchers, academics, consortia, professional bodies and others have signed the campaign's open letter to the UK government to investigate the practices of the academic ebook publishing industry. In October 2021, the UK Society of College, National and University Libraries (SCONUL) produced a position paper delineating the difficulties with ebook provision for libraries. They include the inability to buy all titles in this format—according to Anderson, only 10% of university reading-list items are currently available; the use of bundling, which forces libraries to buy additional titles in order to obtain the one they need; inflated pricing—in November 2021, Pearson Education UK increased the price of all its ebooks by 500%,[127] without providing any justification for the move; and the lack of 'perpetual purchase' options for both concurrent multi-user and single-user access titles.

The last of these is one of the most worrying aspects of the shift to ebooks for libraries. Whereas in the past libraries owned the books they bought, this is no longer the case. Instead, they now merely acquire a licence to use an ebook. That licence may not be perpetual and it can also be withdrawn. Hence, at the end of a limited licence period, publishers are able to increase the price in an arbitrary manner if they wish. Libraries have to pay the increase if they want to continue to access that text, since there are no alternative sources, such as second-hand copies, as there are with analogue books.

The library ebook market is a good example of how the shift from analogue to digital that should have opened up a host of new possibilities has sadly resulted in a loss of basic rights like ownership and control. Although this is most evident in the library sector—particularly during the Covid-19 pandemic, which exacerbated the problems—it applies equally to the general book market.

For example, two of the most famous demonstrations that people do not own or control the ebooks they buy occurred in 2009. The first involved an innovative text-to-speech feature of the Amazon Kindle 2, which could read a text out loud. This was obviously a boon for the visually impaired or those who found it difficult to read printed texts for whatever reason. Yet, just as it had in 2005 with the Google Books case, the Authors Guild of America threw its weight against the new possibilities of digital, claiming the feature was copyright infringement. As the editor and writer Mike Masnick[128] wrote on his *Techdirt* Web site in 2009:

> "The Authors Guild had no claim here. It doesn't violate performance rights, because reading aloud isn't a performance. It doesn't violate copyright, because there's no fixed copy made—and if it did violate copyright, so would reading a book aloud."[129]

Amazon caved in anyway. *The New York Times*[130] reported that Amazon would allow publishers to decide whether the text-to-speech option was available for their titles. However, Amazon did that by remotely disabling the feature for some previously sold ebooks, without asking permission from the people who paid for them.

A few weeks later, Amazon showed again that it retained control over its customers' purchases. It involved an ebook that was apparently sold by a company without the relevant rights to do so. Amazon's response was to delete copies of the book remotely. By a nicely ironic twist of fate, the book involved was George Orwell's *Nineteen Eighty-four*, which depicts a dystopian world where awkward cultural items disappear down a 'memory hole'.[131] As well as underlining that people do not own an ebook when they purchase it from a company like Amazon, this incident also emphasises the difference from the previous, analogue world of books, as *The New York Times* pointed out:

> "Retailers of physical goods cannot, of course, force their way into a customer's home to take back a purchase, no matter how bootlegged it turns out to be. Yet Amazon appears to maintain a unique tether to the digital content it sells for the Kindle."[132]

The New York Times also noted the futility of trying to send a book down a digital memory hole, since free ebook versions of *Nineteen Eighty-four* are readily available in many locations on the Internet. Withdrawing legally purchased copies, as Amazon had, simply drives people to find unauthorised ones. Although Amazon stated that it had changed its policy and would not remove ebooks from a customer's device, it also added 'in these circumstances'.

The fact remains that Amazon—and other ebook publishers—can remove titles instantly and remotely if they wish. Unfortunately, people who thought they owned titles can do nothing about it, because of the DRM used alongside the main file. As Chapter 1 noted, no matter how weak or easy to break the DRM might be, its presence guarantees stronger legal protections against trying to make copies. Author, journalist, and activist Cory Doctorow told *Walled Culture* that the use of DRM by publishers has ironically made them dependent on Amazon.[133] Since readers cannot move ebooks between different DRM platforms, they usually stick to just one, which is typically Amazon's. To serve that large user base, publishers use Amazon's platform for all their books, locking in more readers and helping Amazon to grow even more powerful. It's a positive feedback loop that is yet another consequence of the copyright industry's failure to adapt to the new world of digital abundance.

CHAPTER 3

Aaron Swartz's Manifesto
Making all publicly funded research freely available through open access

The new copyright laws, specifically designed to tame the digital world, saw publishers take advantage of them to increase their control. This meant libraries faced difficulties, and consequently also reduced access to knowledge and culture. Such problems have only emerged in the 21st century, as digitisation projects have sought to convert hardcopy library books to electronic ones and publishers have realised how they can exploit ebook publishing to increase their profits. But long before these shifts and their challenges, some in the academic world were seeking to maximise the benefits of the fledgling Internet system to make access to knowledge as easy and friction-free as possible.

A key moment came in 1978, when a typesetting program called TeX[134] appeared. Written by a brilliant computer scientist, Donald Knuth,[135] TeX was powerful enough to allow articles containing even the most complex mathematics content to be entered and displayed—something that had previously required expensive equipment and specialist professionals. Since TeX was both powerful and free, academics started using it to produce preprints—draft versions—of their papers. Knuth wisely decided to use basic text as the underlying format of TeX. This meant that academics could send preprints via another new technology, email. A culture of sharing manuscripts by email evolved, which later led to their distribution via larger mailing lists.

The process of sharing material became easier in the spring of 1991, when the physicist Paul Ginsparg[136] set up an automated email server while he was a staff member of the Los Alamos National Laboratory. As preprints were uploaded, the server would send out alerts to subscribers, who could then request the full texts. Ginsparg later recalled:

> "It was originally intended for about 100 submissions per year from a small subfield of high-energy particle physics, but rapidly grew in users and scope, receiving 400 submissions in its first half year. The submissions were initially planned to be deleted after three months, by which time the pre-existing paper distribution system [of preprints] would catch up, but by popular demand nothing was ever deleted."[137]

Initially known as 'xxx.lanl.gov', but renamed in 1998 to 'arXiv.org'[138] (pronounced 'archive'), it currently holds more than 2 million papers, in the fields of physics, mathematics, computer science, quantitative biology, quantitative finance, statistics, electrical engineering and systems science, and economics, with an average of 15,000 more added every month. arXiv caught on quickly with science researchers and has become one of the most important ways to disseminate knowledge. However, it differs in certain respects from the traditional journal-based approach that has dominated academic publishing for 350 years since the British Royal Society introduced the first journal devoted to science, *Philosophical Transactions*,[139] in 1665.

Unlike traditional authors, academics do not usually write the articles for a fee. Instead, they are rewarded by receiving recognition from their peers, which in turn aids career advancement and, indirectly, brings financial rewards such as a higher salary and easier access to grants for future work. Academic publishers have exploited this unusual situation to the hilt. Not only are the authors of academic papers unpaid, neither are the referees that provide feedback on whether a journal should publish them, via a process known as 'peer review'.[140] Academics are also frequently asked to work on the editorial boards of academic journals, helping to set objectives, without payment. Often, the editor of a specialist journal is unpaid, since such a post looks good on a curriculum vitae (CV).[141] In addition, senior members of the academic community are expected to shoulder such editorial roles. Furthermore, the need to publish research in well-regarded titles means that publishers are even able to demand payment by the authors for some of the costs of the publication, such as colour photographs. Finally, academics are also expected to assign the copyright of their articles to publishers, supposedly so that the latter can act with full legal powers in defending them from any unauthorised uses.

Academic publishers enjoy some other advantages in this sector. Researchers will push for their institution to pay for academic journals so that they can keep up-to-date with other research in their field, even though most of the publishing work is done for free by their peers. Naturally, such eager demand gives publishers the edge when it comes to setting the price of a publication, since they know that libraries will be under pressure to subscribe to even the most expensive journals.

The fact that academic work, particularly in the scientific field, is about reporting on new findings, means that researchers typically publish their results only once because of the Ingelfinger rule.[142] Originally enunciated in 1969 by the *The New England Journal of Medicine* (*NEJM*), and later taken up by other journals, the Ingelfinger rule stipulated that the *NEJM* would not publish findings that had been published elsewhere. At the time, the rationale was to prevent academics from publishing work multiple times in order to inflate their CV. But it also had the effect of creating a natural publishing monopoly: if an academic wants to read an original piece of research, there is only one place to find it, since the copyright routinely assigned by academics to publishers allows the latter to forbid anyone from disseminating close copies. As with most monopolies, this drives the subscription prices even higher, since libraries have no alternative source for the articles that their users require.

In addition to arXiv, another successful early attempt to use the Internet as a new way of publishing research was the Scientific Electronic Library Online (SciELO), established in Brazil in 1997. It had two primary goals: indexing quality journals published by institutions in Latin America and South Africa, and providing free online access to articles.[143] This was particularly important for developing economies, for which the often high subscription prices of traditional publishing form a major barrier to accessing knowledge. One reason for placing digital copies of papers online was to enable academics around the world to read the latest research in a way that hitherto was not possible.

A similar index of articles in the life sciences, PubMed,[144] was launched in the United States in August 1997.[145] It was run by David Lipman,[146] director of the National Center for Biotechnology Information at the National Institutes of Health (NIH). In 1998, the British publisher Vitek Tracz[147] visited him with an idea, which he later recalled in an interview, published in *Information Today* in 2005:

> "I think perhaps the time has come to create a central repository for research papers. The benefits of having everything available in one place, without any access restrictions, would be enormous. Moreover, with the Web technology available today, publishing can potentially happen independently of publishers. If authors started depositing their papers directly into a central repository, they could bypass publishers and make it freely available."[148]

Lipman said it was an interesting idea, but that he was too busy, not least with running GenBank,[149] the open database of DNA that was coming from the Human Genome Project[150] and elsewhere. But a seed had been planted. Lipman spoke to the head of the NIH, Harold Varmus.[151] In his book *The Art and Politics of Science*, Varmus explains how he came to appreciate the potential of publishing articles online, thanks to advocacy by a young biomedical researcher, Patrick Brown.[152] Varmus had met Brown in December 1998, shortly after Brown had come across Ginsparg's arXiv, which was by then well established:

> "When I returned to my office at the NIH, I looked at Ginsparg's website, continued my conversation with Pat by e-mail, and started thinking about how Internet-based distribution and storage of biomedical

> research articles could dramatically alter the way we worked.
>
> The more I thought about this, the more I was convinced that a radical restructuring of methods for publishing, transmitting, storing, and using biomedical research reports might be possible and beneficial. In a spirit of enthusiasm and political innocence, I wrote a lengthy manifesto, proposing the creation of an NIH-supported online system, called E-biomed."[153]

Varmus envisioned a major repository of reports covering a wide range of biomedical science, including clinical research, cell and molecular biology, medically related behavioural research, bioengineering and related disciplines, which could be accessed for free by anyone. As Varmus said in his 1999 'E-biomed manifesto': 'The single greatest attraction of E-biomed is that all of its scientific content will be available without barriers to any user with Internet access. This will maximize the dissemination and use of research results.'[154] One radical departure from the existing approach to academic publishing was that authors retained copyright in their articles, rather than assigning it to a publisher. The cost of building and maintaining E-biomed would be paid by the NIH.

E-biomed could have had a dramatic impact on global access to knowledge but it met strong resistance from a number of quarters. Varmus wrote that many scientists were strongly attached to their favourite journals and were reluctant to move to a radically new system. 'Shrill opposition' came from scientific and medical societies, which exploited the existing academic publishing system to generate revenue for their activities. Commercial publishers were also 'unhappy'—to the point that they sent their main lobbyist to talk to key politicians in Washington, D.C. One accusation was that Varmus was trying to turn the NIH into a federal publishing company and that he was undermining the free enterprise system.

The ambitious E-biomed was dropped, but a diluted version, PubMed Central, came into being in late 1999. The new digital library allowed Internet users to access articles that were provided on a voluntary basis by any journals, new or established, which were listed in PubMed. In this way, PubMed Central would be conveniently integrated with PubMed, an NIH service that was already respected and time-tested. However, publishers were unwilling to support even this mild attempt to make research more accessible. Varmus later wrote:

> "Those of us who were strong advocates for the new public library regarded the reluctance of publishers to participate as unacceptable obstructionism. After all, the publishers depended on the free services of publicly-funded scientists to produce their journals, but were unwilling to improve public access to the work of those scientists, even on terms—a one-year delay before submission—that would not materially affect their subscription rolls."[155]

There was one publisher who did have the vision to see the potential of PubMed Central: Tracz. He had already suggested creating a central repository for research papers in 1998. Then, he went even further than providing articles from existing titles by founding a publishing house in the United Kingdom called BioMed Central—a clear reference to PubMed Central—with a radically new business model that was later adopted by many publishers. In an interview with journalist Richard Poynder published in *Information Today* in 2005, Tracz recalled:

> "When we started BioMed Central, we didn't know what the business model would be. We believed the data would have to be free, but it also became clear that—for the moment at least—authors couldn't place their papers in the public domain without some processes that cost money. What was also clear was that authors are more interested in publishing than readers are in reading. We also knew that authors have always been prepared to pay for having their papers published by paying page charges and paying for color pictures, etc. So we said: 'OK, we will turn the current model upside down and offer the research articles free to readers and charge for services to authors. We will take their papers, mark them up, find referees to review them, and generally act as an intermediary.' Of course, the charges are not really to authors personally, but rather to the funders of the research or the institutions where the authors work. We soon realized that such a business model could be very effective."[156]

It was a breakthrough moment, since it meant that academic work could be made freely available online, with costs covered by the institutions of the researcher, rather than requiring libraries and individuals to take out what were often costly subscriptions. The concept would prove crucial to important developments in the United States, led once more by Varmus.

In the wake of the rejection of E-biomed, and the lukewarm reception of PubMed Central, Varmus, along with Brown and computational biologist Mike Eisen,[157] wrote what they called a pledge: 'We called our advocacy effort the Public

Library of Science (PLOS)[158] to denote our goal of building a science library that would be open to all.'[159]

They promised not to publish in, edit or review for, or subscribe to, any titles that did not agree to grant 'unrestricted free distribution rights to any and all original research reports that they have published, through PubMed Central and similar online public resources, within 6 months of their initial publication date'.[160] The letter, published in 2000, struck a chord: more than 34,000 scientists from 180 countries signed the pledge. Nevertheless, it had little effect, with fewer than one hundred journals out of the 6,000 that existed in the field of biomedical sciences agreeing to participate. Researchers may have supported the pledge in principle but it was hard for them to follow through: the structure of the academic system meant that researchers needed to publish in prestigious journals to advance their careers. At this point, the institutional inertia was simply too great for them to overcome.

With a surprising pertinacity, the trio behind the idea for the PLOS did not give up. Instead, they decided the best way to overcome the main stumbling block, which was that publishers were unwilling to share their articles, was by becoming publishers themselves.[161] The PLOS was launched in 2001 as a non profit thanks to a $9 million grant from the Gordon and Betty Moore Foundation; its business model was the one devised by Tracz:

> "The essential feature of the financial proposal was the use of authors' fees to cover publication costs, which we estimated to range between one and three thousand dollars [per article]. We viewed such costs as reasonable; they would represent about 1 percent of the average cost of doing the NIH-sponsored research required

> for one manuscript. Furthermore, we thought the publication fees should be considered a part of the cost of doing research; the work would be worth very little if it were not published."[162]

Varmus made an important point: providing wider access to the knowledge they create should be considered one of the key aims for academics, not least because most research is funded by the public through taxation. For the first time, the Internet combined with institution-funded publishing made it possible for ordinary citizens to enjoy benefits of the research their taxes had paid for.

Around the same time, this publishing innovation acquired a name. In December 2001, a group of key people who had been working towards making academic work freely available online met in Budapest. They suggested the term 'open access' (OA) to describe the new form of online distribution. The group's declaration, published in February 2002 as the Budapest Open Access Initiative, begins:

> "An old tradition and a new technology have converged to make possible an unprecedented public good. The old tradition is the willingness of scientists and scholars to publish the fruits of their research in scholarly journals without payment, for the sake of inquiry and knowledge. The new technology is the internet. The public good they make possible is the world-wide electronic distribution of the peer-reviewed journal literature and completely free and unrestricted access to it by all scientists, scholars, teachers, students, and other curious minds. Removing access barriers to this literature will accelerate research, enrich education, share the learning of the rich with the poor and the poor with the rich, make this literature as useful as it can be, and

lay the foundation for uniting humanity in a common intellectual conversation and quest for knowledge."[163]

The definition of 'open access' contained a reference to the role of copyright in this new world:

> "By 'open access' to this literature, we mean its free availability on the public internet, permitting any users to read, download, copy, distribute, print, search, or link to the full texts of these articles, crawl them for indexing, pass them as data to software, or use them for any other lawful purpose, without financial, legal, or technical barriers other than those inseparable from gaining access to the internet itself. The only constraint on reproduction and distribution, and the only role for copyright in this domain, should be to give authors control over the integrity of their work and the right to be properly acknowledged and cited."[164]

The Budapest Open Access Initiative outlined two complementary strategies for achieving open access. One involves placing digital copies of articles in online archives that may be personal, institutional or subject-based, which has become known as 'green open access'. The other model is 'gold open access' and refers to articles published in online journals that can be freely accessed by anyone. The different approaches have provoked fierce debate within the academic community regarding which is better, something that traditional publishers have exploited to their advantage.

The next few years saw further formulations of open access principles. In June 2003, the Bethesda Statement on Open Access Publishing emphasised that '[c]ommunity standards, rather than copyright law, will continue to provide the mechanism for enforcement of proper attribution and responsible use of the published work, as they do now.'[165] In October

2003, the Berlin Declaration on Open Access to Knowledge in the Sciences and Humanities declared: 'For the first time ever, the Internet now offers the chance to constitute a global and interactive representation of human knowledge, including cultural heritage and the guarantee of worldwide access.'[166]

The increasing impetus behind open access was reflected in new requirements by some of the world's major funding bodies. Among them was one of the world's wealthiest charitable foundations,[167] the UK-based Wellcome Trust,[168] which endorsed open access in October 2003. Two years later, in what was a high-profile boost for open access, the trust made publishing in open access titles mandatory for all the work it funded. In 2005, another British funding body, the Research Councils UK (RCUK),[169] stipulated that the work it funded would require open access publication. However, when the final version of the RCUK's policy appeared in June 2006, it had a significant flaw, expressed in the following provision: 'Full implementation of these requirements must be undertaken such that current copyright and licensing policies, for example embargo periods or provisions limiting the use of deposited content to non-commercial purposes, are respected by authors.'

Embargo periods[170] refer to the time that the final version of a paper published in a traditional journal may not be made freely available to the general public in a repository. Thus, the RCUK was allowing publishers to hobble green open access, which is designed to make papers available from repositories immediately. As the leading theorist and historian of open access,[171] Peter Suber,[172] wrote at the time, this was a completely unnecessary concession:

> "Researchers sign funding contracts with the research councils long before they sign copyright transfer agreements with publishers. Funders have a right to dictate terms, such as mandated open access, precisely because they are upstream from publishers. If one condition of the funding contract is that the grantee will deposit the peer-reviewed version of any resulting publication in an open-access repository [immediately], then publishers have no right to intervene."[173]

The successful lobbying that led to this result was not the only evidence that publishers were starting to worry about the potential and impact of open access. In January 2007, the scientific journal *Nature* reported that a group of major scientific publishers had hired Eric Dezenhall, described as 'the pit bull of public relations',[174] to tackle the growing success of the open access movement. He suggested adopting simple forms of messaging such as 'public access equals government censorship'. According to *Nature*, Dezenhall estimated that his services would cost between $300,000 and $500,000. Nothing came of the plan.

Meanwhile, open access began to take hold in the United States. In 2007, the Howard Hughes Medical Institute, one of the world's largest endowed medical research foundations, made open access publication a requirement for the research it funded.[175] The following year, Harvard University became the first major US university to make all its research available as open access as a matter of course. The policy was framed in terms of copyright:

> "Each Faculty member grants to the President and Fellows of Harvard College permission to make available his or her scholarly articles and to exercise the copyright in those articles. In legal terms, the permission granted by each Faculty member is a nonexclusive, ir-

revocable, paid-up, worldwide license to exercise any and all rights under copyright relating to each of his or her scholarly articles, in any medium, and to authorize others to do the same, provided that the articles are not sold for a profit."[176]

As is so often the case in the world of copyright, the publishers pushed for new US legislation to rein in open access. In 2011, the Research Works Act (RWA)[177] was introduced with the aim of ensuring 'the continued publication and integrity of peer-reviewed research works by the private sector'. The bill was partly in reaction to a requirement from 2008 that all articles reporting on research funded by the NIH had to be made available in PubMed Central within a year of publication.

The RWA bill met with little support. An editorial in *Nature* from 2012 summarises the general feeling against the proposal: 'Why is this a ridiculous distraction? Because it tries to reverse a slow but strong political tide that is in favour of access, and because even its supporters believe that it has no chance of passing.'[178]

Although the bill was not enacted it nevertheless caused ripples in the academic world. Suber announced that he would not referee articles[179] for any publisher that did not disavow the Association of American Publishers' support for the RWA. British mathematician and winner of the prestigious Fields Medal Tim Gowers[180] added his support but chose to focus on the major Dutch academic publisher Elsevier[181] in particular. In a blog post, he noted: 'Elsevier supports many of the measures, such as the Research Works Act, that attempt to stop the move to open access.' For this and other reasons, Gowers said: 'So I am not only going to refuse to have anything to do with Elsevier journals from now on, but I am saying so publicly.'[182]

Gowers continued:

> "It occurs to me that it might help if there were a website somewhere, where mathematicians who have decided not to contribute in any way to Elsevier journals could sign their names electronically. I think that some people would be encouraged to take a stand if they could see that many others were already doing so, and that it would be a good way of making that stand public."[183]

Just such a Web site was set up by one of Gowers' readers, Tyler Neylon, called The Cost of Knowledge.[184] It declared that 'the right of authors to achieve easily-accessible distribution of their work' was key, and offered a detailed explanation of the issue.[185] It invited like-minded academics to declare publicly that they would not support any Elsevier journal unless it 'radically' changed how it operated. It was a huge success: a few months after it was launched, 9,000 people had signed;[186] in 2022, the figure was more than 20,000.

Unfortunately, like the earlier PLOS boycott organised by Varmus, the protest failed to achieve its goals. In fact, far from traditional publishers being forced to accommodate open access, they increasingly managed to bend open access to serve their purposes. This was evident in June 2012 with the publication of the Finch Report by the British government's Finch Group, which was 'tasked with proposing a programme of action and [making] recommendations to government, research funders, publishers and other interested parties on how access to research findings and outcomes can be broadened for key audiences such as researchers, policy makers and the general public.'[187]

The report noted: 'The principle that the results of research that has been publicly funded should be freely accessible in the public domain is a compelling one, and fundamentally unanswerable.'[188] Its main recommendation was that 'the UK should embrace the transition to open access'; more specifically, it suggested adopting gold open access rather than the green version: 'a clear policy direction should be set towards support for publication in open access or hybrid journals, funded by APCs [article processing charges paid by institutions], as the main vehicle for the publication of research, especially when it is publicly funded.'[189]

So-called 'hybrid journals'[190] carried articles that were freely available thanks to an upfront payment from a researcher's institution alongside other articles that were not. They soon emerged as a popular way for publishers to adopt open access principles. The theory was that hybrid journals were transitional: as more institutions chose to pay to make articles open access, so the price of a subscription would decrease until it was eventually fully open access and therefore free. A study published in 2015 in the wake of the Finch Report, which was accepted almost entirely by the British government, provided a clear indication of how the academic publishing world was evolving:

> "Open-access publishing options are now widely available: two-thirds of the world's journals offer an OA option of some kind; and more than three-quarters of the journals in which UK authors publish do so. By far the largest group of journals have adopted the hybrid model: just under half of all journals across the world operate in this way, and nearly two-thirds of those in which UK authors publish their work."[191]

Such a summation might seem a win for open access, however it soon became clear that hybrid journals brought a major problem with them. A report from the Wellcome Trust published in March 2014, noted 'the high cost of hybrid open access publishing, which we have found to be nearly twice that of born-digital fully open access journals.'[192] One of the most powerful arguments for moving to open access was that it would lower the costs for institutions because they shifted from paying for subscriptions to paying for publication. This was happening with pure open access titles but the rise of hybrid journals was annulling some of the benefit.

The situation was no better in 2015, when a Wellcome Trust analysis of its journal spending found that the average charge per article for open access publication in a hybrid title was still 64% higher than for titles that were purely open access—despite the fact hybrid titles received revenue from subscriptions too.[193] This and similar experiences elsewhere led to concerns that publishers were 'double dipping' by charging high fees for open access without reducing the overall subscription charges. So publishers were getting paid twice—and getting paid well.

Further evidence of publishers' subtlety and success in attacking open access can be found in another major announcement requiring open access publication of funded work. It came in 2014 from the Higher Education Funding Council for England (HEFCE),[194] which distributes billions of pounds of public money for research each year. The move was seen as positive by many in the open access world because the new HEFCE policy chose green open access rather than the gold open access route that the Finch report had favoured, by opting for the deposition of research articles in repositories.

However, there was a catch in the HEFCE's policy: it allowed publishers to place an embargo period on the release of research articles. This approach was an indirect result of the RCUK's blunder in 2006, when the RCUK could simply have stated that embargo periods were unacceptable. Since funding institutions had conceded the point in the past, they found it hard to refuse the imposition of embargoes by publishers. Yet the real problem lay with researchers routinely assigning copyright to publishers. As the director of European Advocacy for the Scholarly Publishing and Academic Resources Coalition, Alma Swan, said in a blog post about the HEFCE policy in 2014: 'It could have been really bold and required authors to retain the rights they need to provide immediate openness for the final versions of all their articles.'[195]

The fact the policy failed to do so had an important consequence, as noted by the scholarly communication consultant Dr Danny Kingsley[196] in a blog post in 2016:

> "[What] this HEFCE policy change means is that publishers have effectively shifted the HEFCE policy away from a green open-access policy to a gold one for a significant proportion of UK research. This is a deliberate tactic, along with the unsubstantiated campaign that green open access poses a major threat to scholarly publishing and therefore embargoes should be even longer."[197]

Her comment underlines what was becoming clear: traditional publishers had no problem with gold open access. They could charge high prices[198] for publication in their journals, because academics lack price sensitivity,[199] and are unlikely to stop reading a journal just because the subscription is expensive. The ability of publishers to take advantage of the shift to open access was emphasised by a series of what came to be called 'big deals'—bundles of subscriptions to a number of journals, with forced inclusion of titles that were of little interest to researchers. Such big deals were presented as a way to move to open access, but they were more about locking in institutions and shoring up profits.

What publishers really feared was green open access, since it provided researchers and members of the public with full access to articles, but without the publishers being paid. Preprints offered an easy way to offer green open access. As a paper from the International Science Council in 2022, entitled 'The normalization of preprints', pointed out:

> "[If] the record of versions [of a paper as it evolves] includes the final 'author accepted manuscript' this is functionally equivalent to green open access. Indeed, in having access to the full source text, high resolution figures, corrections, comments, and other ancillary files the preprint version may in many cases be more useful than the journal version. If coupled with live links to all cited articles that are not restricted by copyright, to the data they contain, and to text and data mining applications, the resultant interoperability would create new opportunities for a more creative open science."[200]

In fact, in many respects preprints could be even better than the final published versions, and offer one way to overhaul the current system[201] of disseminating research. Alongside the moves by publishers to promote gold open access over the green kind, Elsevier decided to take a more direct approach to deal with what it saw as a serious threat to its business model based on traditional journal publishing. In May 2016, it acquired the Social Science Research Network (SSRN),[202] which is the leading social science and humanities repository, and probably the second-most important preprint collection, after arXiv. Elsevier explained the rationale of the move:

> "SSRN members will benefit from the Mendeley [reference manager[203]] technology platform, its scholarly collaboration network, a leading reference manager and other personal library management tools. Additionally, SSRN members will benefit from access to Mendeley's researcher professional profile capabilities, person to person network communications and 'follow' capabilities. For Elsevier and Mendeley, adding SSRN accelerates its social community strategy, brings opportunities for enhanced author relationships, and provides access to a leading resource for content."[204]

Elsevier's strategy was to subsume preprints into the broader research workflow, relegating them to the preliminary stages that culminated in the 'official' publication in an Elsevier title. The publisher adopted this approach despite the fact that a study conducted in 2019 by researchers at the Los Alamos National Laboratory and the University of California indicated that 'the text contents of the scientific papers generally changed very little from their pre-print to final published versions.'[205] The company aimed to integrate SSRN into its other services, locking researchers even further into the Elsevier ecosystem. SSRN now covers a wider range of subjects than the name 'Social Science Research Network' suggests and is an indication of the company's ambition. Other major publishers are also busily incorporating preprints into their publishing solutions,[206] which increasingly encompass the entire research workflow.[207]

The growing profitability of the new business model based on institutions paying article processing charges (APCs)[208] brought a problem with it in the shape of what are known as 'predatory' open access publishers, 'brown open access'[209] or 'academic spam'.[210] The nature of online publishing means that costs are low even for a journal with numerous articles and this gives unscrupulous publishers an incentive to publish as many articles as possible, regardless of their quality. The result of this state of affairs was illustrated well in 2012 by the acceptance (subject to an APC of $500) of a paper entitled 'Independent, Negative, Canonically Turing Arrows of Equations and Problems in Applied Formal PDE'. Far from being the result of academic research, the paper was nonsense and randomly generated by the Mathgen program.[211] In response to the situation, University of Colorado librarian Jeffrey Beall set up Beall's List to catalogue 'potential, possible, or probably predatory scholarly open-access publishers'.[212] The list named thousands of publishers, indicating the scale of what is an ongoing problem.

Despite such concerns, gold open access became widespread, as more publishers realised that they could ride the wave of enthusiasm for open access while maintaining their profits. The academic publisher to benefit most from the state of play was Elsevier. Research published in 2015 showed that the profit margin of Elsevier's scientific, technical and medical publishing division steadily increased from 30.6% to 38.9% between 2006 and 2013.[213] These figures put the company on a comparable level with Pfizer (42%) and the Industrial and Commercial Bank of China (29%), and way above Hyundai Motors (10%), which were respectively the most profitable drug, bank and car-manufacturing companies at the time according to Forbes' Global 2000 list of 2014.

Gold open access and, to a lesser extent, green open access, dominated the debate about how academic papers should be published. But they were not the whole story. In 2007, Tom

Wilson, a researcher in the field of information science, pointed out that gold open access represented two different ways of gaining immediate access to papers.[214] The first involved institutions paying APCs—what Wilson dubbed 'brass open access'. The other kind, which he called 'platinum open access', required no payment from either the institution or the reader. However, the existence of the latter was then disputed[215] by open access pioneer, cognitive scientist Steven Harnad.[216] In 2012, the director of research at French National Centre for Scientific Research, Marie Farge, came up with the alternative term 'diamond open access'.[217] In 2013, two other academics—professor of Media Systems and Media Organisation, Paderborn University, Christian Fuchs,[218] and senior lecturer in Culture, Policy & Management, City, University of London, Marisol Sandoval[219]—published a paper in which they contrast diamond open access with what they termed 'corporate open access', which was undertaken to generate profits:

> "The article introduces a public service and commons perspective that stresses the importance of fostering and publicly supporting what we term the model of diamond open access. It is a non-profit academic publishing model that makes academic knowledge a common good, reclaims the common character of the academic system and entails the possibility for fostering job security by creating public service publishing jobs. Existing concepts such as 'gold open access' have serious conceptual limits that can be overcome by introducing the new term of diamond open access. The debate on open access lacks visions and requires social innovations."[220]

Even though platinum/diamond open access has been practised for a number of years, its often *ad hoc*, informal or unofficial nature has meant that it received little attention.

To remedy this, a major piece of research on the field was commissioned in 2020 by an important open access group cOAlition S:

> "On 4 September 2018, a group of national research funding organisations, with the support of the European Commission and the European Research Council (ERC), announced the launch of cOAlition S, an initiative to make full and immediate Open Access to research publications a reality. It is built around Plan S, which consists of one target and 10 principles.
>
> cOAlition S signals the commitment to implement the necessary measures to fulfil [the] main principle [of Plan S]:[221] 'With effect from 2021, all scholarly publications on the results from research funded by public or private grants provided by national, regional and international research councils and funding bodies, must be published in Open Access Journals, on Open Access Platforms, or made immediately available through Open Access Repositories without embargo.'"[222]

The in-depth 'OA Diamond Journals Study',[223] published in March 2021, revealed the astonishing scale of this little-known world of diamond open access journals. The study found some 29,000 diamond open access journals, publishing 356,000 articles per year. However, the share of diamond open access journal articles has since dwindled, as APC-based gold open access publishing continues to grow. Some of the statistics gathered emphasise how different the diamond open access world is from that of mainstream, for-profit gold open access:

> "The OA diamond sector is diverse in terms of regions (45% in Europe, 25% in Latin America, 16% in Asia, 5% in the US/Canada) and disciplines (60% [human-

ities and social sciences], 22% science, 17% medicine). In Europe, more than half of them are based in one of the Eastern European countries. The majority of OA diamond journals are small in size, publishing fewer than 25 articles a year. OA diamond journals serve mainly a national authorship (in all disciplines, including science and medicine) but disseminate their output to a largely international audience. OA diamond journals are much more multilingual (publishing in several languages) than APC-based ones (38% compared to 14%)."[224]

Such a geographical and linguistic range is important because it addresses one of the serious failings of commercial gold open access. Initially, researchers in developing economies were unable to access knowledge in academic journals because the subscription prices were too expensive for their institutions; later, the APC costs became a barrier. Although many journals are willing to offer discounted rates for academics unable to pay the full rate, this is not a realistic solution long term. Diamond open access solves that problem by eliminating all costs for readers and researchers alike. Similarly, it is well known that open access titles tend to favour the most commonly spoken Western languages, above all English, as does academic publishing in general.[225] This preference acts as yet another barrier to those working in parts of the world using other languages.

Although diamond open access has many clear advantages over gold and green open access, it is not without its own issues, notably in terms of sustainability, as the 'OA Diamond Journals Study' noted:

"As far as the financial health of OA diamond journals is concerned, just over 40% of journals reported breaking even and 25% stated a loss. Almost one-third of journals reported not knowing their financial status, with over one-third of these reported by both university-owned journals and university presses. Furthermore, 19% stated not knowing their costs of the previous year. While 60% of OA diamond journals depend on volunteers to carry out their work, with 86% reporting either a high or medium reliance on them, they also reported a wide range of funding mechanisms to fund operations and development costs, from in-kind support, voluntary labour, grants, collectively-organised funding, donations, shared infrastructure, membership, funding proportional to the articles published, freemium services, Subscribe to Open, and more. Globally, however, it is to cover small costs: the majority (53%) of journals run on less than 1 [full-time employee equivalent] for their operations and 70% declared less than $/€10,000 annual costs."[226]

Solving the problem is straightforward, at least in theory. In 2016, Björn Brembs, a professor of neurobiology and fervent proponent of free access to academic knowledge, proposed cancelling all academic journal subscriptions and using the money saved to pay directly for publishing:

"The question ... is serious: of the ~US$10 billion we collectively pay publishers annually world-wide to hide publicly funded research behind paywalls, we already know that only between 200–800 million go towards actual costs. The rest goes towards profits (~3–4 billion) and paywalls/other inefficiencies (~5 billion). What do we get for overpaying such services by about 98%? We get a literature that essentially lacks every basic functionality we've come to expect from any digital object."[227]

Since then, many institutions have started to follow Brembs' advice to abandon paying subscriptions, as he details in updates to his blog. Yet there is one obstacle that axing journals and moving to some form of diamond open access would still be unable to overcome, as noted in 2008 by hacker and digital rights activist, Aaron Swartz.[228] In his 'Guerilla Open Access Manifesto', he wrote:

> "The Open Access Movement has fought valiantly to ensure that scientists do not sign their copyrights away but instead ensure their work is published on the Internet, under terms that allow anyone to access it. But even under the best scenarios, their work will only apply to things published in the future. Everything up until now will have been lost.
>
> That is too high a price to pay. Forcing academics to pay money to read the work of their colleagues? Scanning entire libraries but only allowing the folks at Google to read them? Providing scientific articles to those at elite universities in the First World, but not to children in the Global South? It's outrageous and unacceptable."[229]

Swartz had a solution, albeit a radical one:

> "We need to take information, wherever it is stored, make our copies and share them with the world. We need to take stuff that's out of copyright and add it to the archive. We need to buy secret databases and put them on the Web. We need to download scientific journals and upload them to file sharing networks. We need to fight for Guerilla Open Access."[230]

In 2011, he put his words into action and started downloading hundreds of thousands of academic papers from the JSTOR digital library,[231] using a connection at the Massachusetts Institute of Technology (MIT). However, he was caught after retrieving 450,000 papers in 12 hours, having altogether downloaded nearly 5 million articles. It is not known what he intended to do with them—whether to distribute them for free or simply to analyse them. Regardless of the fact that no harm was done and that he was in any case downloading work that had been largely financed by the public, he was charged with a range of offences that carried sentences up to thirty-five years in prison. In January 2013, two years after his arrest and still facing trial despite worldwide pleas to drop the charges, he committed suicide, a victim of the indefensible academic publishing system. He was only twenty-six years old.

Someone who shares Swartz's views on the need to make publicly funded research papers freely available to everyone is Kazakhstani bioengineer turned coder, Alexandra Elbakyan. In her biography, she writes:

> "I was 23 and I returned to Kazakhstan [from the United States] and started working as a freelance programmer. With that experience I was able to quickly in three days start Sci-Hub—a web service that solved a serious problem in science communication. I met this problem while working on my brain-computer interfaces diploma project. That problem is closed access to research literature. Publishers are using paywalls to block access to research articles, asking for high reading fees. A lot of researchers are against that, they created a movement for Open Science or Open Access. Sci-Hub is a PHP script that downloads articles for free to make them open access. Thereby communication in science is restored. Sci-Hub immediately became popular among researchers."[232]

At the time of writing, Sci-Hub[233] holds around 90 million scientific papers, which is a good proportion of all the field's scholarly documents available in digital form. To put that number in context, in 2014, it was estimated that there were 100 million academic documents[234] on the public Web. According to the site's statistics: '77% of the documents available through Sci-Hub were published between 1980 and 2020, and 36% between 2010 and 2020. The coverage is > 95% for all major scientific publishers. The total size of [the] Sci-Hub database is about 100 [terabytes].'[235] In 2016, an article entitled 'Who's downloading pirated papers? Everyone' appeared in the academic journal *Science*. It looked at the profile of Sci-Hub's users:

> "The Sci-Hub data provide the first detailed view of what is becoming the world's de facto open-access research library. Among the revelations that may surprise both fans and foes alike: Sci-Hub users are not limited to the developing world. Some critics of Sci-Hub have complained that many users can access the same papers through their libraries but turn to Sci-Hub instead—for convenience rather than necessity. The data provide some support for that claim. The United States is the fifth-largest downloader after Russia, and a quarter of the Sci-Hub requests for papers came from the 34 members of the Organization for Economic Cooperation and Development, the wealthiest nations with, supposedly, the best journal access. In fact, some of the most intense use of Sci-Hub appears to be happening on the campuses of US and European universities."[236]

Sci-Hub's popularity derives from a number of factors. For researchers in developing countries, it is often the only way they can reliably access key papers without having to depend upon the possibly fleeting mercy of publishers making copies available freely or cheaply. For academics in wealthier nations, Sci-Hub is attractive because it is easier to use than negotiating complex authentication systems that seem designed to make accessing knowledge hard. Finally, one of the chief reasons that so many people use the site is that Sci-Hub realises a long-held dream of creating a single point of access to almost all scientific knowledge.

Such popularity combined with ease of use make Sci-Hub the top enemy for academic publishers. Leading the attack on Sci-Hub was Elsevier, which sought and obtained an injunction[237] against the site in 2015, when it was located at sci-hub.org. Elbakyan simply moved to a new domain, and then on to others[238] as subsequent court orders closed those down too. In 2017, a US court awarded Elsevier millions in damages,[239] although it seems unlikely the company will ever see any of it, given Elbakyan's geographical location in Russia and lack of assets. In 2019, Elsevier seemed to be opening up another front in its war against Sci-Hub: the company sent a legal threat to the site Citationsy—a citation manager—alleging that merely linking to Sci-Hub was copyright infringement. That argument was undercut by the fact that Elsevier itself pointed to Sci-Hub,[240] emphasising just how useful and important the latter site has become.

Elbakyan has always been hesitant[241] to give details of how exactly she manages to download so many papers. Her caution has allowed Elsevier to paint Sci-Hub[242] as an 'international network of piracy and copyright infringement by circumventing legal and authorized means of access to [Elsevier's] ScienceDirect database.' However, that is not a charge that can be made against another site containing a vast collection of academic papers, ResearchGate,[243] which claims to hold 135 million publication pages. Unlike the shoestring

Sci-Hub, ResearchGate is extremely well funded: in November 2015, it received investments totalling \$52.6 million from some well-known names, including Bill Gates, and the Wellcome Trust.[244]

ResearchGate's basic premise is encapsulated as: 'Share your research, collaborate with your peers, and get the support you need to advance your career.'[245] In other words, researchers are encouraged to upload their own papers and millions have done so. But an analysis in March 2017 by scientist and open science activist Jon Tennant[246] found that about half of his admittedly small sample of articles on the site were not compliant with publishers' policy on posting on other sites.[247] As ResearchGate says on this issue:

> "As a general matter, if you are an author publishing in a journal, you may be allowed to publish certain versions of your article, but not others, and privately share certain content with others. However, many journals restrict publication of final versions and impose limitations on private sharing."[248]

A few months after the post by Tennant, publishers woke up to the fact that ResearchGate was hosting millions of academic papers without their authorisation—just like Sci-Hub. The International Association of Scientific, Technical and Medical Publishers (STM)[249] proposed a solution for ResearchGate in the form of an upload filter that would determine whether researchers were permitted to post their own papers to ResearchGate.[250] When this proposal went nowhere, the Coalition for Responsible Sharing was formed by a group of publishers, businesses and societies. It wanted to act as gatekeeper for all academic papers—and thus knowledge—announcing:

> "Following unsuccessful attempts to jointly find ways
> for scholarly collaboration network ResearchGate to
> run its service in a copyright-compliant way, a coali-
> tion of information analytics businesses, publishers and
> societies is now left with no other choice but to take
> formal steps to remedy the illicit hosting of millions of
> subscription articles on the ResearchGate site."[251]

The coalition was threatening to send out millions of take-down notices to remove academic papers uploaded by the papers' authors. In addition, two of the coalition's publishers, the American Chemical Society and Elsevier, filed a lawsuit in a German regional court, asking for 'clarity'[252] on the legality of ResearchGate's activities. On 31 January 2022, the Regional Court of Munich found that ResearchGate is responsible for material that is made available on its site in contravention of agreements between publishers and authors.[253]

It is those agreements between publishers and authors that lie at the heart of the debate. Academic publishers generally pay nothing for the papers written by academics, and nothing for the work of referees that vet them. Yet in addition to this free labour, publishers typically insist that the authors assign the copyright in the article to the publisher, thereby losing control of it. This transfer means that publishers are able to refuse to allow researchers to post their own articles to ResearchGate, even though the researchers themselves want their work to appear on the site in order to be shared and discussed as widely as possible. The assignment also enables publishers to pursue sites like Sci-Hub, despite its global popularity, and the great benefits it brings to societies around the world that are otherwise unable to afford the high subscription prices to gain access to what may be life-saving information. Finally. it is because of copyright assignment that publishers are legally able to stop the public from freely accessing taxpayer-supported research.

This absurd situation has arisen because thirty years ago, copyright was an obscure detail that was almost completely irrelevant to researchers. They were happy to assign copyright to publishers because the latter demanded it, and their actions seemed to incur no penalties. But copyright has come to be embedded at the heart of the Internet's operation and is the key obstacle to greater access to knowledge. Indeed, the outdated practice of assigning copyright blocks hundreds of millions of papers from being shared universally and freely.

If researchers refused to hand over their copyright, their work would have a far wider audience and a bigger impact on the world, which is surely what every academic hopes for. Knowledge about an individual's work would lead to greater recognition, improve career prospects and probably lead—albeit indirectly—to greater financial rewards. There is no downside to doing this, except for the publishing houses that have grown lazy and fat on 35% profit margins. If the situation were to change perhaps publishers would have to innovate rather than litigate, which in turn might engender further benefits for society, the realm of knowledge and beyond. A shift to researchers retaining copyright would be a simple but powerful adjustment that is long overdue. Evangelising and propagating that cultural sea change should be a priority for the academic world in order to realise the enormous potential of the switch from analogue to digital that is fully underway in every sphere of life.

CHAPTER 4

Internet Users at Risk

Napster, three strikes and the Great Internet Blackout

Passing new legislation like the DMCA and Information Society Directive, both designed to stop people making copies of digital material under copyright, was only the beginning; there followed over a decade of attempts to use the harsh new laws to stop files being copied and shared. The main battles took place in the area of digital music, where the US copyright industry's assumption that it was in control of the situation thanks to the passing of the DMCA was to prove a colossal mistake.

In December 1998, the recording industry announced the Secure Digital Music Initiative (SDMI),[254] a consortium of more than 200 record companies, software houses and consumer electronics manufacturers that were working together to devise a new digital music format. From the copyright industry's point of view, the initiative's most important characteristic was the first word of its name: 'secure'. Above all, the SDMI format would ensure that people could not make copies of music files and share them over the Internet. This obsession with policing what members of the public could or could not do with the files they owned meant that the industry repeated the mistakes of the DAT format, whose key feature was also a technical mechanism to restrict copying. In fact, the industry's overarching interest in maintaining control made deciding on a format harder, and it spent many months arguing over the sought-after restrictions.

The delay proved fatal to the SDMI because in the meantime the MP3[255] file compression format, which had no copy protection, became so popular that the recording music industry were then unable to prevent people from sharing music in this form. The MP3 algorithm allows digital music tracks of a CD to be compressed around ten times, using readily available software for desktop computers.

Two things happened as a result. First, it was then possible to build new portable digital music devices that were small but held a dozen or so MP3 files. The most famous of these was Diamond Multimedia's Rio PMP300 player,[256] which introduced many people to the convenience of the MP3 format. Needless to say, the recording industry's reaction to this new technology was to sue. In October 1998, the Recording Industry Association of America (RIAA)[257] asked for a temporary restraining order to prevent sales of the Rio; a few weeks later, the judge denied the application. On appeal, the higher court ruled that the Audio Home Recording Act did not apply to a hard drive based MP3 player like the Rio.[258]

Secondly—and more importantly—the MP3 files were small enough that they could be uploaded and shared across the Internet, despite the relatively slow speeds available from the modems[259] in use at the time. Online services then arose to take advantage of this powerful new capability. Among them was the MP3.com[260] site, launched by entrepreneur Michael Robertson[261] in 1997. It originally offered free downloads of non-major label music in the MP3 format. In 2000, MP3.

com launched My.MP3.com, which allowed users to register their personal CDs and then stream digital copies from the Web site. This saved them the effort of uploading the relevant MP3 files first, which would have taken hours. Once more, the recording industry sued.

An even more important digital music service was launched by Shawn Fanning[262] and Sean Parker[263] in June 1999, Napster.[264] Unlike the centralised MP3.com, Napster took advantage of an approach to file sharing called peer-to-peer (P2P)[265] that is unique to the Internet. P2P allows users to run a program on their system that can access digital files held on other computers running the same software, anywhere on the Internet. Napster stored no digital material itself; it merely provided a directory service allowing its users to find the MP3 songs they were looking for on other users' systems. The service also facilitated the transfer of files between computers, making the process as easy and frictionless as possible. It is a good example of something that is only possible in a connected, digital world.

Unsurprisingly, Napster fast became extremely popular. Within nine months of its launch, Napster had 10 million users; within eighteen months, there were nearly 80 million registered users. Clearly, this presented an opportunity for copyright companies to use the power of the Internet to reach new audiences by offering similar services. Cory Doctorow explains in a *Walled Culture* interview why Napster was such an important moment in digital history:

> "Napster was a remarkable thing. It emerged at a moment in which 80% of the music that had been recorded was not available for sale at any price. You just couldn't buy it in the new market as a record or as a tape or as a CD. Maybe you could find a used copy, but

there was no one actually making it as a commercial object. And in a year or less, Napster turned all of that music into articles that could be sourced online at the click of a button.

It even had a plan for turning that into money. They had basically surveyed their audience and found that the median Napster user was prepared to spend $15 a month to keep Napster up. They said to the record labels: 'just tell us who owns what and we'll send them the money. It'll be the equivalent of people buying a CD every month for the rest of time.' And the music publishers said: 'No, we're going to sue you. We're going to put you out of business.'"[266]

In March 2001, an injunction was issued that effectively prevented copyright music being swapped across the Napster network. As legal scholar and expert on digital copyright Lawrence Lessig[267] writes in his book *Free Culture*:

"When Napster told the district court that it had developed a technology to block the transfer of 99.4 percent of identified infringing material, the district court told counsel for Napster 99.4 percent was not good enough. Napster had to push the infringements 'down to zero.'

If 99.4 percent is not good enough, then this is a war on file-sharing technologies, not a war on copyright infringement. There is no way to assure that a p2p system is used 100 percent of the time in compliance with the law, any more than there is a way to assure that 100 percent of VCRs or 100 percent of Xerox machines or 100 percent of handguns are used in compliance with the law. Zero tolerance means zero p2p. The court's ruling means that we as a society must lose the benefits of p2p, even for the totally legal and beneficial uses they serve, simply to assure that there are zero copyright infringements caused by p2p."[268]

It was yet another example of the copyright world preferring to shut down the exciting possibilities of new technologies rather than lose even 1% of its control. That might have been possible when using analogue devices but in an online, digital world it was not so simple. Napster had shown that the P2P approach to file sharing not only worked but scaled to tens of millions of users. Even before Napster was closed down, there were other implementations of its approach. One such file-sharing service was Madster,[269] which allowed users to send files via instant messaging services such as AOL Instant Messenger.[270] Users could share files with a limited set of people on a buddy list, which enhanced the privacy of all involved. The copyright industry successfully sued Madster, which had to shut down.

Gnutella,[271] originally just a client program[272] that accessed an online service, and later a general protocol (that is, technical specification) supported by many other compatible clients that implemented the same specification, also enhanced privacy, but in a more sophisticated fashion. Napster's weak point was the central server that acted as a directory for the file transfers between users. Gnutella dispensed with the directory and adopted a truly distributed system for finding music files. It was therefore much harder to track who was sharing music, since there was no central point to monitor who was active. Many of the Gnutella clients were released as open source software.[273] This means anyone can take the underlying source code[274] and write their own, modified and possibly superior versions, without needing to ask permission or to pay. Moreover, those writing open source clients do not need to be a formal company or even in one location.

As a result, the Gnutella ecosystem proved much more resistant to legal action seeking to shut it down than its antecedents.

The same is true of the BitTorrent[275] protocol, and the client programs that support it. BitTorrent is one of the most popular ways of transferring large files, which it breaks up into numerous smaller pieces that are sent independently, possibly from different locations. This feature has made it a favourite for sharing unauthorised copies of digitised films, which are typically much larger than MP3 music files.

The rise of these decentralised approaches forced the recording industry to shift its focus. A post on the Electronic Frontier Foundation (EFF) Web site explains how instead of quashing startups like MP3.com or Napster, companies started suing members of the public.[276] In September 2003, the RIAA announced the first 261 lawsuits against individuals it claimed were sharing unauthorised copies of music. One was a twelve-year-old girl living with her single mother. In order to settle the case, she was forced to apologise publicly and pay $2,000. A grandmother in Massachusetts was accused of downloading hardcore rap music. Although the RIAA ultimately withdrew the lawsuit, it was unapologetic. An RIAA spokesperson said: 'When you fish with a net, you sometimes are going to catch a few dolphin,'[277] evidently condoning the slaughter of dolphins. The lawsuits continued to multiply, as the EFF details:

"The RIAA filed 5,460 lawsuits during 2004, ringing in the new school year with a wave of suits against university students and bringing the total number of lawsuits to 7,437. By the end of 2005, the total number of suits had swelled to 16,087. In February 2006, at which point 17,587 had been sued, the RIAA stopped making

> monthly announcements regarding the precise number of suits being filed. As a result, it is now impossible to get an exact count of the total number of lawsuits that have been filed. The lawsuits, however, have continued, with the RIAA admitting in April 2007 that more than 18,000 individuals had been sued by its member companies, and news reports showing the number as of October 2007 to be at least 30,000.'[278]

If the case went to trial, the damages could be enormous. Perhaps the most famous example from this time involved Jammie Thomas, a single mother of two. In 2007, she was found liable for $222,000 in damages for sharing twenty-four songs on the P2P service Kazaa.[279] The judge, ordering a new trial for Thomas, called 'the award of hundreds of thousands of dollars in damages unprecedented and oppressive', and took the opportunity to 'implore Congress to amend the Copyright Act to address liability and damages in peer-to-peer network cases such as the one currently before this Court.'[280] On retrial, Thomas was found liable for even more: $1.92 million.[281]

When even judges call for a reform of the 'oppressive' copyright system, it is evident that something is deeply wrong. Moreover, the punishments in these cases were so manifestly disproportionate that the recording industry began to suffer serious reputational damage for bullying single mothers and grandmothers over the download of a few files. Cory Doctorow recalls that at one point a considerable percentage of the federal civil docket was just the record labels suing children. 'It was ugly and foul and stupid and counterproductive,'[282] he says.

Consequently the industries came up with a new approach to tackling the unauthorised sharing and downloading of copyright material, what came to be known as the 'graduated response'. Rebecca Giblin,[283] a professor at Melbourne Law School, has written a history of graduated response schemes that outlines their 'three strikes' approach.[284] Under these measures, users would not be taken to court if they were suspected of downloading unauthorised copies of material. Instead, they would be given a series of warnings or 'strikes'—typically three—before action was finally taken. That usually involved a fine, but originally the copyright industry hoped that repeat offenders would be thrown off the Internet entirely by their Internet Service Providers (ISPs),[285] despite the growing importance of the online world in everyday life. Indeed, the recording industry's main organisation, the International Federation of the Phonographic Industry (IFPI),[286] wrote in its 2007 digital music report:

> "Disconnection of serious copyright offenders by ISPs is the easiest and most practical response to illegal file-sharing. ISPs have been very slow to help the music industry crack down on internet P2P piracy."[287]

The outcry over lawsuits against vulnerable members of the community had taught the industry that it could never risk bringing lawsuits to inflict such extreme punishments on individuals directly. Instead, it pushed for national legislation that saw courts impose penalties for repeated unauthorised downloads of copyright material. The first country to bring in such a law was New Zealand in 2008, followed by South Korea and Taiwan in 2009. But the country that tried—and failed—to implement the three strikes idea most fully was France.

The French graduated response law is known as Hadopi,[288] an acronym for 'Haute Autorité pour la diffusion des oeuvres et la protection des droits sur internet' (High Authority for the Dissemination of Works and the Protection of Rights on the Internet). It refers both to the law and government agency that implemented it. As Marc Rees, editor in chief of the French computer title *Next INpact*[289] told *Walled Culture*: 'For right holders, Hadopi was an absolutely perfect system because it enabled them to offload the defence of their interests on the public budget, the state budget.'[290]

The first version envisaged throwing alleged infringers off the Internet for up to a year. It was blocked by France's Constitutional Council, which is an indication of how extreme its approach was. The second version came into operation in 2010. Alleged infringers were warned twice; if another allegation was made within a year of the second warning, the subscriber's Internet connection could be suspended. A fine of €1,500 could also be imposed. The first notices were sent out in September 2010; by December of that year, copyright companies were issuing between 25,000 and 50,000 infringement allegations per day, according to Rebecca Giblin.[291] At the end of July 2013, Hadopi had issued 2 million first notices and 200,000 second notices. There were 710 investigations to ascertain whether those who had been accused three times should be referred to the prosecutors.

In June 2013, the first and only disconnection order was issued, for fifteen days.[292] But it seemed that the judgment was unenforceable, because the disconnection only applied to Web access—other services like email, private messaging, the telephone line or TV services had to be preserved somehow. Three months later, the French Hadopi law was changed, dropping the option to disconnect people.[293] As a result, even the one disconnection called for never happened. Summarising the situation in 2013, Giblin wrote:

> "France has been described as 'very much the gold standard for graduated response public law.' However, when the data is carefully considered, there is scant evidence that the law actually reduces infringement. Since the dearth of infringement actions in its first three years of operation cannot be explained by a reduction in infringement, the most likely remaining explanation is simply that it is not very well equipped to identify and process the most egregious repeat offenders."[294]

Giblin went on to consider to what extent graduated response maximises authorised uses and found 'there's little persuasive evidence showing a causal link between graduated response and increased legitimate usage.'[295] Finally, she looked at whether the three strikes approach helped to stimulate the local music industry. Of New Zealand, the first country to adopt a graduated response, she wrote:

> "Every case has involved infringements of music performed by international artists such Beyoncé, Coldplay and Elton John. Not a single local New Zealand artist has featured. This can be at least partly explained by the fact that the biggest international artists are most likely to attract the most interest from illegal downloaders, and thus have a greater chance of detection. However, the clear message is that infringers are only at risk if they step on the toes of powerful international rightholders. Other content owners and creators, who may also be facing serious challenges from widespread infringement, effectively receive less protection than the majors."[296]

By 2020, France's Hadopi had been in existence in various forms for a decade. Working from Hadopi's annual report for that year, *Next INpact* calculated that in total the agency had imposed €87,000 in fines.[297] The cost of running Hadopi was picked up entirely by French taxpayers and came to €82 million. In other words, a system that had failed to stop people downloading unauthorised copies of copyright material, cost nearly a thousand times more to run than it generated in fines. It would be hard to think of a more complete failure.

During peak enthusiasm for the graduated response around the world, many other countries flirted with the idea, including the United States and the United Kingdom. But the copyright industry was active on other fronts, too. The European Union's Telecoms Package,[298] which was designed to update the European Union telecoms framework of 2002 in the light of the rise of the Internet, acquired amendments designed to boost punishments for copyright infringement, including the use of three strikes.[299] When the legislation was passed in 2011, another amendment placed limits on how this could be done. However, by then the problems with graduated response were becoming evident. Moreover, the United Nations (UN) Special Rapporteur on the promotion and protection of the right to freedom of opinion and expression, Frank La Rue,[300] said he was 'alarmed by proposals to disconnect users from Internet access if they violate intellectual property rights'.[301]

The copyright industry had already started to divert its energies elsewhere, in search of more effective and less contentious approaches to taming the Internet. In 2011, a major new bill was introduced in the United States, titled the 'Stop Online Piracy Act' (SOPA).[302] The battle against it and the similar Preventing Real Online Threats to Economic Creativity and Theft of Intellectual Property Act (PIPA)[303] bill of the same year, was an important moment in the wider appreciation of the impact of copyright on everyday use of the Internet. The idea behind SOPA, PIPA and the earlier Combating

Online Infringement and Counterfeits Act (COICA)[304] was to isolate Web sites that allegedly violated copyright law. This included requiring ISPs to block access by the public; preventing search engines from linking to them; and barring advertising networks and payment services from conducting business with them. It represented yet another approach to stopping people from downloading material online, this time one that focused on the sites rather than the users.

Although the US bills were ostensibly aimed at foreign Web sites, the fear was that any company or organisation with a server overseas, or that used a foreign domain name, could be at risk. As people soon realised, the powers they proposed could easily be misused to censor sites and threaten free speech; mistakes could see servers hosting thousands of sites blocked erroneously, or because a single infringing file had been uploaded. Even small sites would be forced to monitor all the material on their Web pages constantly, which was an impossibly onerous burden. If passed, the new legislation would chill innovation and prevent the launch of services because of fears that they might come within the scope of the bans. SOPA and PIPA represented an assault not only on the Internet culture of innovation, but also on the way that the Internet worked. The attacks were a move driven entirely by the demands of the copyright industry, with no input from the digital world.

However, by the end of 2011 the Internet community had become more self-confident and organised. One of the sites that helped crystallise organisation and resistance was *Techdirt*.[305] In 2022, the site's founder and editor, Mike Masnick, recalls how the resistance took shape:

> "The very first meeting that I was aware of involving a bunch of the different activists looking to stop

SOPA, it was the folks at Fight for the Future (calling in from Massachusetts to a meeting held at Mozilla) who suggested having an internet blackout (though this was targeted at the markup day in November, and was kind of a test run for what happened in January). People agreed—and some pointed to a similar kind of blackout that was done back in the 90s, but I actually thought it was an awful idea. I thought that there was no way that enough people would care or do anything to make it matter. And, my fear was that if it fizzled, it would demonstrate how weak this coalition was, and how easy it would be to keep passing even worse legislation over and over again.

I was wrong. People did get energized and all sorts of people from all different backgrounds and viewpoints came together to speak up and make it clear—loudly—that this was not to be."[306]

The Internet blackout of 18 January 2012 involved well-known sites such as the English-language Wikipedia pages as well as 115,000 smaller Web sites that went dark[307] for the day. Major companies including Google carried information about the protest. This unprecedented online rebellion spilled into the offline world, with dramatic impact on the politicians who had originally supported the bills wholeheartedly. In 2022, writer, editor and democracy activist Micah L. Sifry reflected on the protest campaign:

"An estimated ten to fifteen million people expressed their opposition directly: Congress' phone lines, fax lines and in boxes were all flooded. A million people signed a petition organized against the bills organized by the Electronic Frontier Foundation. Another 4.5 million signed a petition on Google's home page. In New York City, two thousand techies took off their

> lunch hour to rally outside the offices of Senators Chuck Schumer and Kirsten Gillibrand. Sponsors of the two bills, which was heavily backed by Hollywood and other copyright-centric industries, began visibly flipping their positions. Two days later, the bills were withdrawn from consideration."[308]

US politicians were shocked that so many people cared so deeply about two pieces of proposed legislation. The outpouring of anger over SOPA and PIPA was a seminal moment for the Internet community, which came together as never before to have a real and important effect on the world. It was also a turning point in the history of copyright legislation, which could no longer be considered as a dry, abstract body of laws that barely touched ordinary people, and which could thus be introduced and passed with little concern for public opinion. The SOPA protests demonstrated that millions of people in the United States and elsewhere cared about how copyright affected the online world, and would no longer be ignored. Director of digital rights advocacy group Fight for the Future,[309] which played a major role in organising the SOPA blackout,[310] Evan Greer,[311] said:

> "[It was] the largest online protest in human history, when millions of people drove phone calls to Congress in a single day and took a piece of legislation that was considered sure to pass and framed as an anti-piracy measure, rebranded it and helped people understand that, in fact, this was a piece of Internet censorship legislation. And effectively turned it into arguably the most unpopular piece of legislation in modern history. Congressional staffers to this day tell me that their bosses say to them, don't do anything that's going to get us in trouble with those crazy Internet kids."[312]

An important knock-on effect of the SOPA blackout and the withdrawal of the copyright bills was its impact on the Anti-Counterfeiting Trade Agreement (ACTA).[313] Blayne Haggart,[314] associate professor of Political Science, Brock University, writes in his book *Copyfight*:

> "Despite its name, ACTA was mainly concerned with digital-copyright issues; content industries received privileged access to the negotiations, while telecoms were generally shut out. ACTA represented a classic example of forum shifting; it was essentially an attempt to avoid having to make the compromises that characterized the [WIPO] Internet treaties by moving talks to a more flexible and easily controlled venue; any result could then be exported to non-signatory countries. With respect to its copyright provisions (it also covered issues such as counterfeiting and medicine patents), ACTA was an obvious attempt by the United States to continue pushing and expanding the Internet treaties, which were then about a decade old."[315]

The general public had no access to these negotiations nor was it even made aware of ACTA's existence until 2008, when a discussion paper was uploaded to WikiLeaks.[316] The leak of a consolidated text of ACTA[317] in March 2010 revealed that the European Union was proposing that ACTA should require criminal sanctions[318] for inciting, aiding and abetting copyright infringements 'on a commercial scale'. That included 'significant wilful copyright or related rights infringements that have no direct or indirect motivation of financial gain'. In what was an unprecedented move, this could include personal use.

The leak led to an official release of the text the following month. A conference of ninety academics and public interest groups from six continents analysed the proposals in detail, and issued what they called an 'Urgent ACTA Communiqué'.[319] They noted that in addition to the criminal enforcement requirements, ACTA would:

> "Encourage internet service providers to police the activities of Internet users by holding Internet providers responsible for the actions of subscribers, conditioning safe harbors on adopting policing policies, and by requiring parties to encourage cooperation between service providers and rights holders;
>
> Encourage this surveillance, and the potential for punitive disconnections by private actors, without adequate court oversight or due process;
>
> Globalize 'anti-circumvention' provisions which threaten innovation, competition, free (freedom-respecting) software, open access business models, interoperability, the enjoyment of user rights, and user choice."[320]

Despite the serious concerns raised by numerous groups worldwide, the negotiations continued behind closed doors. A text was agreed and the agreement was signed in October 2011 by Australia, Canada, Japan, Morocco, New Zealand, Singapore, South Korea and the United States. In January 2012, Mexico, the European Union and twenty-two member states signed too. But the agreement would only come into force once six of the signatories had formally ratified the deal. This meant that the battle to stop ACTA, with its damaging copyright provisions, was not over.

Protests against ACTA began in Poland where thousands of people took to the streets to demonstrate against the agreement.[321] The Polish prime minister Donald Tusk[322] called this expression of people's feelings 'blackmail' and said Poland would sign ACTA anyway.[323] In February 2012, further protests took place in many countries across Europe, and Bulgaria, Czech Republic, Latvia and Poland[324] went on to halt ratification. In April, the Member of the European Parliament (MEP) steering the ACTA legislation in the European Parliament, David Martin,[325] announced: '[In] the end I think the hopes of ACTA are outweighed by the fears; my recommendation is that we reject ACTA'.[326]

At the end of May, three European Union Parliament committees came out against it.[327] In June, they were joined by two more.[328] Finally, on 4 July 2012, the European Parliament rejected ACTA by 478 votes to thirty-nine, with 165 abstentions. Without parliament's support, the European Union could not ratify ACTA and without the European Union, ACTA was dead.[329] Reacting to the dramatic turn-around in the fortunes of ACTA, European Parliament President Martin Schultz[330] said:

> "The debate on ACTA demonstrated the existence of European public opinion that transcends national borders. All over Europe, people were engaged in protests and debates. The mobilisation of public opinion was unprecedented. As the President of the European Parliament, I am committed to dialogue with citizens and to make Europe more democratic and understandable."[331]

Inspired by the success of the SOPA fight, people had taken to the streets in Europe to protest against ACTA, which would have brought in bad copyright legislation when European Union Member States were forced to implement ACTA's measures. As with SOPA, it was a turning point. For the first time, large numbers of ordinary—and mostly young—people in Europe had taken direct action against proposals that would have harmed the digital world that had become so important to them. Nevertheless, the shock defeats of

SOPA and ACTA did not prevent the copyright industry and its supporters in governments around the world from pushing for new laws that would enshrine yet more unbalanced approaches to copyright. But at least they were now aware that it was no longer possible to assume that ordinary people cared little about abstruse issues of copyright law, and that they must expect real resistance to their plans to bend it even further to their advantage.

CHAPTER 5

From Scare Tactics to Censorship
Big Content's wrongful takedowns and Web site blocking

Online platforms often give access to digital material that is under copyright. If any of that content is infringing, then the platform would potentially be liable as well as the person who uploaded it. Online companies want to be immune to the consequences of any copyright infringement committed by their users. However, companies in the copyright industry demand the ability to protect their copyright material.

To address this tension, the DMCA provides online companies with a 'safe harbour'. The Online Copyright Infringement Liability Limitation Act (OCILLA)[332] was passed as part of the DMCA legislation. It is often referred to as 'DMCA 512' because it added Section 512 to Title 17 of the United States Code[333] that outlines US copyright law. It aims to strike a balance between the concerns of the online and copyright worlds by creating safe harbours for intermediaries provided they fulfil certain conditions. Importantly, companies that are able to meet these conditions do not need to actively seek out infringements on their systems: general monitoring is not required.

There are four distinct safe harbours. One is for companies that are serving as a 'mere conduit' of material (Internet access providers); another is when they store material temporarily while it is transmitted over the Internet (cacheing); held longer term (hosting); and finally, one for a company that links users to other sites, such as a search engine. To enjoy the benefits of one of these safe harbours, an online service must also have no knowledge of any infringing content, not benefit from it financially and—crucially—take down infringing material when it becomes aware of it.

The 'notice and takedown' system foresees that the copyright industry will send takedown notices when they discover infringements on a site to the relevant Internet companies, asking for removal. The person who uploaded the material can send a counter-notice. Such a response may trigger a lawsuit from the company claiming copyright. If it does not, the site owner may restore the material that was taken down.

Although the safe harbour approach is designed to provide a balanced solution to the requirements of both the copyright companies and the online service providers, it masks a deeper inequality that is typical of the copyright world. Takedown notices are generally sent by lawyers or specialists who carry out this operation all the time, often thousands of times a day, using automated systems. They know the details of the law and are only required to provide a statement that they have a 'good faith belief' that the use of the copyright material is unauthorised. Associate director of Policy and Activism at the Electronic Frontier Foundation (EFF), Katharine Trendacosta,[334] explains the detrimental impact of takedown notices:

> "[US] case law has said that as long as the people who sent the takedown have a good faith belief that it's in-

fringement, they can send the takedown without violating the statute for bogus takedowns. And that's a problem, because what it means is, if you are sending takedowns, you are better off not researching what's allowed and what isn't. You're better off believing that someone saying something bad about your work is infringement when that is definitely not it. Because then you can argue in court that that's what you believed, and it counts.'[335]

The recipients of takedown notices are usually ordinary members of the public. They are unlikely to have any legal training yet must respond to a formal legal notification if they wish to send a counter-notice. In addition, their counterclaim must include contact information. For an individual, that will mean personal contact details—probably the last thing that an individual wishes to hand over to a company threatening them with legal action. Finally, the counter-notice must include a statement 'under penalty of perjury' that the material was taken down by mistake. Many will quail at the thought that they risk being convicted of perjury and this stands in stark contrast to the mere 'good faith belief' required from the sender of a takedown request. Consequently, most people will simply accept that their material is removed, even if it was legal, for instance under fair use.

Given the hidden bias of takedown notices in favour of the copyright industry, it is no wonder that they have been used increasingly. Research in 2014 noted: 'From a mere 7,374 notices and 27,035 takedown requests in 2010, by the end of 2012, a total of 435,063 notices and more than fifty-four million takedown requests have been issued'.[336] Since then, the numbers have ballooned. The principal recipient of DMCA takedown requests is Google, because of the central importance of its search engine to most people's use of the

Internet. At the time of writing, Google had received more than 5.7 billion takedown requests.[337] Another indication of how widely takedown notices are used is provided by the Lumen project of the Berkman Klein Center for Internet & Society at Harvard University, which collects and analyses requests to remove material from the Internet: 'As of the end of 2021, the project hosts over eighteen million notices, referencing close to four and a half billion URLs.'[338]

In 2017, a report consisting of three studies examined how the notice and takedown system has been working in practice.[339] The first study explores a major shift in how takedown notices are sent, which explains in part the huge rise in the numbers:

> "[Some] rightsholders have transformed their notice sending practices by adopting automated systems to detect infringing content and send takedown notices. For some OSPs [online service providers], this automation increased the annual number of notices they received to hundreds of thousands or even millions of requests. Some OSPs responded by sacrificing human review of the vast majority of takedown requests and deploying their own automated processing methods to accomplish takedown more efficiently."[340]

However, this is problematic because automated processes are unable to appreciate the subtleties of copyright law. In particular, it is hard for them to recognise when a claimed infringement is a fair use of copyright material. This difficulty is confirmed by the second study in the 2017 report, which looked at takedown requests to Google Web Search. It found that 31% of them were 'potentially problematic':

> "One in twenty-five of the takedown requests (4.2%) were fundamentally flawed because they targeted con-

tent that clearly did not match the identified infringed work. This translates to approximately 4.5 million requests across the entire six-month set that could be expected to suffer from this problem.

Nearly a third (28.4%) had other characteristics that raised questions about their validity."[341]

The third study analysed takedown requests sent to Google Image Search. It found yet more problems:

"Strikingly, nearly 53% of the Google Image Search takedown requests were from one individual sender, Ella Miller. All of these requests appeared to be improper subject matter for DMCA takedown—none were copyright complaints.

Overall, including the Miller requests, seven out of ten (70%) of the Google Image Search takedown requests presented serious questions about their validity.

Even without the Miller requests, 36.3% of the remaining Google Image Search takedown requests were questionable."[342]

Although the studies reflect the situation some years ago, there is no reason to believe things have improved since. DMCA takedowns have been used abusively from the earliest days, even for outright fraud.[343] In 2009, patent lawyer Jeffrey Cobia[344] wrote an article listing numerous examples of abuse that fall into three broad categories.[345] The first is where fair use material is taken down unjustly; the second is where the person sending the takedown notice has no right to do so and thus violates the rights of the legitimate owner of the material; and the third where DMCA takedown notices are used for censorship. The *Lumen* blog cites an instance of where copyright law was used as a tool for censorship in 2016:

> "Annabelle Narey, the head of a programme at an international children's charity, posted a negative review of a building firm's construction work on Mumsnet, a popular website for parents in the United Kingdom. Shortly after, an individual by the name of 'Douglas Bush' sent a DMCA notice to Google for delisting this review on Mumsnet since it was allegedly 'copied' from Bush's original review on a different website. The DMCA by Bush is available in the [L]umen database… However, Narey countered this claim and stated that hers was the original review. Since Bush's review is no longer available online, it is probable that the review was backdated and the following DMCA notice was likely a tactic to remove legitimate content from Google since it was a negative review."[346]

What is unusual about this case is not that the original DMCA claim was made, but that Narey bothered to send a counter-notice given that most people do not. Hence it is tempting to use the DMCA to censor perfectly legitimate online material and the practice has become all-too common.[347] Indeed, the reputation management[348] sector has evolved to take advantage of this possibility. Online reputation management (ORM) specialists use DMCA takedown notices as a way of intimidating sites by persuading them to remove material that is inconvenient for their clients. In early 2022, the *Rest of the World* technology news site reported:

> "The [reputation management] industry has thrived, in part thanks to the effectiveness, ease, and low cost of making complaints using the DMCA. Hosting providers often lack the capacity or interest to investigate every complaint, and, under the law they can be held lia-

> ble for contributing to the infringement of copyright, if it's later proven, which can be very costly. Often, they simply comply with these requests."[349]

One case that was eventually settled out of court in 2019 involved someone allegedly going much further than simply sending false takedowns and it underlines why the DMCA system is tilted against people who are accused of infringing on copyright. An individual called Christopher L. Brady allegedly filed false DMCA claims regarding the ownership of videos on YouTube. It is then claimed that he sent messages to the people he had filed takedowns against, allegedly promising to withdraw them in exchange for money. For many, paying up probably appeared an easier option than filing a counter-notice. In this instance, opting to send a counter-notice had serious consequences, as the EFF relates:

> "According to YouTube's complaint,[350] shortly after [one] of the users Brady targeted did the thing they are supposed to do in the face of a bogus claim—send a counter-notice—they were swatted. (Swatting is [a] harassment technique that consists of calling in a fake emergency to 911, resulting in a large number of police officers, often with guns drawn, showing up to the target's home.) In other words, it's suspected that Brady was able to swat someone only because of the information contained in the counter-notice. Personal information from a counter-notice being used for harassment purposes even further disincentivizes people from taking advantage of their legal right to respond to bad takedowns. And counter-notices have been shown to be fairly rare."[351,352]

If submitting personal contact information in a counterclaim leads to harassment like swatting, then few will be brave enough to file one. Even the possibility that personal information will be abused—say, for stalking—will have a chilling effect on the process.

Despite the problems with takedowns, the DMCA's approach has been widely copied worldwide and the European Union's e-Commerce Directive of 2000 is just one example. Other countries adopting a similar approach include Chile, Singapore, Australia, Morocco, the Dominican Republic, Colombia, Panama, Peru and South Korea. They implemented DMCA-compatible rules to meet the conditions required by various US trade deals[353] in what is another example of how copyright law is changed without being subject to any parliamentary oversight as would be customary in passing legislation in a democracy. The lack of such public scrutiny means there is no opportunity for ordinary citizens to have any input.

Takedowns target particular items and sometimes remove legitimate material in the process. However, takedowns have limitations; when a site lies outside a court's jurisdiction, it is unlikely to obey its judgments. This situation has led companies to seek court orders to block foreign sites. The risk of lawful material being adversely affected is greater in such circumstances but that has not prevented the growing use of site blocking as a strategy, particularly in Europe.

Denmark was in the vanguard for Web site blocking.[354] From 2006, Danish ISPs were ordered to block foreign sites such as *www.allofmp3.com* and *www.mp3sparks.com*. In 2008, a court ordered the blocking of the site at *www.thepiratebay. org*, which became one of the most famous sites offering access to unauthorised copyright material and one of the most frequently blocked. On appeal, Denmark's Supreme Court considered the main methods of blocking a site, and chose Domain Name System (DNS) blocking.[355] When somebody tries to access a site, the human-readable domain name, for example *www.thepiratebay.org*, is converted into an Internet Protocol address (IP address), which consists of four numbers in the form 192.168.0.1. DNS blocking stops that conversion but if the Internet address is known the block can be bypassed by entering the Internet address directly into the browser.

DNS is not the only approach available. In 2004, the Société d'Auteurs Belge—Belgische Auteurs Maatschappij (Belgian Association of Authors, Composers and Publishers, SABAM[356]) management company representing the interests of certain groups of copyright owners in Belgium brought a case against Belgian ISP Scarlet Extended that explored whether another site-blocking technique, based on deep packet inspection (DPI),[357] could be used. DPI looks in detail at the digital traffic flow over a network to establish whether it contains unauthorised copyright files. Although it is the most effective way of finding and then filtering such material, from a user's point of view it is also the most intrusive, since it carries out continual surveillance of Internet activity. Such pervasive digital surveillance raises the possibility of human rights abuses, so the case was referred to the Court of Justice of the European Union (CJEU).[358] In November 2011, the CJEU handed down one of the most important European Union legal rulings concerning the Internet:

> "[The] Court finds that, in adopting the injunction requiring Scarlet to install such a filtering system, the national court would not be respecting the requirement that a fair balance be struck between the right to intellectual property, on the one hand, and the freedom to conduct business, the right to protection of personal data and the right to receive or impart information, on the other.

> Accordingly, the Court's reply is that EU law precludes an injunction made against an internet service provider requiring it to install a system for filtering all electronic communications passing via its services which applies indiscriminately to all its customers, as a preventive measure, exclusively at its expense, and for an unlimited period."[359]

Four months before the CJEU's judgment, a British court had ordered the Newzbin2 site to be blocked using a combination of DPI and IP address blocking,[360,361] whereby the numerical Internet address is checked for every communication. IP address blocking is problematic, because there may be more than one Web site running on a server with a single IP address. Blocking that IP address blocks all the Web sites hosted there, even if some are perfectly lawful. In the wake of the Scarlet Extended v. SABAM ruling, British courts dropped DPI, to impose DNS and IP blocking. The move was taken despite the porous nature of DNS blocking and the possible indiscriminate harm IP address blocking could cause. Such harm came about during 2013 in Australia when an order by the Australian Securities & Investments Commission (ASIC)[362] to shut down a single site accidentally took down 250,000 others.[363] The move was already controversial, since ASIC invoked a little-known fifteen-year-old law to order the block.[364]

In 2014, a worrying development in Italy saw Internet sites blocked by the national telecoms regulator, Autorità per le Garanzie nelle Comunicazioni (Authority for Communications Guarantees, AGCOM[365]), without the need for a court order.[366] This made using Internet blocks cheaper, quicker and easier, thus encouraging their wider use. A similar rapid site-blocking mechanism was introduced by Portugal in 2015.[367]

Yet even without such streamlined processes, Internet blocks have come to be used extensively around the world, except that is in the United States, since one of the main features of the SOPA proposal defeated in 2012 was this form of Internet site blocking. As the Information Technology & Innovation Foundation (ITIF)[368] observed in 2018:

> "[At] least 42 countries have either adopted and implemented, or are legally obligated to adopt, measures ensuring that ISPs block access to copyright-infringing websites. Some countries have had measures in place and used them for some time, others have the means to block websites but have not done so, while others are moving to enact website blocking. For example, in the European Union, at least 17 member states (including the United Kingdom, France, Belgium, the Netherlands, Germany, Denmark, Norway, Ireland, Sweden, Italy, Spain, Portugal, and Greece) have enacted website blocking, while others have relevant laws in place, but have not used them (such as Bulgaria, Croatia, Cyprus, the Czech Republic, Malta, Poland, and Romania). As of April 2018, it is estimated that over 1,800 websites and over 5,300 domains used by such sites have been blocked in the European Union (mainly in the United Kingdom, Denmark, Italy, and Portugal)."[369]

The ITIF claimed that such Internet blocking can reduce unauthorised downloads without 'breaking the Internet'. The foundation reiterated the claim in 2022, on the tenth anniversary of the SOPA defeat, suggesting that it is 'time to revisit website blocking'[370] and introduce US legislation to enact it. Although blocks of specific sites do not generally harm the rest of the online system, studies and court rulings in the United Kingdom, Italy, Spain, the Netherlands and elsewhere all show that site blocking is ineffective.[371]

Moreover, blocks can cause collateral damage by taking down sites other than that targeted. This was demonstrated in 2012 in the case of *Yıldırım v Turkey*[372] considered by the European Court of Human Rights (ECHR).[373] It concerned a block imposed by a Turkish court on an Internet site, hosted by Google Sites[374] in Turkey, whose owner had been accused of insulting the memory of a Turkish politician. The Turkish court was asked to extend the blocking order to all Google Sites, because it was claimed that this was the only way to shut down the offending site. Another user of Google Sites in Turkey, Ahmet Yıldırım, unable to access his Web site when the wider block was implemented, brought a case to the ECHR and won. The *UK Human Rights* blog reported:

> "In the case of Yildrim v Turkey the European Court of Human Rights decided that a Court order blocking access to 'Google Sites' in Turkey was a violation of Article 10 [of the European Convention on Human rights, concerning freedom of expression[375]]. The measure was not 'prescribed by law' because it was not reasonably foreseeable or in accordance with the rule of law."[376]

Perhaps the most extreme demonstration of how Internet site blocks can harm both the proprietors of a site and its users is the case of Megaupload.[377] One of the largest file hosting and sharing sites on the Internet, Megaupload was founded in 2005 by flamboyant German-Finnish entrepreneur Kim Schmitz, who changed his name to Kim Dotcom[378] the same year. At one point, Megaupload had revenues of $175 million and 50 million visitors daily. The company was hugely successful and at its peak, it was estimated to be the thirteenth most popular site on the Internet, accounting for 4% of all online traffic.

On 5 January 2012, indictments were filed in the United States against Dotcom and other Megaupload executives, alleging crimes that included racketeering, conspiring to commit copyright infringement and conspiring to commit money laundering. Dotcom was residing in New Zealand at the time. He described what happened next in a statement released in 2017 concerning the events that took place in the early morning of 20 January 2012:

> "[Seventy-two] police officers including the heavily armed Special Tactics Group (STG) and the Armed Offenders Squad (AOS) descended on the Dotcoms' family home in Coatesville to make a number of arrests at the request of the United States in an Internet copyright matter. Landing two helicopters just outside the family home, the entry team sprang to action, wielding M4 Bushmaster rifles.
>
> The forces entered the Dotcom home and held the Dotcom family, staff and guests at gunpoint. The officers caused considerable damage to the Dotcom property as they stormed through the house, around the grounds and over the roof. Mona Dotcom, who was 7 months pregnant with twins, and the Dotcom children were traumatised. Neither the Dotcoms nor their guests were allowed to talk to each other or their lawyers for an unreasonable period."[379]

The scale and ferocity of the raid were more in keeping with taking down international terrorists or drug lords, rather than dealing with alleged copyright infringement. In addition, the US Department of Justice seized Megaupload's domain names and closed down its sites.

As the extraordinarily complicated legal battles over Dotcom's arrest and the attempt to extradite him to the United

States unfolded,[380] it became evident that the case against Dotcom and Megaupload was not straightforward. At the time of writing, it is unclear whether Dotcom will be extradited and whether the court cases against him will proceed. What is certain however is that millions of Megaupload users have lost access to the files they stored on the service's many servers. In March 2012, the EFF filed a brief on behalf of US user, Kyle Goodwin, who lost access to his files. In December that year, a report by technology news site *Ars Technica* explained:

> "When the Feds shut down the file-sharing locker earlier this year, they seized more than 1,000 servers that Megaupload was leasing from hosting company Carpathia, including 525 servers in Virginia alone. Government authorities have been using the servers in the investigation of Dotcom and his company. Earlier this week, Carpathia announced that the 25 petabytes of Megaupload data stored on its servers have been costing the company $9,000 a day, and Megaupload has no way of paying its bills with its assets frozen.
>
> According to the EFF, authorities told Carpathia that after it completed examining the servers and had copied portions of the data, the hosting company could delete the files and repurpose its servers. Carpathia [has] noted ... that it would like to allow Megaupload users to recover their data, but has struggled to find a way to do so."[381]

Aside from the inconvenience the case has caused millions of people who, like Goodwin, had stored their files on its servers, the ongoing saga of the Megaupload takedown is a potent symbol of the exaggerated response that governments have made regarding claims of alleged copyright infringement. In this instance, there was a dangerous, costly show of force involving helicopters and seventy-two police officers, some of them wielding weapons. Such dramatic action was also unnecessary, as Dotcom said later: 'They could have easily knocked at our door at a reasonable hour and advised me of my arrest.'[382] Sadly, being reasonable is rarely how the world of digital copyright functions.

CHAPTER 6

How the European Union Passed Copyright's Worst New Law

Spying on the Internet with upload filters

Given the fast pace of change in the digital world, it is sensible for governments to bring in new copyright laws that try to take account of the important innovations that are being made. The problem is that new legislation has traditionally been an opportunity for the copyright industry to present a laundry list of demands, with the expectation that the government in question would implement them. But in the 21st century, the dynamics have changed. As the massive demonstrations against SOPA and ACTA showed, ordinary people not only cared about copyright and its effect on their daily lives, they were even prepared to take to the streets to protest about it.

At the end of 2012, the European Commission decided it needed to revisit its copyright law, the 2001 Information Society Directive. The commission announced it would begin a 'stakeholder dialogue' in early 2013, to gather input for a possible revision of the region's copyright laws.[383] The report on the consultation was published in July 2014, and provides clear evidence of public engagement:

> "The public consultation generated broad interest with more than 9,500 replies to the consultation document and a total of more than 11,000 messages, including questions and comments, sent to the Commission's dedicated email address. A number of initiatives were also launched by organized stakeholders that nurtured the debate around the public consultation and drew attention to it."[384]

The initiatives mentioned included those from 'Fix Copyright!' and 'Copywrongs.eu'—a further indication that people were keen to address the imbalances in existing copyright law. Some 5,600 citizens took the trouble to respond—despite the lack of an easy online interface[385] to do so: responses required a document to be completed then emailed. Other respondents included 2,400 creators, 300 institutional users and around 1,300 from the copyright industry. It is striking how divided the responses were, with those from ordinary users typically diametrically opposed to those of the copyright industries. For example, on the key question of whether linking and browsing should be subject to the authorisation of the copyright holder, users responded:

> "The vast majority of end users/consumers consider that hyperlinks to a work or other protected subject matter should not be subject to authorisation by the rightholder. They emphasise that the ability to freely link from one resource to another is one of the fundamental building blocks of the internet. Users do it every day when they post a Facebook update, put a tweet on Twitter, write a blog post, comment, etc ... Almost all end users/consumers consider that browsing should not require rightholders' authorisation as it is akin to

reading. Reading, viewing or simply listening to a work has never been subject to copyright and this should not change."[386]

Whereas the copyright industry held the opposite view:

"The vast majority of publishers, producers and broadcasters consider that the use of hyperlinks should be subject to the rightholders' authorisation, at least in specific circumstances ... Many respondents in this category also consider that browsing should be subject to the rightholders' authorisation. Some indicate that browsing should be lawful under the condition that the work itself was made available with the rightholders' consent. However, they say, it should not be assumed that all 'cache' memory copies are temporary or incidental under the exception set out in Article 5(1) of the InfoSoc Directive. Many believe that the facts of each case ought to be analysed in court. They also suggest that the rightholder should be able to decide whether a work is accessible for indexing by search engines."[387]

Respondents had two, completely incompatible visions. Ordinary citizens aimed to maximise the potential of the Internet, whereas the copyright industry sought to control it down to the last hyperlink. This dynamic played out over the next five years, as the three players in the European Union's legislative process—the European Commission,[388] the European Council,[389] and the European Parliament[390]—formed their views of what should be in a new copyright directive.

As part of the preparations for the legislative process, a Member of the European Parliament (MEP),[391] Felix Reda,[392] wrote a comprehensive report analysing the problems with copyright and proposing solutions. Reda represented the Pirate Party[393] and his approach reflected the concerns of ordinary citizens not the copyright industry. Although the final version of the report was heavily amended, the draft version contains some innovative ideas.[394]

These included strengthening the public domain—those works for which copyright has expired or to which copyright never applied. Reda advocated following the US model,[395] which required all works created by employees of governments, public administration and the courts to be in the public domain. The draft report suggested making the EU copyright exceptions laid down in the Information Society Directive mandatory, not optional. It proposed allowing libraries to lend out ebooks and prohibiting DRM from preventing people from making use of copyright exceptions provided by law.

The report also recommended the recognition of a right to create remixes and use copyright material in memes, which would appeal in particular to creatives such as the young artists who appear on the videogame live-streaming site Twitch[396] as the director of advocacy group Fight for the Future,[397] Evan Greer, has explained:

> "[There's] this entire generation of new types of artists and creators who are Twitch streamers, who are talking about video games while they play them, [and] online content creators that are making reaction videos of popular movies. And all of that requires reusing, recycling, resharing, existing art to create new art."[398]

Despite the popularity of such practices—and the fact that they do not interfere with the commercial exploitation of works—under the law of most EU countries they are infringing. Many more people might reuse material creatively in this way if the law were changed. Another recommendation was to grant a copyright exception for what is known as 'freedom of panorama'.[399] Reda explained:

> "Freedom of Panorama means that anyone can take pictures of public buildings and distribute them without permission of the architect—but it is not or only partially implemented in many [EU] member states.
>
> Example: While it is legal to take a picture of the Eiffel Tower during the day (because its copyright has expired) that is not the case at night, because there is an independent copyright protection of the Eiffel Tower's light show.
>
> Due to the territoriality of copyright, an image legally taken under Freedom of Panorama in one country may be illegal to distribute in another. For people sharing their holiday pictures after traveling to another member state, this is incomprehensible."[400]

The lack of general freedom of panorama illustrates how copyright legislation has failed to keep up with technology. When photographs were purely analogue, it was hard to share many of them, and so copyright issues regarding the architecture in the background of an image rarely arose. But thanks to smartphone cameras, people take pictures of their everyday lives in urban settings. The surrounding architecture appears in their photos that are then often posted online. There is no meaningful copyright infringement in such actions, but that is not what the outdated laws say in many parts of the European Union.

Despite the bold ideas in the draft report, the final version saw many of them removed. Reda outlined why:

> "The big political groups not only turned their backs on these ideas that enjoy vast public support according to the consultation—they specifically insisted that the mention of the unprecedented number of responses by end users be deleted from the report. This was the most

> successful political participation effort on copyright is-
> sues ever—and we must keep reminding politicians of
> the results. It is unacceptable that so many voices are
> ignored."[401]

Moreover, even though 500,000 Europeans had signed a petition calling for the freedom of panorama right to be written into law, it was taken out of the final European Parliament report. As a result, it is still copyright infringement
in some parts of the European Union to share pictures that
show buildings. The former chief executive officer and executive director of the Wikimedia Foundation,[402] Katherine
Maher,[403] described in a *Walled Culture* interview why it is a
challenge to get people interested in freedom of panorama:

> "[So] many people go to Paris and take a photo of the
> Eiffel Tower and post it on their social media feeds, and
> nobody comes after them for it, despite the fact that
> it's in violation of all sorts of Terms of Use. And so I
> think freedom of panorama tends to be a really tough
> conversation to have with people because there's not a
> tangible impact on their lives in most instances."[404]

Since everyone ignores what is an absurd aspect of copyright
and nothing happens, there is no pressure to alter the situation.

In the public consultation on the proposed copyright legislation, one of the topics many people were passionate about
was text and data mining (TDM).[405] This is the ability of
computers to aggregate large quantities of data and use advanced software techniques to sift through it to find information and patterns. People within the field who responded
to the EU consultation had clear ideas of how to maximise
the benefits from TDM:

> "Researchers and institutional users consider that text and data mining should not be subject to licences. They believe that a legislative change is needed to introduce a specific mandatory exception for text and data mining in EU copyright law. They consider that the exception should cover both commercial and non-commercial scientific research, as confining it to non-commercial uses would create legal uncertainty and impede the full development of the potential of text and data mining. According to them, technological protection measures [such as DRM] and contracts should not be permitted to override the exception. These respondents also consider that researchers should be entitled to share the results of mining with fellow researchers as long as such results are not substitutable for the original works which have been mined."[406]

Initially, the European Parliament committee leading the work on the Directive on Copyright in the Digital Single Market (or EU Copyright Directive) had intended to extend a new TDM copyright exception to everyone.[407] Unfortunately, Therese Comodini Cachia,[408] the MEP who was writing the report in the lead committee and who backed the move left the European Parliament. The MEP who then assumed the task, Axel Voss,[409] did not follow through with the idea of a TDM copyright exception for all. In the final version of what came to be known as Article 3 of the Directive,[410] the copyright exception for TDM was only for 'research organisations and cultural heritage institutions' and 'for the purposes of scientific research'. Even then, the new exception came with a loophole that allowed the owners of the input text and data 'to apply measures to ensure the security and integrity of the networks and databases where the works or other subject-matter are hosted'. This might mean throttling the rate at which networks and databases could be accessed or asking for the input of a CAPTCHA[411] test at regular intervals during download. All of which limited the utility of the new TDM exception.[412]

Under Article 4 of the directive commercial applications of TDM were allowed but could be blocked by the publishers of the text and data, without giving a reason. As a result, startups in the European Union in particular are disadvantaged compared to rivals in the United States and Asia, since companies in Europe typically need to pay for licences to carry out TDM. It also makes it less likely that journalists use TDM in investigations, which is a pity given it is an important tool for revealing information others want to hide. Such restrictions illustrate of how the copyright industry's obsession with requiring licences for any kind of use of copyright material is to the detriment of wider society and fails to reap the full benefits of technological innovation.

The same desire to control how people make even minimal use of material can be seen in a feature of the EU Copyright Directive that was not present in Reda's initial report, but added later at the behest of some of the European Union's largest newspaper publishers. It concerned something known by numerous names: 'link tax', 'snippet tax', 'publishers' right', 'neighbouring right', 'ancillary copyright' and, in German, '*Leistungsschutzrecht*'.

As the term 'ancillary copyright' suggests, this is an extension of copyright in favour of companies. It concerns 'snippets' of short extracts from news publications that typically arise as a result of searches made with sites such as Google. Even though the snippets are already covered by copyright, publishers wanted extra protection for them to force search sites to pay when snippets appear in search results. That is despite the fact that snippets link to the original article on a newspaper's site and thus drive traffic to it. In effect, publishers wanted to be paid to receive free exposure leading to additional visitors. What is remarkable is that the idea had already been tried in various forms across the European Union and failed in all of them.

In 2005, Agence France Presse (AFP)[413] sued Google over linking to its stories[414] so Google removed the AFP material from Google News. However, AFP customers that paid to syndicate news stories were up in arms because Google no longer indexed their site and hence they lost revenue. In 2006, a court ordered Google to remove all French- and German-language Belgian news stories[415] from Google News and its main cache. Five years later, a Belgian appeals court ruled that Google should pay for its past links to newspaper Web sites and also remove them.[416] As *Techdirt* pointed out at the time, if newspapers do not want Google linking to them, all they need to do is to configure a file called robots.txt[417] to tell Google not to index their site. The fact that publishers avoid doing so suggests they want Google to link to their sites because it drives traffic. Yet they also think they deserve to be paid for this. Indeed, when Google called the Belgian publishers' bluff and removed the links, traffic to the sites fell and the publishers then gave 'permission' to Google to reinsert them, at the same time promising not to sue the search engine again.[418]

In 2014, German publishers made even more extreme demands. The VG Media industry group (now Corint Media[419]) wanted 11% of gross worldwide revenue[420] on any search result that included one of their snippets. Once more, Google responded by dropping the snippets from its search results (but left the title and link). Yet again, the publishers caved in. They granted Google a 'free licence' to use snippets[421] but did not do so for other news aggregators, thus strengthening Google's position in the sector.

Despite these humiliating climbdowns, around the same time the Spanish Parliament passed a law that was even more demanding in that it made payment for snippets an 'inalienable right'. So publishers could not allow snippets from their publications to be displayed in search engines for free even if they wanted to do so. Google responded by shutting down Google News in Spain.[422] Google pointed out that Google News carries no advertising, so being forced to pay for snippets of newspapers was economically unviable. The Asociación de Editores de Diarios Españoles[423] (Spanish Newspaper Publishers' Association) reacted with alarm[424] at the possible decline in traffic. Their concerns were not unfounded and Spanish publishers suffered terribly as a result of losing traffic. An economic study commissioned in 2015 by the Asociación Española de Editoriales de Publicaciones Periódicas (Spanish Association of Publishers of Periodical Publications) found that there had been a decline in the number of visitors[425] to the eighty-four major Spanish online newspapers.

Article 15 of the EU Copyright Directive[426] (known as 'Article 11' during the legislative process) adopts the same approach as these failed experiments in trying to force platforms like Google to pay for using snippets. But Cory Doctorow points out in a blog post: '[The] problem isn't Big Tech stealing publishers' content; it's that Big Tech is stealing publishers' money.'[427]

Internet sites such as Google and Facebook dominate the mainstream online advertising market, a sector that used to be the mainstay of print newspaper revenues. Likewise, Amazon has become a major destination for advertising budgets that previously would have appeared in print newspapers and magazines.[428] In 2021, Amazon gained $31 billion in revenue from advertising, which is as much as that gained by the entire global newspaper industry.[429] The snippet tax is the wrong solution to a real problem; the right solution is reforming how the online advertising market works.

Although the introduction of an ancillary copyright was controversial, the resistance it encountered was nothing compared to the most problematic aspect of the EU Copyright Directive[430]: Article 17 (known as 'Article 13' during the legislative process). Presented by the European Commission in September 2016, Article 17 had two big new ideas. First, that online services based around large quantities of user-uploaded material, such as YouTube and Facebook, would be required to obtain a licence for copyrighted items uploaded by their users. This was the latest manifestation of a strategy that the European Commission and copyright industry had been advocating for some years. In 2013, a series of 'Licences for Europe'[431] stakeholder dialogues were held. They were based on the assumption that modernising copyright meant bringing in licensing for everything that occurred online. One of the four 'discussion' groups covered user-generated content. Tellingly, 75% of the participants came from the copyright industry,[432] underlining the fact that the views of ordinary users were considered unimportant.

The second idea behind Article 17 was more radical. In order to 'ensure the functioning of [licensing] agreements concluded with rightholders' the online services would be required to 'take measures', such as 'the use of effective content recognition technologies'. Article 17 would require sites where large amounts of content were uploaded by users to install filters that would block commercial material. In 2017, a paper on 'content detection tools', 'The Limits of Filtering',[433] noted that this was a move calculated to roll back the 'safe harbour' for online service providers (OSPs) provided by the DMCA and similar laws, which had formed the foundation for new Internet services during the previous twenty years:

> "The DMCA's limited liability regime prompted an unprecedented boom in internet activity to the benefit of users, OSPs, and creators alike. Although the DMCA has succeeded admirably in fostering the growth of the internet, some policymakers and copyright industry lobbyists have advocated for drastic changes to the copyright system to force OSPs to implement content filtering technologies in order to obtain the protections of the safe harbor and potentially punish them if and when those filters fail."[434]

The copyright industry framed these filters—and thus Article 17—as necessary in order to address what it called the 'value gap'. The term cleverly suggested that the main issue was that struggling creators were losing out, while skating over the fact that the media companies involved were highly profitable. In 2019, lawyer Annemarie Bridy[435] (who has since joined Google as copyright counsel) explained the idea:

> "The 'value gap' is a slogan that music industry trade groups created to sell policy makers on the idea that copyright safe harbors are not a sound policy choice for the whole internet but a legal loophole that allows YouTube to unfairly exploit the music industry's valuable intellectual property. According to the International Federation of the Phonographic Industry (IFPI) and other industry groups, safe harbors create a value gap between what content-sharing services like YouTube pay per stream of copyrighted music and what dedicated music streaming services like Spotify pay.

> The fact that copyright law treats YouTube and Spotify differently, they argue, distorts the digital music marketplace by suppressing streaming royalty rates across the board."[436]

Bridy pointed out that the claimed equivalence between music streaming services like Spotify and platforms like YouTube that are based on material uploaded by users is false:

> "Spotify is a closed distribution platform; it directly chooses and controls the whole universe of content it makes available to subscribers. It therefore knows exactly what content will be available on its service at any given time. No random subscriber in Paris—France or Texas—can upload a cat video to Spotify at three o'clock in the morning on a Sunday. YouTube, by contrast, is open to all comers all the time.
>
> Open services like YouTube face uncertain and continuous exposure to legal claims arising from their users' activity, including copyright infringement. Safe harbors were created because policy makers knew that infringement is inevitable on open, public-facing platforms. Closed services like Spotify don't enjoy the protection of safe harbors, not because they are being treated unfairly but because they don't need it. Considering the nature of the services in question, the comparison at the heart of the value gap campaign is inapt."[437]

One reason why the concept of the 'value gap' caught on with politicians was because it confirmed their belief that the big Internet companies, especially Google and Facebook, were greedy and too powerful to the extent that at times they seemed to act as if they were beyond the reach of the law. This did not make them popular with lawmakers. Members of the public, too, felt increasingly impotent in the face of these trillion-dollar companies' indifference to their complaints and concerns, and supported the idea of them being chastened.

As the EFF's Katharine Trendacosta[438] has explained, the copyright world shrewdly 'weaponised the way that people don't like those companies to make arguments for things that have nothing to do with the reasons those companies are bad—nothing to do with Amazon's abuse of its workers, nothing to do with Google and Facebook gutting the ad market.'[439] The supposed value gap had nothing to do with the real problems of these global platforms but that did not prevent it from becoming a convenient rallying cry.

In response to the European Commission's proposal for licensing and filtering, fifty-seven human rights and digital-rights organisations wrote an open letter asking MEPs to withdraw the measure:

> "Article 13 [17] of the proposal on Copyright in the Digital Single Market include obligations on internet companies that would be impossible to respect without the imposition of excessive restrictions on citizens' fundamental rights.
>
> Article 13 [17] introduces new obligations on internet service providers that share and store user-generated content, such as video or photo-sharing platforms or even creative writing websites, including obligations to filter uploads to their services. Article 13 [17] appears to provoke such legal uncertainty that online services will have no other option than to monitor, filter and block EU citizens' communications if they are to have any chance of staying in business."[440]

As is usual when the European Union crafts laws, the European Commission presented its draft document and the European Parliament then offered its own ideas.[441] These came in the form of amendments to the initial proposal put together by a lead committee—in this case, the Committee on Legal Affairs (JURI)[442] with the input of several other committees. As noted above, the person on the committee initially given the job of steering the copyright reform through the European Parliament, known as the 'rapporteur', was Therese Comodini Cachia, but she left the European Parliament in the middle of the process. The person who took over, Axel Voss, chose to ignore the explanations of why upload filters would not work, and gave the 'green light for censorship machines'[443] in his proposed text, as his fellow MEP Felix Reda put it in a 2018 post:

> "In doing so, [Voss] is dismissing calls from across the political spectrum to stop the censorship machines.[444] He is ignoring one and a half years of intense academic and political debate pointing out the proposal's many glaring flaws.[445] He is discarding the work of several committees of the Parliament which came out against upload filters,[446] and of his predecessor and party colleague MEP Comodini, who had correctly identified the problems almost a year ago. He is brushing off the concerns about the proposal's legality several national governments have voiced[447] in [the European] Council. And he is going against the recently published coalition agreement[448] of the new German government—which is going to include Voss' own Christian Democratic Party—where filtering obligations are rejected as disproportionate."[449]

Article 17 requires sites to obtain a licence for every kind of material subject to copyright, unless covered by one of the limited legal exceptions. Even if it were possible to license all music and every video, there are no structures in place that would allow sites to obtain blanket licences for everything else that might be uploaded in the form of text, images, computer software, 3D models, music scores, ballet scores and so on. Hence, the prime requirement of Article 17—to license everything—is impossible. Consequently, the second part of Article 17 becomes key and most large sites will be required to use upload filters.

One problem with implementing this approach is the vast quantity of material uploaded by users to platforms. In 2020, more than 500 hours of video were uploaded to YouTube every minute.[450] The only way to check those uploads for possible copyright infringements is to use an automated system. YouTube introduced Content ID as its upload filter in 2013[451] and by 2018 it had cost more than $100 million[452] to implement. But it soon became apparent how even an expensive system built by some of the world's top engineers, can have flaws in practice. In 2017, Reda put together an instructive page listing some notable Content ID fails.[453] They included:

> "A claim that a 12 second recording of cats purring contained works copyrighted by EMI Music.
>
> A recording of a Harvard Law School lecture on copyright was taken down because it used short extracts of pop songs to illustrate legal points.
>
> NASA's recording of a Mars landing was identified as a copyright infringement, even though everything created by parts of the US government is automatically in the public domain.
>
> When the animated sitcom *Family Guy* used a clip from an old computer game, the YouTube video from which

they took it was removed as supposedly infringing on *Family Guy*'s copyright."[454]

In further demonstrations of the problems with automated upload filters, Content ID has also taken down tens of thousands of videos documenting atrocities in Syria and a debate on torture in the European Parliament.

But the problem with upload filters is not just a matter of a few erroneous takedowns. Security expert Alex Muffett[455] built a software emulator to show the effect of imperfect filters operating on large numbers of uploads. His model allowed him to investigate how serious the overblocking would be for various levels of accuracy.[456] For example, if filters were correct 98.5% of the time, then around 150,000 legitimate uploads would be blocked in order to stop 1,000 that were infringing if, on average, one in 10,000 uploads was unauthorised.

The complexities of copyright law, which strain even lawyers and judges, are impossible to code perfectly into algorithms that can be used to filter out supposedly infringing material. This means that legitimate uses of copyrighted material for, say, parody and criticism may be taken down because they appear to be infringements to a dumb automated filter. It is unlikely that real-world filters could achieve 98.5% accuracy in this situation, in which case the degree of overblocking would be even worse than Muffett's figures suggest.

There are a few upload filters available commercially for music and video content. However, Article 17 requires upload filters for every kind of material that is subject to copyright. So sites will need upload filters that work for not only music and video, but also text, images—including drawings, paintings and maps—computer software, 3D models, music scores, ballet scores and more. At the time of writing, they do not exist, and it seems unlikely that many companies will make the significant investments needed to create even flawed implementations. Even if they did, companies would need to charge such high licensing fees for their use that most sites would be unable to afford them. Anecdotal evidence about the pricing of one of the few companies already offering filtering services for audio and video suggests that fees are of the order of the tens of thousands of dollars per month.[457]

In addition, once in place, EU governments might well push to use upload filters to block other kinds of material: they are the perfect censorship machines. That is what happened in the United Kingdom. When the telecoms company BT set up filters to block pornographic material from reaching its users, the courts allowed copyright companies to demand that the filters be used to block access to other sites.[458]

Practicalities aside, there are legal concerns about Article 17's upload filters. The European Union's e-Commerce Directive states:

> "Member States shall not impose a general obligation on providers ... to monitor the information which they transmit or store, nor a general obligation actively to seek facts or circumstances indicating illegal activity."[459]

This was confirmed by a ruling by the Court of Justice of the European Union (CJEU) in 2011, Scarlet Extended v. SABAM, mentioned in the previous chapter, which stated:

> "EU law precludes the imposition of an injunction by a national court which requires an internet service provider to install a filtering system with a view to preventing the illegal downloading of files.

> Such an injunction does not comply with the prohibition on imposing a general monitoring obligation on such a provider, or with the requirement to strike a fair balance between, on the one hand, the right to intellectual property, and, on the other, the freedom to conduct business, the right to protection of personal data and the freedom to receive or impart information."[460]

Article 17 itself re-affirms: "The application of this Article shall not lead to any general monitoring obligation." However, the issue of what constitutes "general monitoring" remains unclear.[461]

Article 17's upload filters may also run counter to one of the European Union's most innovative and important laws, the General Data Protection Regulation (GDPR),[462] widely regarded as the strongest data protection law in the world. Article 22 of the GDPR states: 'The data subject shall have the right not to be subject to a decision based solely on automated processing.'[463] Filtering is an automated decision process that has major negative consequences for citizens in the European Union, and is unable to 'safeguard the data subject's rights and freedoms and legitimate interests' as required by the GDPR, and thus may be illegal under that law.

As the wide range of potential problems with upload filters became apparent, supporters of Article 17 tried to pretend they would not be required. In June 2018, before a crucial vote in the European Parliament, the rapporteur for the new law, Voss, stated: 'No one is and no one will ever filter the Internet.'[464] The main supporters of the Copyright Directive in the European Parliament sent an email to fellow MEPs, lamenting the 'unprecedented spam campaign flooding our inboxes regarding the Copyright Reform.'[465] Worried by some of the points the emails raised, the missive continues 'we thought it wise to explain why all these spam emails are factually incorrect and do not reflect the actual text on Articles 11 [15] and 13 [17] that were voted for in [the] JURI Committee.'[466]

The email insists that Article 17 'will not filter the internet'. However, nonsensically it says 'specific copyright protected content will be identified on the basis of information provided by the artists to the platforms (digital fingerprint)', which is how filters work. Filtering sites involves filtering the Internet, or at least parts of it. Moreover, only a few days before the email was sent out, a senior member of the JURI Committee, the French MEP Jean-Marie Cavada, tweeted triumphantly about the inclusion of upload filters in the proposed text, which translates as '#CopyrightDirective: creation of a neighbouring right [for publishers] and automatic filtering of online content, a big step forward!'[467]

The MEPs' email also employs the word 'spam', in what amounts to an acknowledgement that they had received an unprecedented number of emails from EU citizens, many of which came via sites set up for the purpose. Such sites are often the only avenue open to ordinary citizens to express their view, because they are unversed in the workings of the EU legislative process. The active participation of so many people in the consultation proved how important copyright in the digital world had become to the public. So it is odd that such democratic engagement was not celebrated but cursorily dismissed as spam, perhaps indicating an indifference to citizens' opinions.

The same insistence that the new copyright directive would not herald the introduction of upload filters came from the Independent Music Companies Association (IMPALA),[468] which represents European businesses in the sector. In an open letter to MEPs ahead of a crucial European Parliament vote taking place on 5 July 2018, it wrote: 'There is no "Censorship machine", "upload filter", or "robocopyright".'[469]

Despite such attempts to deny upload filters were necessary, MEPs were unconvinced. They voted not to proceed to the final negotiation stage, but to reopen the debate. They may have also been swayed by input from the UN special rapporteur on Freedom of Opinion and Expression, David Kaye,[470] who raised the issue in a letter to the European Commission in June 2018:

> "I have concluded that 'States and intergovernmental organizations should refrain from establishing laws or arrangements that would require the 'proactive' monitoring or filtering of content, which is both inconsistent with the right to privacy and likely to amount to pre-publication censorship.' I have explained that '[a]utomated tools scanning music and video for copyright infringement at the point of upload have raised concerns of overblocking, and calls to expand upload filtering to terrorist-related and other areas of content threaten to establish comprehensive and disproportionate regimes of pre-publication censorship.' In particular, automated filtering may be ill-equipped to perform assessments of context in the application of complex areas of law, such as copyright and counterterrorism."[471]

Seventy of 'the Internet's original architects and pioneers', including Vint Cerf[472] (chief Internet evangelist for Google[473]), Tim Berners-Lee[474] (director of the World Wide Web Consortium[475]) and Jimmy Wales[476] (Wikipedia founder[477]), sent an open letter to the president of the European parliament.[478] They were similarly concerned by the likely impact of Article 17:

> "By requiring Internet platforms to perform automatic
> filtering all of the content that their users upload, Ar-
> ticle 13 [17] takes an unprecedented step towards the
> transformation of the Internet from an open platform
> for sharing and innovation, into a tool for the automat-
> ed surveillance and control of its users."[479]

Discussions in the European Parliament continued, the draft
text was tweaked, and MEPs voted again on 12 September
2018. The legislation was approved even though, as Reda
pointed out, it made 'nothing but cosmetic changes to the
controversial plans for upload filters and a 'link tax''.[480] The
European Parliament stated:

> "Any action taken by platforms to check that uploads
> do not breach copyright rules must be designed in such
> a way as to avoid catching 'non-infringing works'.
> These platforms will moreover be required to estab-
> lish rapid redress systems (operated by the platform's
> staff, not algorithms) through which complaints can be
> lodged when an upload is wrongly taken down."[481]

There is no mention of upload filters, rather there is a bland
reference to 'any action', as if it was optional and even trivial. It is easy to demand that 'action' must avoid catching
non-infringing works, yet this overlooks the fact that the
only action that fulfils the general requirements of the new
law is filtering uploads, which are imperfect and thus will
inevitably block lawful material. The statement is a peculiar
framing of what was agreed, since it implies that even the
impossible can be done if the law requires it.

The rapporteur Voss said he was very glad that the legislation had passed 'despite the very strong lobbying campaign
by the internet giants'.[482] Those in favour of the new measures adopted the stance that 'internet giants' were the main

lobbyists,[483] but this was not the case as an in-depth report on the issue published by the Corporate European Observatory lobbying watchdog in December 2018 discovered. It revealed that the copyright industry carried out most of the lobbying at the highest level:

> "Since November 2014 there were 765 declared encounters between lobbyists and the [European] Commission with 'copyright' as a subject. Over 93% of these were with corporate interests, but the list of main actors might be quite surprising: the lobbyists with the highest access were in fact not big tech, but the collecting societies, creative industries (including big film and music studios) and press publishers."[484]

Catherine Stihler,[485] CEO of Creative Commons,[486] was an MEP representing Scotland at the time. She remembers how intense lobbying activity was around the proposed copyright law: 'I have never seen anything quite like this. Either you were with them or you were the complete enemy, there was just no in-between.'[487]

When the so-called 'trilogue'[488] discussions started between the European Parliament, the European Council and the European Commission to harmonise the draft versions of the text they took place behind closed doors,[489] as usual. In January 2019, arguments were still raging among the European Union's national governments about whether the proposed text concerning upload filters protected users' rights sufficiently.[490] In early February, the German government reversed its position, which had been to block progress unless smaller companies were shielded. Later, it emerged that the German volte-face was part of some political horse-trading to obtain France's approval of the controversial Nord Stream 2 gas pipeline from Russia[491] (cancelled in 2022 because of

Russia's invasion of Ukraine). As part of the deal, Germany agreed that smaller companies would only be exempt from the requirement to establish filters for their first three years of trading.[492] It was as if the European Union wanted to punish its startups for surviving to the next stage of their evolution. Germany's agreement to abandon small companies allowed the trilogue negotiations to proceed.

Yet the climbdown by German negotiators did not go unnoticed. Millions of people signed an online petition[493] against Article 17 and its upload filters. Thousands of people took to the streets[494] in Cologne, Berlin[495] and beyond.[496] In Cologne, people carried placards reading '*Ich bin kein Bot*' (I am not a bot) in a reference to German MEP Sven Schulze's[497] claim that the thousands of emails he received from people voicing their opinions against the upload filters were part of a 'fake' campaign[498] conducted by bots. He arrived at this erroneous conclusion because many of the emails came from the gmail.com domain—a demonstration of his poor understanding of how Gmail works and how widely used it is. The Internet community staged other protest measures included blacking out the German, Danish, Czech and Slovak versions of Wikipedia, and holding an Internet blackout day.[499]

Meanwhile, the European Commission became more strident. The trilogue negotiations were completed on 13 February 2019. The day after, the European Commission published a post on its official *Medium* account that called those who were against the idea of upload filters a 'mob'.[500] The article was removed shortly afterwards and replaced by the note: 'We acknowledge that its language and title were not appropriate and we apologise for the fact that it has been seen as offending.'[501] At the same time, the European Parliament's Twitter account was also disseminating propaganda, including the misleading claim on a video that 'platforms will not be required to put filters in place'.[502]

Then just before the final plenary vote in the European Parliament was to be held, Germany's commissioner for data protection, Ulrich Kelber, raised an issue regarding privacy and upload filters. Given even flawed filters will be hard to create, there are likely to be only a few major providers serving the EU market. Kelber warned in a statement:

> "[Introducing upload filters would] result in an oligopoly consisting of a few vendors of filtering technologies, which would then be instrumental to more or less the entire Internet data traffic of relevant platforms and services. The wealth of information those vendors would receive about all users in the process is evidenced by, among other examples, current media coverage of data transfers by eHealth apps to Facebook."[503]

UN special rapporteur Kaye weighed in once more on the issue, this time just before the plenary vote in the European Parliament. He said: 'Such sweeping pressure for pre-publication filtering is neither a necessary nor proportionate response to copyright infringement online'.[504]

He urged the European Union to reconsider because:

> "Misplaced confidence in filtering technologies to make nuanced distinctions between copyright violations and legitimate uses of protected material would escalate the risk of error and censorship. Who would bear the brunt of this practice? Typically it would be creators and artists, who lack the resources to litigate such claims."[505]

Article 17 would hurt the very people its supporters claimed to be helping the most. Similarly, 240 EU-based Internet companies wrote an open letter to the European Parliament pointing out that far from supporting the local digital economy, Article 17 would boost that of its rivals:

> "Although the purpose of these regulations is to limit the powers of big US Internet companies like Google or Facebook, the proposed legislation would end up having the opposite effect. Article 13 [17] requires filtering of massive amounts of data, requiring technology only the Internet giants have the resources to build. European companies will be thus forced to hand over their data to them, jeopardizing the independence of the European tech industry as well as the privacy of our users. European companies like ours will be hindered in their ability to compete or will have to abandon certain markets completely."[506]

Another round of street protests was organised across the European Union[507] to coincide with the final vote in the European Parliament on 23 March 2019. Large numbers of people took part and estimates vary from 150,000 to 200,000 protesters in Germany alone.[508] Yet some politicians still refused to recognise that ordinary people cared deeply about the risks to the Internet. One German MEP, Daniel Caspary,[509] even saw the protests as sinister, alleging that:

> "Now an attempt is apparently being made to prevent the adoption of the copyright law with bought demonstrators as well. Up to 450 euros are being offered by a so-called NGO for participation in the demo. The money seems to come at least partly from big American Internet corporations. When American corporations try to prevent legislation with the massive use of disinformation and bought demonstrators, our democracy is threatened."[510]

In reality, as Emanuel Karlsten reports,[511] the digital rights organisation EDRi[512] awarded €450 in travel expenses to twelve activists who wanted to join the protests in Strasbourg. Moreover, the details of how such grants were made was available on a public Web site.[513] The claim that the protestors were 'bought demonstrators' is indicative of the reflexive contempt that some supporters of the EU Copyright Directive had for ordinary citizens daring to express their views by taking to the streets.

The final plenary vote in the European Parliament took place on 26 March 2019. Before the main vote, another vote was held to determine whether amendments should be allowed at this late stage. It failed by just five votes, 317 to 312. Had the vote passed, it would have opened up the possibility of deleting one or both of the Articles creating upload filters and the snippet tax. Yet even at this point in the passage of the legislation through the European Parliament, there was a dramatic twist. After the vote, the Swedish Democrats stated there had been a mix-up, as Karlsten reported on *Medium*:

> "Today we had three push-button votes on the Copyright Directive. On one of the votes, we pressed the wrong button: the vote on the order in which we would vote. If it had gone through we could've voted on deleting Article 13 [17], which we wanted."[514]

As Karlsten notes: 'Parliament was stopped by only a single vote from voting on the decision to delete Articles 11 [15] and 13 [17] of the Directive. One wrongly-pushed button fewer, and the result for all of Europe could've been very different.'[515]

Subsequently, other MEPs also revealed that they had pressed the wrong button too,[516] believing they were voting for something else. Unfortunately, under European Parliament rules, it is not what MEPs meant to do that counts, thus the preliminary vote stands, and the possibility that Article 15 and Article 17 could be deleted was never explored. The EU Copyright Directive passed by 348 to 274 votes.[517]

Although a terrible disappointment for opponents of the law, the EU Directive on Copyright in the Digital Single Market was by no means complete. As an EU Directive, its measures had to be implemented before June 2021 in national laws for each of the twenty-seven member states of the European Union.[518] This meant that there were twenty-seven skirmishes over what should appear in the local legislation and so twenty-seven opportunities to ameliorate some of the worst aspects of the legislation, including the upload filters and snippet tax.

Even before such battles began, some hope that upload filters might be removed came from an unexpected quarter. In April 2019, just after the final vote on the EU Copyright Directive, seven Member States expressed their concerns about the proposals.[519] Five of them issued a joint statement saying they believed 'the Directive does not strike the right balance between the protection of right holders and the interests of EU citizens and companies. It therefore risks to hinder innovation rather than promote it and to have a negative impact [on] the competitiveness of the European Digital Single Market.'

Then, in June 2019, the Chancellery of the Prime Minister of Poland tweeted about possible legal action:

> "Tomorrow #Poland brings action against copyright directive to CJEU. Here's why. #Article13 #Article17 #ACTA2."[520]

Details of the legal action at the CJEU did not emerge until August 2019. Poland wanted to remove the requirement in Article 17 that upload filters should be used when it is not possible to obtain a licensing agreement. If the CJEU decided it was impossible to remove this stipulation, Poland wanted to delete Article 17 altogether.

While Poland's challenge was heard at the CJEU, the member states began preparing national legislation to implement the EU Copyright Directive. Despite supporters of the law insisting that upload filters would not be required, once the law was passed they admitted upload filters would be indispensable. For example, the EU commissioner most responsible for instigating work on the EU Copyright Directive, Günther Oettinger,[521] conceded that 'upload filters can not be completely avoided'.[522] The French Minister for Culture, Franck Riester, even went so far as to promote their use.[523]

When France's proposed implementation was published in December 2019, it was even worse than the EU Copyright Directive itself. For example, as Reda explained in a detailed analysis of the text, the upload filtering provision would not only apply to platforms that profit directly from user uploads of copyrighted content, but also to those that do so indirectly, thus widening its scope.[524] Moreover:

> "The French draft law clarifies that rightsholders should be completely free in deciding whether to give a license to a platform, shutting down any efforts such as those discussed in Germany to avoid upload filters by introducing some kind of mandatory licensing solution. Whenever a rightsholder decides not to offer a platform a license, it will therefore have to use upload filters."[525]

France wanted its law to be as one-sided as possible. Online platforms would be obliged to seek licensing deals, but copyright companies would be free to refuse, thus forcing Internet companies to use the flawed upload filters. The French law was also stacked against users:

> "It's clear from the creatively named 'user rights' section of the draft law that copyrighted content gets blocked by default and users can only benefit from copyright exceptions if they complain after their content has already been blocked. Of course, getting your reaction gif or live stream unblocked a couple of days after the fact is completely useless, which explains why very few users ever make use of such complaint mechanisms where they exist. Under the French proposal, platforms have to offer a mechanism to deal with user complaints about blocked content (so the procedure is clearly 'block first, ask questions later')."[526]

Worse, the French proposal made it even easier for those claiming to own copyrights to use the law to block and censor material:

> "Rightsholders, unlike what the directive says, do not have to justify their initial requests to block content, but only have to respond once a user challenges the blocking of one of their uploads. During this dispute resolution, the content stays blocked. This opens the door to copyfraud, where companies falsely claim to hold rights in other people's creations, and the original author has to complain to have their own work unblocked. Although the directive says that all decisions by a platform to block content must be subject to human review, the French proposal only requires this in cases where a user complains after their content has already been blocked. Outrageous mistakes by fully automated upload filters are likely to become a lot more common under this proposal.

To add insult to injury, when users or rightsholders want to complain about the result of the redress mechanism offered by the platform, they are supposed to turn to a new regulator called ARCOM, which is the direct successor of HADOPI, the organization best known for administering the infamous 'three strikes' rule [discussed in Chapter 4], which could block users from accessing the Internet if they repeatedly violated copyright law. This is hardly a regulator that is known for impartially weighing the competing interests of users and rightsholders."[527]

In contrast, Germany tried to achieve balance in its implementation. Originally, it planned to allow users to 'pre-flag' the material they were uploading, as lawful, with the aim of stopping things such as memes and parodies being blocked. It would also prevent the filtering of an important class of material released under Creative Commons (CC) licences,[528] which aim to provide creators with greater flexibility regarding how their work can be used than the rigid requirements of copyright. Unfortunately, Germany's initial pre-flagging idea was dropped,[529] but the replacement implementation still had some admirable provisions, as a post on the *Communia* blog explained:

"[The] German implementation relies on the concept of 'uses presumably authorised by law,' which must not be blocked automatically. For an upload to qualify as 'presumably authorised by law,' it needs to fulfil the following cumulative criteria:

The use must consist of less than 50% of the original protected work,

The use must combine the parts of the work with other content, and

> The use must be minor (a non-commercial use of less than 15 seconds of audio or video, 160 characters of text or 125 kB of graphics) or, if it generates significant revenues or exceeds these thresholds, the user must flag it as being covered by an exception."[530]

Although the idea is sound, the actual limits are absurd. For example, the name of the EU Copyright Directive[531] in German is longer than 160 characters. Another important feature of the German version is the right of non-commercial associations to take legal action against platforms that block legal content repeatedly. In addition, users will be able to claim damages against false copyright claims. These are powerful options for users and fill a glaring gap in previous takedown systems such as the DMCA. The German legislation also brought in copyright exceptions for memes, remixes, mashups, fan fiction and fan art—all of which were missing in the EU Copyright Directive.

EU member states were required to pass their national versions of the EU Copyright Directive before a deadline of 7 June 2021 yet few did so, in what is a reflection of the difficulty of implementing a badly drafted law.[532] To help the process, the European Commission was supposed to provide an advisory document on how to implement Article 17. It finally appeared after the official deadline, and contained a flawed idea that hinted at the ongoing influence of copyright lobbyists.

The European Commission suggested that copyright companies would be able to earmark material they felt 'could cause significant economic harm' if uploaded without permission. Such a capability circumvents the principle that automatic blocking should be limited to 'manifestly infringing uses'. Since there were no requirements on what material could be designated as potentially harmful, this provided copyright companies with a loophole to avoid the user protections that supposedly made Article 17 balanced.[533]

Evidently, there was a serious divergence of views as to how the EU Copyright Directive should be implemented. This division was helpful to Poland in its legal challenge to Article 17, since even supporters of the provision could not agree on its implementation.[534] Nevertheless, on 26 April 2022, the CJEU dismissed Poland's action, stating:

> "[The] obligation, on online content-sharing service providers, to review, prior to its dissemination to the public, the content that users wish to upload to their platforms, resulting from the specific liability regime established in the Directive, has been accompanied by appropriate safeguards by the EU legislature in order to ensure respect for the right to freedom of expression and information of the users of those services, and a fair balance between that right, on the one hand, and the right to intellectual property, on the other."[535]

On the plus side, the CJEU's ruling imposed major constraints on the use of upload filters:

> "[A] filtering system which might not distinguish adequately between unlawful content and lawful content, with the result that its introduction could lead to the blocking of lawful communications, would be incompatible with the right to freedom of expression and information and would not respect the fair balance between that right and the right to intellectual property."[536]

However, no filtering system can 'distinguish adequately between unlawful content and lawful content'[537] because algorithms are unable to gauge reliably whether uploaded material is an infringement or a legal use of material for the purposes of say, parody or criticism. As the editor-in-chief of French technology news site *Next INpact*, Marc Rees, put it: 'Algorithms are as dumb as toasters.'[538]

The CJEU's ruling continued:

> "[The] providers of online content-sharing services cannot be required to prevent the uploading and making available to the public of content which, in order to be found unlawful, would require an independent assessment of the content by them in the light of the information provided by the rightholders and of any exceptions and limitations to copyright."[539]

This implies that online platforms can only block material if it is obviously infringing—for instance, if it is identical to a copyrighted work. When the CJEU's advocate general[540] Henrik Saugmandsgaard Øe[541] offered his preliminary opinion on the case in 2021 he came to the same conclusion:

> "[Sharing] service providers must only detect and block content that is 'identical' or 'equivalent' to the protected subject matter identified by the rightholders, that is to say content the unlawfulness of which may be regarded as manifest in the light of the information provided by the rightholders. By contrast, in all ambiguous situations—short extracts from works included in longer content, 'transformative' works, etc.—in which, in particular, the application of exceptions and limitations to copyright is reasonably foreseeable, the content concerned should not be the subject of a preventive blocking measure."[542]

Crucially, the CJEU emphasised:

> "Member States must, when transposing Article 17 of the Directive into their national law, take care to act on

> the basis of an interpretation of that provision which
> allows a fair balance to be struck between the various
> fundamental rights protected by the charter of funda-
> mental rights."[543]

Unfortunately, the CJEU fails to give any guidance on how exactly 'fair balance' can be achieved.

At the time of writing, several nations were still introducing legislation[544] to implement the EU Copyright Directive, so legal challenges to the exact wording in many jurisdictions are likely. In addition to the issue of what constitutes 'fair balance', Article 17 is replete with vague phrases including 'best efforts', 'high industry standards of professional diligence', 'expeditiously', 'sufficiently substantiated' and 'without undue delay'. Exactly how nations interpret such subjective valuations in local legislation will be closely scrutinised and challenged where appropriate.

The EU Copyright Directive was supposed to unify copyright law across the twenty-seven member states and bring it into the digital age. It has failed to do either. The directive does not take into account how citizens or companies in the European Union depend on the Internet as part of their everyday activities. Upload filters are incompatible with the way millions of people and businesses employ creative material online. They introduce unnecessary obstacles to the use of the Internet essentially because the copyright industry stubbornly refuses to adapt to the digital world, decades after it entered the mainstream. Instead, the directive seeks to shore up the outdated business models of powerful copyright companies. Ironically, along the way the directive makes it harder for digital startups in the European Union to compete internationally and locally.

Moreover, the vastly different interpretations of the directive by France and Germany illustrate that far from forging a large, vibrant digital single market, the ill-conceived and deeply flawed EU Copyright Directive will achieve the opposite by causing it to fragment into numerous smaller markets with different rules that take different and even incompatible approaches to digital copyright.[545] This state of affairs is bad news for small companies and startups in particular. Worse, the negative consequences of the EU Copyright Directive are even more serious than these kind of competitive issues suggest.

CHAPTER 7

Digital Monopolies

Relentless lobbying plus regulatory capture leave artists and the public powerless

The introduction of the EU Copyright Directive was important for two reasons. First, because it is a prime example of how the copyright industry is seeking to use legislation to impose analogue approaches—in this case, a presumption of the need for licensing—on the digital Internet. It was only able to do that by conducting a dishonest campaign about what the EU Copyright Directive would do and how it would do it. Secondly, the EU Copyright Directive is being put forward as the benchmark for digital copyright laws around the world. It is a good example of the copyright ratchet: the fact that once a law is passed in one jurisdiction that strengthens copyright in some way, it is invoked as a reason to strengthen copyright laws elsewhere, supposedly to create a level playing-field.

The EU Copyright Directive was used as a template soon after its creation. Pointing to the ancillary copyright created by Article 15 of the EU law, Australia brought in its own system that forces Google and Facebook to pay for sending traffic to newspaper sites.[546] Canada aims to do the same.[547]

In the United States, a new bill has been proposed called the 'Strengthening Measures to Advance Rights Technologies Copyright Act of 2022' or 'SMART Copyright Act of 2022',[548] which builds on Article 17 of the EU law. Legal scholar Eric Goldman[549] explained in a blog post:

> "The bill would authorize the Copyright Office to designate technology as 'designated technical measures' (DTMs) that all [user-generated content] services must implement, and copyright owners could sue any services that don't properly implement DTMs. In practice, copyright owners will force the entire Internet industry to adopt technology preferred by copyright owners—including mandatory filtering technology—and make the Internet services pay for it."[550]

As Goldman notes, the SMART Copyright Act would essentially place the US Copyright Office in charge of mandating new technologies to control what people can do online—for example, by requiring upload filters:

> "[The] SMART Copyright Act would give the Copyright Office a truly extraordinary power—the ability to force thousands of businesses to adopt, at their expense, technology they don't want and may not need, and the mandated technologies could reshape how the Internet works. That's an enormous amount of power to put into the hands of any government agency. It's especially puzzling to give that enormous power to the Copyright Office given its relatively narrow focus. The Copyright Office is not expert at Internet technology, content moderation, or the inherent tradeoffs in publication processes. If Congress really thinks DTMs are worth pursuing, that's a massively consequential decision for the Internet. It's an important enough decision that Congress should solicit a multi-stakeholder study

conducted by an entity with broader expertise than just copyrights, and Congress should vet and approve the recommendations itself through regular order rather than letting an administrative agency make such important decisions without further supervision from Congress."[551]

Alongside those clear knock-on effects of the EU Copyright Directive, there are some more subtle aspects that reflect deeper problems caused by attempts to impose outdated copyright approaches on the digital world. At their heart, they have the same underlying cause: monopoly power, which the EU Copyright Directive bolsters to a dangerous degree.

The ancillary copyright of Article 15 creates a right for news publishers to demand licensing fees for even minimal use of their material by online services. It is one that is likely to benefit established news publishers at the expense of new entrants, as research commissioned by the Spanish Association of Publishers of Periodical Publications revealed was the case with Spain's earlier snippet tax, introduced prior to the EU legislation:

> "The evidence available so far shows that the impact on traffic has been negative and that less consolidated publishing titles, such as digital native newspapers, have been the worst affected. This is not only because the total number of publication readers has been reduced but, in the case of online readers that would be attracted anyway (that is, who would visit the publications websites in some other way), they will surely end up visiting known publications with established brands, to the detriment of small and new publications."[552]

As Cory Doctorow pointed out in an interview on the *Walled Culture* blog, this is also bad news for the broader Internet ecosystem:

> "[The] fallout from a link tax is that smaller platforms, independent platforms that we hope might someday challenge Google and Facebook and the other major platforms will never get off the ground because they can't navigate the compliance."[553]

In Australia, the main media companies are profiting from the country's new snippet tax law, while smaller companies are struggling when negotiating with the digital giants.[554] The effect of ancillary copyright is to strengthen the larger companies, while weakening smaller ones and new entrants. In the United States, newspapers want lawmakers to go further. In 2017, the News Media Alliance (NMA),[555] which represents almost 2,000 news organisations, called on the US government to allow them to negotiate collectively through a special exception to laws against precisely this kind of collusion:

> "Antitrust laws are intended to address the injury inflicted by dominant monopolistic companies. Yet when it comes to the media, existing laws are having the unintended consequence of preventing news organizations from working together to negotiate better deals that will sustain local, enterprise journalism that is critical to a vibrant democracy. News organizations are limited with disaggregated negotiating power against a de facto duopoly that is vacuuming up all but an ever-decreasing segment of advertising revenue."[556]

Denmark's media companies have formed just such a 'copyright collective'.[557] But as Matthew Ingram of the *Columbia*

Journalism Review pointed out, there is an astonishing sense of entitlement at the core of the NMA proposal:

> "In effect, it is suggesting that mainstream newspaper companies are the only entities capable of producing quality journalism, and therefore they deserve a get-out-of-jail-free card so they can engage in what amounts to collusion. And they are hoping Congress will see Google and Facebook as the enemy.
>
> Here's a thought: What if these newspaper companies had spent a little more time trying to compete over the past decade or so, instead of relying on their historic market control to keep their profits rolling in? What if more had tried to improve their websites and their mobile versions, so that users wouldn't install ad blockers, or turn to other solutions like Facebook Instant Articles?"[558]

The industry's special pleading found sympathetic listeners among some US politicians, who have put forward the Journalism Competition and Preservation Act (JCPA).[559] As a letter to Congress[560] from the digital-rights advocacy group Public Knowledge[561] outlined, the JCPA would not alter the underlying copyright law. Hence, news publications would have no extra powers to prohibit Google and Facebook from linking to articles: 'a cartel of news sites is exactly as powerless to prevent Facebook or Google from linking to its members' content as a small site would be negotiating on its own'. However:

> "[This] bill could be interpreted by courts to implicitly change the scope of copyright, expanding the exclusive rights that news publications enjoy in their material beyond what any copyright owner has ever enjoyed. To the extent that this creates a new substantive right to

> demand that material not be linked to, this is unwise; to the extent that it interferes with fair use rights, particularly of the rights of users of platforms, it is unconstitutional and violative of our international obligations.
>
> The ability of one website to connect ('link') to other websites, without needing to negotiate to do so, is a foundational component of modern internet infrastructure. Linking is not, and has never been, an act within the scope of copyright. It is not within the statutory or common-law ambit of copyright law, as merely linking to a piece of external content is not a reproduction, display, performance, or distribution of that content. As such, rightsholders do not—and should not—have the ability under copyright law to prevent third parties from linking to their publicly available content. (Notably, the vast majority of rightsholders do not want such a right, and those that do already have technical methods which allow them to do so.)"[562]

The letter lays bare how copyright maximalism in the form of a snippet tax would attack the very foundation of the Internet: the ability to link freely. The fact that the JCPA provides an exemption from antitrust laws, which are meant to prevent such a dangerous concentration of power, is proof of how extreme the idea of ancillary copyright idea is. Even a study from the US Copyright Office concluded that ancillary copyright for press publishers is not the right solution to their problems.[563]

The most problematic element of the EU Copyright Directive is Article 17, originally numbered Article 13. It has two core elements. The first is that online services based around large quantities of user-uploaded material would be required to obtain a licence for those uploads. The second is a requirement to inspect and filter every upload if a licence is not obtained—even if that is because a company holding copyright refuses to give a licence.

The belief that the solution to every copyright problem online is licensing assumes that people or organisations can always be found to grant those licences, and that the process is not onerous. This is naive, as is demonstrated by the fate of the UK government's Copyright Hub. It was one of the few parts of the review of copyright and related areas[564] conducted in 2011 that was implemented. Drafted by Professor Ian Hargreaves,[565] most of the report's sensible recommendations on updating copyright for the digital age and strengthening the rights of users, were ditched because of resistance from the copyright industry. However, one key element of the report concerned copyright licensing, which drew widespread support from the same group. The report detailed the existing licensing approach:

> "Examples of inefficiency in copyright licensing are not difficult to find. The BBC has said that it took nearly five years to assemble the rights necessary to launch its popular iPlayer service. Among a group of young technology SMEs the Review met at a meeting at TechHub, half claimed to have had difficulty licensing others' IP across all rights. One SME, providing on demand streaming of radio shows and DJ mixes, reported it took about nine months of lobbying music collecting societies to make any headway on licensing. Others said that licensing discussions are inconsistent, with some users offered access to licences and others denied without clear explanation. Some were met with threats of legal action rather than a business discussion about terms. Others reported that it was simply impossible to get the information needed on what terms might be available, since there was no precise clarity about

who should be contacted and how to discuss licensing needs."[566]

The report proposed resolving the issue with a Copyright Hub, consisting of 'a network of interoperable databases to provide a common platform for licensing transactions' that would make obtaining licences for material simpler and cheaper than the methods used at the time. An article on Wikipedia about the project explains:

> "The idea was to make it easy and free for anyone to attach an identifier to any piece of content, and then to create a record with the Copyright Hub which would link that identifier to an authoritative record of information about the piece of content and its owner. The technology would also allow automated licensing processes to take place, making authorisation and creation of records of permission a very low cost process."[567]

The Copyright Hub was founded in 2013 with funding from the UK government. It was launched in July 2015,[568] and the Copyright Done Right[569] site was established. Ambitious plans were made, including the creation of browser extensions to allow Internet users to license copyright material. The Copyright Hub became part of the Ardito project,[570] which aimed to connect online content to rights information:

> "The vision of the project is that any user should be able easily to access such rights information. To fulfil this objective, we need a Rights Data Network (RDN), a network of connected e-infrastructures to automate the exchange of information about rights between owners and users.
>
> We do not start from scratch. The Linked Content Coalition [LCC] initiative has defined the technical framework. The RDI [Rights Data Integration] Project has

> demonstrated unequivocally how such a Rights Data Network could implement the LCC framework; and the Copyright Hub has provided a first implementation of how this works in practice. The time to go live with actual services in the market place is now."[571]

Nevertheless, no 'actual services in the market place' appeared. The Final Report of the RDI Project was released in 2016 and said: 'The RDI project has produced a set of tools and prototypes which the project partners, including the LCC and the Copyright Hub, now expect to take forward into production systems'.[572] Far from doing so, the LCC has not issued any kind of update on its work since April 2013,[573] while the Copyright Hub Web site has disappeared from the Internet. At the time of writing, The Copyright Done Right site was live, but on the page 'Want to get involved?'[574] there were no ways to do so; on the 'Check out our wonderful supporters',[575] nobody was listed. Nowhere on the site gives substantive information about how the Copyright Hub works.[576] The most serious attempt to make copyright licensing easier for the digital age has proved a damp squib and ended in failure.

Alongside innovative but unsuccessful attempts to reshape copyright licensing in the form of the Copyright Hub and related projects, there are more traditional systems, such as collective management organisations, also known as copyright collection societies. A report on the topic by the World Intellectual Property Organization (WIPO) in 2002 explained:

> "In the framework of a collective management system, owners of rights authorize collective management organizations to monitor the use of their works, negotiate with prospective users, give them licenses against ap-

> propriate remuneration on the basis of a tariff system
> and under appropriate conditions, collect such remu-
> neration, and distribute it among the owners of rights
> … although a collective management system serves pri-
> marily the interests of owners of copyright and related
> rights, such a system also offers great advantages to us-
> ers who, thus, may have access to the works they need
> in a simple manner from one single source, and—since
> collective management simplifies negotiations with us-
> ers, monitoring uses and collecting fees—at low trans-
> action costs.'[577]

Yet the history of such collective right organisations (CROs)[578] is not a happy one. The nature and scale of the problem is indicated by two reports published by Infojustice, an initiative by the American University Washington College of Law, in 2013 and 2018. The episodes in the first report 'reveal a long history of corruption, mismanagement, confiscation of funds, and lack of transparency [by CROs] that has deprived artists of the revenues they earned'.[579] Countries where CROs have been engaged in one or more of these activities in the 21st century include Australia, the Bahamas, Brazil, Canada, China, Columbia, Ghana, Italy, Kenya, the Netherlands, Nigeria, Romania, Senegal, South Africa, Spain, Sweden, Russia and the United States. In addition, CROs have demanded that people pay for licences in absurd circumstances as the Infojustice report of 2013 reveals.[580]

In 1995, the US CRO ASCAP (American Society of Composers, Authors, and Publishers) demanded that each of the 2,300 camps represented by the American Camping Association (including the Girl Scout camps), obtain a blanket licence for the public singing of songs.

Soza (Slovenský Ochranný Zväz Autorský/Slovak Performing and Mechanical Rights Society), a Slovakian CRO, has sought money from villages when their children sing. One case involved children singing to their mothers on Mothers' Day.

SABAM (Société d'Auteurs Belge/Belgische Auteurs Maatschappij/Belgian Authors' Society), a Belgian CRO, sought expanded protection for readings of copyrighted works. One consequence of their action was that it would require librarians to pay a licence to read books to children in a children's library.

SABAM sought a licensing fee from truck drivers who listened to the radio alone in their trucks.

The British CRO PPL (Phonographic Performance Limited) sought a fee from a hardware store owner who listened to the radio in his store while cleaning it after he had closed.

The Performing Rights Society in the UK sought performance licensing fees from a woman who played classical music to her horses.

Of particular note is the German CRO GEMA[581] (Gesellschaft für musikalische Aufführungs- und mechanische Vervielfältigungsrechte/Society for musical performing and mechanical reproduction rights). From 2009 to 2016, music videos for major artists were unavailable on YouTube in Germany, because of the high licensing fees GEMA demanded. For example, in 2009 GEMA asked Google to pay 17 cents per video view.[582] The dispute has since been resolved. GEMA enjoys an extraordinary legal privilege, the GEMA-Vermutung, which allows GEMA to assume that all songs must be licensed through the organisation unless it can be shown that they are in the public domain or owned by non-members.

The abuse by some CROs of their monopoly positions was serious enough for the European Union to intervene by introducing a new law to deal with it. As an 'FAQ' section on the Directive on Collective Management of Copyright[583] of 2014 explained:

> "[The] functioning of some collective management organisations has raised concerns as to their transparency, governance and the handling of revenues collected on behalf of right-holders. Cases of risky investment by certain collective management organisations of royalties that should have gone to rightholders highlighted the lack of oversight and influence of rightholders on the activities of a number of collective management organisations, contributing to irregularities in their financial management and investment decisions."[584]

The second Infojustice summary of CROs behaving badly,[585] published in 2018, showed that despite the new directive, little had improved since 2013 in the European Union and beyond. Stories of mismanagement and worse could be found in Australia, Belgium, Bulgaria, Greece, Iceland, Japan, Kenya, Latvia, Macedonia, Nigeria, Paraguay, Peru, Russia, South Africa and the United Kingdom. One case in Spain was particularly shocking:

> "In November 2014, Pedro Farre, the former head of corporate relations for the Spanish Society of Authors and Publishers (SGAE), received a 30-month sentence after the National Court found him guilty of embezzlement and faking work-related documents. The court found that Farre had paid $50,000 during trips to brothels, then created and submitted false receipts for catering services for SGAE clients to receive reimbursement. During the legal proceedings, Farre claimed that he visited the brothels to determine if they were performing music without a license."[586]

Because CROs are either effectively or even explicitly monopolies, they are open to the kinds of inefficiencies and corruption to which monopolies are prone. It is one of the reasons why copyright functions so badly in the modern world, since such outdated licensing systems are ill-equipped to deal with the rapid developments that are common to the digital sphere.

The situation has worsened in the European Union since the advent of the EU Copyright Directive, which requires large-scale digital platforms with user-uploaded material to license everything where possible. Even assuming that mismanagement and corruption is not a big problem in the EU CROs—a generous assumption given the field's track record—there is another issue. According to the European Commission, in 2014 there were 250 collective management organisations in the European Union, and the current number is probably similar.[587] Consequently, digital platforms will need to sign licensing agreements with hundreds of bodies across the European Union, which is unlikely to be a quick or easy process. Matters are even more challenging than such a figure suggests. The vast majority of CROs in the European Union, and of CROs globally, are for the main categories of music, film, TV and text, where consolidation and concentration has already taken place. There are many other areas of copyright where CROs are few or non-existent such as computer software, images, maps, music scores, ballet scores and 3D files. For these classes of uploads, it will be hard to obtain the licences required by the EU Copyright Directive.

The inevitable consequence of the inefficiencies of CROs when they can be found, and the fact that they may not be available at all for certain kinds of material, is that digital platforms will be forced to resort to upload filters to block swathes of unlicensed copyright material. The implications of this situation were not explored when the Copyright Directive was passing through the European Union legislative system because proponents refused to admit that upload filters were inevitable until after the law was passed.

The effects of mandating upload filters are far-reaching. Few online platforms will be able to afford to create their own upload filters. Licensing software from specialist companies may be an option, but given the cost of creating upload filters that meet the requirements of Article 17, the licensing fees will probably be high. Startups may well view this as a good reason not to bother launching in the European Union. In an interview with *Walled Culture*, Cory Doctorow pointed out: 'a monopolist's first preference is to not be regulated at all, but their second preference is to have regulation that only they can comply with.'[588]

Whether homegrown like YouTube's Content ID or licensed from a third-party, any upload filters that are put in place will inevitably be imperfect. Copyright law has become so complex that even lawyers and judges struggle to delineate what is meant or required. In this situation, the only logical response for a company is to err on the side of caution. As the EFF's Katharine Trendacosta observed:

> "If you're Google, your fear isn't that a famous YouTuber sues you, because even in that case, they don't have a ton of money. Your fear is that Disney sues you, in which case, you're up against a company that has the money and time and resources to really fight you on this. So it's better to design filters that make that side happy, rather than one that works for users and for creators."[589]

When an online service provider is faced with the prospect of massive copyright claims should it fail to block infringing material, it will prefer to overblock, at least to the degree that the CJEU's 2022 ruling on upload filters allows.[590] So the everyday reality of Article 17 is a copyright law that diminishes the rights of Internet users.

The erosion of users' rights was already underway in the United States after the passage of the DMCA in 1998, as Annemarie Bridy pinpointed in 2015 in her paper, 'Copyright's Digital Deputies: DMCA-Plus Enforcement by Internet Intermediaries'.[591] Bridy asserted that online intermediaries such as Google had gone beyond what the law required in order to forestall legal attacks from the copyright industry—what she called 'DMCA-plus' enforcement. Such caution gave the copyright industry exactly what it wanted: more stringent copyright enforcement but without the need to introduce new legislation requiring it. The losers, once more, are ordinary citizens:

> "The dilemma for intermediaries that volunteer to undertake DMCA-plus enforcement is that each new commitment they make raises the bar for what the copyright industries and policy makers regard as minimum standards. The more intermediaries give, it seems, the more is expected of them. In the DMCA-plus enforcement world, the gap between what the law requires and what intermediaries are promising to do is growing. As that gap widens, there is reason to be concerned about the expressive and due process rights of users and website operators, who have no seat at the table when intermediaries and copyright owners negotiate 'best practices' for mitigating online infringement, including which sanctions to impose, which content to

remove, and which websites to block without judicial intervention."[592]

It is not just a matter of overzealous application of a fixed and well-defined law. The upload filter is a demonstration of how technology is used to enforce existing rules, and what legal expert, academic and activist Lawrence Lessig[593] phrased as 'code is law'.[594] The algorithms that are used to determine if an upload will be accepted will in practice define what constitutes Article 17. Regardless of what the EU politicians intended when they were writing the legislation, what the algorithms permit is what matters for the millions of people who use sites such as YouTube or Facebook. The EFF's Trendacosta explains the chilling effect this has had on the quality of user uploads to YouTube:

> "[If] it's a video to teach you how to do something, or to teach you a film technique, they're not going to use the best example, they're going to use the one that Content ID doesn't take down. So you're actually as a user and a viewer getting a lesser product, because you are being given only what can make it pass the filter, not what those people actually have a right to use."[595]

Digital platforms have always had complete power to control how people use their platforms—through terms of service, community guidelines, and technical design. The copyright industry may have intended to curtail the power of US online giants with the EU Copyright Directive, but the resulting legislation leaves them with the ability to determine how people in the European Union use some of the most popular sites online largely undiminished.

YouTube is dominant in ways that few people realise, and not just in the video sector. The third quarter 2021 results for Alphabet, the parent company of Google and YouTube, show YouTube advertising revenue went from \$5 billion to \$7.2 billion, year on year.[596] According to *The Hollywood Reporter* in September 2021 YouTube's chief business officer, Robert Kyncl, told a conference: 'We are roughly neck-and-neck with Netflix on revenue, actually we are slightly larger and growing faster.'[597]

Kyncl also revealed that video represents 25% of YouTube 'watch time', 50% is YouTube creators and 25% is music. YouTube is a formidable player in the music streaming sector. Figures from 2020 indicate that it has more than 30 million Music and Premium paid subscribers.[598] This tally is well below Spotify's figure of around 180 million paid subscribers, but streaming music represents only one strand of YouTube's business.

An analysis in *Music Business Worldwide* puts the numbers in perspective.[599] In 2019, the global recorded music industry generated around \$20 billion in sales; in 2020 it generated \$21.6 billion. According to the article, the figure for 2021 was predicted by Goldman Sachs to be around \$23.5 billion. YouTube ads probably generated \$30 billion for the same period, making this part of Alphabet considerably larger than the entire recording industry.

Among traditional recorded music companies, growth and consolidation is taking place thanks to the rapid uptake of streaming. In September 2021, the Universal Music Group (UMG)[600] went public on Amsterdam's Euronext exchange with a valuation of €45 billion.[601] In the prospectus for its initial public offering (IPO),[602] it wrote:

> "Even with its strong growth in recent years, UMG believes streaming is still in the early stages of global penetration and there remains a substantial opportunity for further expansion driven by growth in the number of

paid subscribers of digital streaming services, including in established streaming markets which still have room for meaningfully increased adoption. Similarly, in new, high growth markets, the continuing migration of consumers online provides potential for significant growth of ad-supported streaming. This trend is also driven by continued technological innovation across devices and formats, such as voice-controlled speakers, connected cars, intersections with social media and gaming, audio-visual product evolution, which is deepening fans' engagement and consumption of music. These are also early days of the expansion of streaming music licensing into new lifestyle categories such as digital health and fitness, which have considerable potential for growth."[603]

But as Fight for the Future director Evan Greer has highlighted, the rise of streaming has brought with it a new problem for musicians:

"[The] analytics of streaming show that people like to listen to the oldies more than they like to listen to new artists. The back catalogues have essentially become more and more profitable. So more and more interest and focus from the entire industry and also from investors is going towards buying up these catalogues, with less focus on new, often living artists. There is just a deep devaluation in the impetus to create new art or to create art that is significantly different from what is already doing well. That suppression of creativity based on the analytics that old stuff makes more money is really harmful to society and culture at large, not just creatives themselves."[604]

UMG is one of the companies busily acquiring the song catalogues of famous modern musicians such as Bob Dylan,[605]

Neil Diamond and Sting.[606] Although it is the world's largest music company,[607] UMG is becoming more reliant on Spotify.[608] In 2018, Spotify contributed 14% of UMG's revenue; in 2021 it was 18%. Spotify is riding the streaming music wave that UMG believes is the future. At the time of writing, Spotify had yet to show a profit, but was nevertheless expanding into related areas, notably podcasts. Spotify's co-founder and CEO Daniel Ek told *Forbes* magazine: 'Everyone underestimates audio. It should be a multi-hundred-billion-dollar industry. Audio is ours to win.'[609]

Ek has set his sights on not just podcasts, but also news, live talk, audiobooks and education. In addition, he wants to fill a gap and provide audio creators with the tools they need. It is an ambitious strategy but one that stands a chance of succeeding given Spotify's track record. Nor does Spotify have to face direct competition from artists, as Greer outlines:

> "[If] we had a copyright system that was geared more toward individual creators rather than big content holders, then you could have a system where there's a much lower barrier of entry to create something like a competitor to Spotify. [One] where it's easy for artists to allow their music to be streamed and to be paid, or have people donate or have different ways to compensate artists for their creativity. Rather than a model that's basically where copyright is making Spotify and Apple Music and Amazon close to monopolies."[610]

Consolidation is taking place in other parts of the copyright world. At the time of writing, the publishing giant Penguin Random House[611] was trying to acquire one of its close competitors, Simon & Schuster.[612] Such a move would turn the 'Big Five' in US book publishing—Hachette Book Group,[613] HarperCollins,[614] Macmillan Publishers,[615] Penguin Random

House and Simon & Schuster—into the 'Big Four'. Even the US Justice Department was worried by that concentration of power and filed a civil antitrust lawsuit in November 2021 to block the merger:

> "As alleged in the complaint filed in the U.S. District Court for the District of Columbia, this acquisition would enable Penguin Random House, which is already the largest book publisher in the world, to exert outsized influence over which books are published in the United States and how much authors are paid for their work."[616]

Another sector where major mergers are taking place is video gaming, as reported by *The Hollywood Reporter* in January 2022:

> "[Two] gaming megadeals have put Wall Street focus squarely on what increasingly feels like an M&A free-for-all. Microsoft unveiled a $68.7 billion takeover of gaming publisher Activision Blizzard on Jan. 18, eight days after Take-Two Interactive's $12.7 billion deal to acquire mobile game powerhouse Zynga (Words With Friends)."[617]

The article explains that Microsoft's acquisition—its biggest ever—helps it become the 'Netflix of gaming'. Other players in this rapidly growing sector include the Chinese tech giant Tencent, Sony (which announced it was buying Bungie, for $3.5 billion[618] in January 2022) and Netflix itself. The synergies between streamed games and cinema may also spur companies like Disney to join the fray. *The Hollywood Reporter* revealed that the Activision acquisition makes Microsoft the third-largest video game company in the world, with revenues of $24 billion, just behind Sony ($24.4 billion) and Tencent ($29 billion).

The gaming sector is large—$200 billion in 2021—and growing rapidly.[619] This compares to $259 billion for the global publishing market in 2019,[620] and $101 billion for the world's entertainment market in the same year.[621] The global music industry, which includes the live, recorded and publishing sectors, is projected to increase from $62 billion in 2017 to $131 billion in 2030.[622]

In *The Captured Economy*, Niskanen Center scholars Brink Lindsey[623] and Steven Teles[624] explain why there is a natural 'winner takes all' dynamic in the world of copyright, and a tendency for market power to become concentrated. The vast majority of books, songs, films and games generate few sales, while a few become hits:

> "If there were no copyright law, the artist and original distributor of one of these lucky jackpot winners would receive income from sales, but so too would other distributors that moved in once it was clear that the work was in high demand. Because of copyright, all sales are captured by a single distributor, and the price per unit sold is substantially higher as well because of the lack of competition. Since copyright law gives distributors monopolies over popular works, the income generated by those works is much more highly concentrated than it otherwise would be."[625]

The natural concentration of power not only raises prices and boosts profits to abnormal levels, it also encourages lobbying for new laws that further consolidate the dominant position of monopolists. Such behaviour is known as rent-seeking, which Wikipedia defines as 'the effort to increase one's share of existing wealth without creating new wealth.'[626] For most publishing, recording and film companies, copyright is central to their business model. They will fight fiercely in order to preserve or even strengthen it. By contrast, those who are hurt by copyright's intellectual monopoly may not even realise it, because copyright represents only a comparatively small extra cost for them. In particular, the public domain has no natural defenders,[627] and certainly none that can match the lobbying might of the copyright industry. As a result, Lindsey and Teles note:

> "[Rent-seekers] rarely fail to recognize their common interest, and they are willing to invest in politics up to the value of the benefit they are protecting. Those stakes ... are in the billions of dollars, which means that even a small segment of wealthy rent-seekers can justify participating in politics."[628]

This is the history of copyright over the last few decades. Massive lobbying by the music, film and publishing industries has seen politicians pass laws time and again that extend copyright in multiple ways, and strengthen the penalties for infringing upon it, including criminal ones.[629]

It is not just the legislative process that the copyright industry has succeeded in bending to its will. One of the most powerful positions in the world of copyright is the General Counsel of the US Copyright Office. The latter claims that it 'promotes creativity and free expression by administering the nation's copyright laws and by providing impartial, expert advice on copyright law and policy for the benefit of all.'[630]

Yet as *Techdirt* journalist Mike Masnick opined in January 2022, this is not true:

> "[The] organization is dominated by former (and, if the past is any indication, soon to be again), lobbyists and lawyers of the biggest copyright abusers on the planet. So it's difficult to take the Office seriously as a steward

for the public good (as they are supposed to be), when it's currently headed by the former top lawyer at [International Federation of the Phonographic Industry], who, before that, was the top IP lawyer for Time Warner. And, when she then decides to hire Disney's top 'IP lawyer' to become General Counsel of the Copyright Office (as has just been announced), it becomes really difficult not to be cynical.

This is what regulatory capture looks like.

But even worse, actions like this are why the public doesn't believe in copyright. Over and over again all we see is abuse of copyright, and then the government puts the same people who have abused copyright in charge of copyright at the Copyright Office, it makes the public cynical and (reasonably) distrustful of the intentions of the Copyright Office. That's disappointing, as there are plenty of people who have expertise in copyright law who would be great for the Copyright Office. But, for some reason, they never get hired into the top jobs unless they've spent time working for one of the giant Hollywood or recording industry organizations."[631]

When copyright had only marginal impact on ordinary life, it might have been argued that regulatory capture was not an issue for most people.[632] Given that copyright is central to the online world, with almost every action online involving copyright of some sort, the collateral damage of the successful lobbying by publishers, recording companies and film studios has a disastrous impact on not only members of the public but on creators themselves.

CHAPTER 8

Copyright Absurdities

Disobedient computers, rotting films, and Katy Perry's battle over an ostinato

A chasm has opened up between copyright law and the day-to-day workings of the digital world. Many absurd situations have arisen as a result. For example, removing the need for formalities means that copyright obtrudes into almost every action in the online world. People must actively seek to tone down copyright if they wish to avoid its core aim to prevent material being shared freely. The Creative Commons (CC) licences[633] provide a popular way to do so. By choosing to apply one of the standard CC licences to their work, people have tried to counter the belief that sharing is inherently bad. As one of the legal experts who created the CC licences, Lawrence Lessig, told the *Walled Culture* blog:

> "There are many photographers and musicians that began to make their work available because they wanted people to freely be able to build upon it. These are lots of different contexts where people began to see that they didn't actually want perfect control. What they wanted was some acknowledgments, and that's the re-

quirement of citing who it is you've gotten the work from."[634]

Nevertheless, the distortions of 20th-century copyright law have succeeded in poisoning the communal well. Author and digital-rights activist Cory Doctorow, who among other things was the European director of Creative Commons, has explained that early versions of CC licences contained a small flaw that exposes millions of people who use material released under them to legal risk:

> "The original version of the CC licence stated that the license would 'terminate automatically upon any breach.' That meant that if you failed to live up to the licence terms in any substantial way, you were no longer a licensed user of the copyrighted work. Any uses you had made of that work were no longer permitted under the licence, so unless you had another basis for using it (for example, if your use qualified as 'fair use'), then you were now infringing copyright."[635]

This should not be a problem for something that is a tiny oversight and essentially trivial. But the statutory damages for 'wilful infringement' in the United States can be $150,000 for each work infringed. Even the mere threat of being ordered to pay such a sum will terrify most people into accepting any deal to avert a fine. That is the business model of the 'copyright troll', a company or a person who claims that someone is infringing on their copyright, and offers a 'licence' for a smaller sum—typically a few hundred dollars—to spare people the risk of incurring a fine of thousands of dollars if they go to court.[636] 'Copyleft trolls', as Doctorow calls those exploiting the flaw in the early CC licences, are worse than traditional copyright trolls:

> "It's even more of a pure predator play than the copyright troll racket, because the targets of these extortion demands are people who understand (correctly) that they are allowed to use the work they are being threatened over. The basis for the threat isn't that they infringed copyright—rather, it's that they made the equivalent of a typo, like failing to dot an 'i' or cross a 't'."[637]

Evidently, the copyright system is not only broken, it can even be used as a weapon against those trying to fix it.

Copyleft trolls are not the only threat to CC licences. The copyright industry is trying to extend, strengthen and widen the reach of copyright via legislation, regardless of whether it makes sense to do so, and often ignores the significant harms this inflicts on the rights of the general public. One such example is WIPO's proposed Protection of Broadcasts and Broadcasting Organizations Treaty,[638] or Broadcasting Treaty, which aims to give broadcasters a new right to material they broadcast, even if they did not create it. In 2019, one of the main digital organisations following international policymaking, Knowledge Ecology International, warned:

> "The proposal would give broadcasters effectively perpetual rights over content that they do not create, own or license, including works where there is no underlying copyright or where the copyright holders have not been paid and/or license their works for use by the public at no cost, such as under Creative Commons licenses."[639]

This means that if a broadcaster showed works released under a CC licence—or material that was in the public domain[640]—it would have a legal right to restrict its free use. The treaty would create yet another layer of legal protection designed to prevent sharing even where the original creators desire it, or where the work is in the public domain and should not be subject to any restrictions.

The hefty penalties available under the US DMCA have led to another absurd situation whereby in effect people do not own products they buy if the latter contains software that has even minimal technical protections. In such circumstances, people are forbidden from repairing these items, whether that is a TV, a fridge, or a car, because the software is protected by the DMCA and cannot be modified. One famous example of this anomaly appeared in 2015 with respect to tractors made by US machinery manufacturer John Deere.[641] The company told the US Copyright Office:

> "In the absence of an express written license in conjunction with the purchase of the vehicle, the vehicle owner receives an implied license for the life of the vehicle to operate the vehicle, subject to any warranty limitations, disclaimers or other contractual limitations in the sales contract or documentation."[642]

Hence, farmers do not own the John Deere tractors they purchased, they merely have a licence to use them. An article in *Wired* from the time pointed out the absurdity of the company's logic that seeks to eviscerate the notion of ownership:

> "The company argues that allowing people to alter the software—even for the purpose of repair—would 'make it possible for pirates, third-party developers, and less innovative competitors to free-ride off the creativity, unique expression and ingenuity of vehicle software.' The pièce de résistance in John Deere's argument: permitting owners to root around in a tractor's programming might lead to pirating music through a vehicle's entertainment system. Because copyright-marauding farmers are very busy and need to multitask by

simultaneously copying Taylor Swift's *1989* and harvesting corn?"[643]

Given that software is covered by copyright, any device containing software can potentially be protected by legislation such as the DMCA and the European Union's Information Society Directive. The consequences of this will affect objects that form the Internet of Things (IoT),[644] which links together a range of domestic devices from thermostats to home security systems by imbuing them with computational power. As security expert Bruce Schneier[645] wrote in *The Atlantic* in 2015:

> "We'll want our light bulbs to communicate with a central controller, regardless of manufacturer. We'll want our clothes to communicate with our washing machines and our cars to communicate with traffic signs.
>
> We can't have this when companies can cut off compatible products, or use the law to prevent competitors from reverse-engineering their products to ensure compatibility across brands. For the Internet of Things to provide any value, what we need is a world that looks like the automotive industry, where you can go to a store and buy replacement parts made by a wide variety of different manufacturers. Instead, the Internet of Things is on track to become a battleground of competing standards, as companies try to build monopolies by locking each other out."[646]

Copyright legislation makes it easy for manufacturers to thwart this kind of necessary interoperability. Unless the situation is addressed, the full potential of the IoT will never be realised. This has far-reaching consequences, as Cory Doctorow has warned:

> "I worry a lot more about steaming towards this world in which everything is computerised. In which your house is a giant computer you put your body into, and then you fill your body up with computers, implants and so on, and you surround it with computers, and we design those computers specifically to disobey the person whose life they hold in their hands. That seems to me to be just a foundationally bad idea."[647]

Strong copyright protection not only leads to people losing control of things: it can also lead to the complete physical loss of them. Celluloid films are especially vulnerable for a variety of reasons, as writer Meg Shields has pointed out on the *Film School Rejects* blog:

> "Every movie 20th Century-Fox made before 1932 was lost when a fire broke out in inadequately ventilated storage. Later, in the mid-60s, massive swaths of MGM's silent film history went up in smoke.

> The ability of nitrate film to clear out a vault was perhaps only rivaled by the studios themselves, who regularly destroyed old prints to make space for new releases. Studios saw no financial incentive to keep silent films after the advent of sound, and it took the clout and coin of big names like [Griffith], Chaplin, and Pickford to properly safeguard their filmographies. An estimated three-quarters of silent movies have been destroyed, including more than 90 percent of pre-1929 films."[648]

It is estimated that half of all US films made before 1950 have been lost.[649] Copyright restrictions prevented copies being made of the films, which could have preserved them for posterity. As Lawrence Lessig has said: "That's just an unintended consequence of the particular system of copyright that we've adopted that benefits nobody, harms culture and people generally.'[650]

Surprisingly, digital films suffer from the same issues of neglect and the inability to make plenty of backup copies, as filmmaker Charlie Shackleton wrote in *The Guardian*:

> "A physical film print, properly stored, can last for hundreds of years. Digital media, for all its flexibility, is vastly less stable, requiring constant migration to evade data degradation and format obsolescence. One infamous cautionary tale concerns Pixar's efforts to release *Toy Story* on DVD for the first time in 2000. Though just five years had elapsed since the film's cinema release, the original animation files had become so thoroughly corrupted that animators were forced to recreate as much as a fifth of the film from reference copies. It's safe to assume films that didn't spawn multi-billion dollar franchises have not fared better."[651]

Shackleton lamented the rise of video-streaming giants such as Netflix and Amazon Prime, which, ironically, have limited access to cinematic culture, despite the potential for enabling more people to watch a wider range of films. Writer Timothy Lee explained the extent of the problem in 2021 on the *Full Stack Economics* blog:

> "Fifteen years ago, you could find almost anything on Netflix, from the latest blockbusters to classic movies to popular television series. In total, Netflix had around 60,000 titles available.
>
> Today, Netflix's streaming service only has about one-tenth as many titles available. While it has some amazing original content, the back catalog is unimpressive."[652]

Lee suggested this is happening 'not because of technological or economic constraints—it's because the law gives copyright holders more control over streaming of older movies than it did over DVD rentals.'[653]

The situation is just as bad for another modern art form, the video game. Once more, the DMCA and similar laws elsewhere are to blame. Copyright's legal overreach makes academics reluctant to risk transferring video-game code from older media such as floppy discs to newer, more reliable systems, for example cloud storage,[654] in order to make backups. It also stops them from creating software emulators of the hardware needed to run old games. As a result, even when copyright protection on a game expires—in a century or so—there is a risk that copies of old video games will be unplayable because the media on which they are stored has degraded, or there is no hardware available on which to run them. In the United States, there is a way around this problem. However, it is not being adopted because of resistance by the Entertainment Software Association (ESA),[655] the industry body that lobbies on behalf of video game publishers, as an article in *The Washington Post* explained:

> "In U.S. copyright law, exemptions exist for specific use cases, such as academic research, that would otherwise violate the technical protections of copyrighted works. Proposals for exemptions are reviewed every three years by the U.S. Copyright Office. In 2018, academics scored a victory that granted them an exemption to preserve games that are no longer commercially available. In 2021, a push for remote access to preserved games for academics failed.
>
> In response to the push for copyright exemptions by the academics, the ESA has stated that increasing such

access would 'risk the possibility of substantial market harm' for publishers."[656]

Ironically, the ESA's desire to control every possible use of video games means that in the long term it is likely that many masterpieces of the genre will not be preserved in a playable form, and the creativity of the industry will be lost forever.

The academic world also suffers because of copyright legislation and not just regarding the publication of academic papers. An apparently minor copyright squabble between researchers regarding p-values has had an outsized negative effect on research culture. Wikipedia explains the concept of a p-value:

> "In null-hypothesis significance testing, the p-value is the probability of obtaining test results at least as extreme as the results actually observed, under the assumption that the null hypothesis is correct. A very small p-value means that such an extreme observed outcome would be very unlikely under the null hypothesis. Reporting p-values of statistical tests is common practice in academic publications of many quantitative fields."[657]

These p-values are typically used to evaluate whether the results of an experiment could have happened by chance, or whether there is an alternative explanation such as the hypothesis being investigated. Wikipedia notes that different p-values can be used but 'by convention' a p-value cut-off of 0.05 is generally picked. The reason for the convention is because of a spat over copyright, as scholars Brent Goldfarb (Robert H. Smith School of Business, University of Maryland) and Andrew King (Questrom School of Business, Boston University) explained in a paper in 2014:

> "We were surprised to learn, in the course of writing this paper, that the $p < 0.05$ cutoff was established as a competitive response to a disagreement over book royalties between two foundational statisticians. In the early 1920s, Kendall Pearson, whose income depended on the sale of extensive statistical tables, was unwilling to allow Ronald A. Fisher to use them in his new book. To work around this barrier, Fisher created a method of inference based on only two values: p-values of 0.05 and 0.01."[658]

Fisher himself later admitted that using a range of p-values was better than his approach based on just two figures, 0.05 and 0.01. But by then, the use of the 0.05 figure had become part of the established scientific method adopted by researchers. As a result of copyright, and a statistician's refusal to share some basic calculations, the academic world has been producing research using a suboptimal analytical approach for decades.

The story of how academia arrived at the p-value is an example of how an apparently minor issue has major impact. The same is true of the private copying levy,[659] which Wikipedia describes as 'a government-mandated scheme in which a special tax or levy (additional to any general sales tax) is charged on purchases of recordable media.'[660] It is an instance of the copyright industry demanding payment for even potential copies, since there is no way of knowing what the level of private copying is.

In theory, it's a simple scheme to compensate creators for private copies individuals make and then store on recordable media. However, the copyright industry has convinced the French government to create a complex and burdensome system.[661] The sums collected are substantial: in 2017, the French levy raised nearly €270 million.[662] Three-quarters of the levy goes to French collecting societies, adding to the concentration of power and money in those organisations. The remainder of the money is used to finance festivals and support organisations such as Hadopi, the government agency that administered the three-strike system, now part of Arcom[663] (France's Audiovisual and Digital Communication Regulatory Authority). As a result, the levy has become another way for the copyright world to cement its position and propagate its ideology.

The fact that so many ultimately ineffectual laws were passed shows the extent to which the legislative process has been warped by the copyright world. That is also clear from the attempts to use international treaties like ACTA to impose harsh new copyright laws—including criminal sanctions for infringement—across the world without any democratic input or even scrutiny.

A good example of how international trade deals ride roughshod over the rights of citizens to the benefit of the copyright industry is provided by New Zealand. The country is something of an outlier: its copyright term is life plus fifty years, rather than the more common life plus seventy years found in most countries. At the time of writing, an in-principle trade deal between New Zealand and the United Kingdom proposes changing the former's copyright term of life plus fifty years become life plus seventy years. What is remarkable is that extending copyright makes no sense,[664] and the New Zealand government likely knows it, as a blog post by international copyright lawyer Michael Wolfe, from the Tohatoha Aotearoa Commons,[665] has explained:

> "New Zealand considered longer copyright terms as part of the negotiations around the Trans-Pacific Partnership Agreement [TPPA—another trade deal]. The

verdict then? That term extension was an economic loser of a provision that would cost around [NZ]$55m annually. New Zealand's current, albeit stalled, review of the Copyright Act reached the same conclusion, taking term extension off the table for lack of any compelling evidence that it would provide a public benefit."[666]

Despite that fact, which is backed up by research carried out in other countries, New Zealand intends to sign the trade deal with the United Kingdom and to lengthen its copyright term by twenty years. At the time of writing, Canada, too, looks likely to extend its copyright term, ignoring evidence that doing so fails to create an additional incentive for creativity.[667] Rebecca Giblin, ARC Future Fellow and professor within the Melbourne Law School, told *Walled Culture* about the issues with extending copyright:

"That twenty-year term extension that was rolled out in Europe, the United States and Australia, to extend copyright from the life plus fifty years to life plus seventy years, in nearly all cases that benefited the owner of the copyright, not the creator of the copyright. So those additional rights went to the person or the company that happened to own those rights, rather than the one that actually created it in the first place."[668]

Another example of how copyright has brought no benefits for the average creator is evident from the major acquisitions taking place across all the industries involving copyright material. Although the companies and investors involved are enjoying a golden age as a result, this is not the case for creators, who are becoming the cultural equivalent of impoverished peasants tilling fields for the benefit of the aristocracy.

For example, in 2018 the US Authors Guild conducted a survey of US authors[669] that revealed a median author income of $6,080, down from $8,000 in 2014, $10,500 in 2009 and $12,850 in 2007. Earnings from book income alone fell even more, declining 21% to $3,100 in 2017 from $3,900 in 2013 and just over 50% from 2009's median book earnings of $6,250. As a result, authors were finding ways to supplement their writing income, for example speaking engagements, book reviewing or teaching. Respondents who identified themselves as full-time book authors still only earned a median income of $20,300, even including these other sources of income—a figure that is well below the US federal poverty line for a family of three or more. The Authors Guild offered the following explanation for such dismal figures:

> "Among the factors contributing to the pressure on authorship, the Guild cited the growing dominance of Amazon over the marketplace, lower royalties and advances for mid-list books (which publishers report comes from losses they are forced to pass on), including the extremely low royalties paid on the increasing number of deeply discounted sales and the 25 percent of net ebook royalty. The blockbuster mentality of publishers who grant celebrity writers massive advances and markets them wildly at the expense of the working writers is also certainly a factor."[670]

The situation is just as bad in the world of recorded music. In 2021, the Digital, Culture, Media and Sport Committee of the UK Parliament[671] published its second report on the Economics of Music Streaming.[672] As with the world of publishing, companies in the music industry are flourishing, while musicians struggle to earn a decent living. The committee found what it called an 'oligopsony in asset acquisition':

> "An oligopsony occurs when a market is dominated by a small number of large buyers. This theoretically concentrates demand (and therefore market power) in the hands of the buyers, which can effectively keep prices down at the expense of the sellers. When applied to the music industry, this means that the terms under which the major music groups in particular acquire the rights to music favour the majors at the expense of the creators. As has been discussed, the major music groups are disproportionately benefitting from music streaming relative to creators. This has resulted in record high levels of income and profit growth and historic levels of profitability for the major labels whilst performers' incomes average less than the median wage."[673]

Alex Sayf Cummings,[674] a history professor at Georgia State University, has described streaming in a *Walled Culture* interview as 'an amazing paradise for listeners' but 'not a great thing' for artists: 'It basically replicates the conflict that had always existed, which is that record labels rip off artists and take the lion's share of the proceeds.'[675]

The problem is exacerbated because the most successful artists—the top 1%—receive a disproportionately large fraction of the total earnings in a sector. Hence, everyone else receives a worse deal than the average figure for the industry suggests. This important aspect of copyright was explored in 2020 in the paper 'Copyright and the 1%'[676] by law professor Glynn Lunney,[677] Texas A&M University School of Law.

Lunney explained why a world where the income from copyright is more evenly distributed among the most and least popular artists is different from one with almost all the revenue going to a few superstars. He called this an 'L-shaped' distribution because there is a huge peak of income at one end and almost nothing elsewhere. There is no 'middle class' of creators, only superstars and paupers. As Lunney said: 'Artists are either superstars, and so do not need copyright. Or they are flops to whom no one wants to listen, and so are beyond copyright's help.'[678]

Lunney went on to explore some detailed real-world data from the PC video game industry, where he finds just such an L-shaped distribution: the top 1% of games by popularity capture nearly half the players, and the top 10% capture around 90%. In 2021, a leak of data about video gamers who stream live on the Twitch platform[679] found the same extremely skewed shares: the top 1% made more than half of all the money paid.[680] In the world of podcasting, the L-shape is even more extreme: during January 2019, the top 1% of podcasts received 99% of downloads.[681] In his paper, Lunney concluded:

> "No one ever argues for copyright on the grounds that superstar authors and artists need more money. Yet, if the L-shaped distribution of demand for PC videogames is representative for works of authorship generally, overpaying superstars may be all, or mostly all, that copyright in its present form does. While copyright undoubtedly provides some incentives for average artists, and their works undeniably generate some social value, 90% of copyright's incentives flow to the top 10% of works. Given that distribution, the losses copyright generates by overpaying superstars, already firmly ensconced in the wealthy 1%, far outweigh whatever benefits in efficiency or fairness that copyright generates by offering, relatively speaking, token incentives to the average or marginal artist or author."[682]

Data from different industries suggests that aside from the lucky 1% of artists who reap substantial benefits from the current copyright system, most creators are struggling. This is in part because the big copyright companies can use their monopolies 'to extract so much wealth from artists and continue to perpetuate the myth that artists must starve in order to make great art',[683] according to Fight for the Future's campaigns and communications director, Lia Holland.[684] For some, the situation is even more difficult: the concept of copyright is inimical to their creativity. Kevin Greene,[685] professor of law at Southwestern Law School in Los Angeles, has pointed out that several aspects of copyright are a poor fit for the way many artists create:

> "The [US] Copyright Act requires that a work of authorship must be 'fixed in any tangible medium of expression, now known or later developed, from which [it] can be perceived, reproduced, or otherwise communicated, either directly or indirectly with the aid of a machine or device.' Although 'race-neutral,' the fixation requirement has not served the ways Black artists create: 'a key component of black cultural production is improvisation.' As a result, fixation deeply disadvantages African-American modes of cultural production, which are derived from an oral tradition and communal standards."[686]

The same is true for much creativity outside the Western nations that invented and then vastly expanded copyright's reach, and which then imposed the system and its values on other countries regardless of whether it was an appropriate framework for their cultures.

Copyright is not just a bad fit for creativity. The obsession with exclusive ownership of material means that there is a constant threat hanging over creators in the form of lawsuits alleging that elements were 'stolen'. For example, in the United States there is a long-running saga concerning the work of artist Andy Warhol,[687] who often drew on pre-existing images for his own inspiration. The case concerns War-hol's paintings of the musician Prince, which are based on a photograph taken by Lynn Goldsmith. Art market Web site Artnet explained the history behind the work:

> "Goldsmith initially shot the image of Prince while on assignment for *Newsweek* in 1981, but it was never published. In 1984, *Vanity Fair* licensed one of her por-traits of the singer for an illustration by Warhol. The artist ultimately made an entire series based on the pho-to (which he did not license himself). Goldsmith only learned about the works in 2016, when *Vanity Fair* re-published them after Prince's death without crediting her."[688]

Litigation ensued. The Andy Warhol Foundation filed a pre-emptive suit in April 2017, asking the court to rule that the 'Prince Series' did not violate the copyright of Gold-smith's photograph. A year later, a New York federal court ruled that there was no infringement, then in 2021, an ap-peals court reversed that judgment. The US Supreme Court has announced that it will hear the case, which is an indica-tion that it thinks important legal issues need to be resolved.

This kind of litigation is particularly problematic in the world of pop music because the sums involved can easily run into millions. In 2022, Dua Lipa[689] faced two lawsuits alleg-ing copyright infringement in the same song.[690] Similarly, in 2020, Taylor Swift[691] defended two different lawsuits over a single hit.[692] In 2022, music and entertainment magazine *Billboard* reported on a win for Katy Perry[693] against a copy-right infringement action brought against her song 'Dark Horse'[694] (2013), by Marcus Gray,[695] who alleged she had taken ideas from his track 'Joyful Noise' (2009). A federal appeals court upheld an earlier ruling that the musical element concerned was too basic to be protected by copyright:

> "The portion of the 'Joyful Noise' ostinato [repeated musical phrase] that overlaps with the 'Dark Horse' ostinato consists of a manifestly conventional arrangement of musical building blocks ... Allowing a copyright over this material would essentially amount to allowing an improper monopoly over two-note pitch sequences or even the minor scale itself."[696]

Although this is a welcome ruling, it is still absurd that a case could even be brought over whether two-note pitch sequences could be turned into a copyright monopoly. In another court case in 2022, alleging copyright infringement by Ed Sheeran,[697] music industry news site *Music Business Worldwide* reported that the judge said:

> "The use of the first four notes of the rising minor pentatonic scale for the melody is so short, simple, commonplace and obvious in the context of the rest of the song that it is not credible that Sheeran sought out inspiration from other songs to come up with it."[698]

As Sheeran pointed out afterwards:

> "There's only so many notes and very few chords used in pop music. Coincidence is bound to happen if 60,000 songs are being released every day on Spotify—that's 22 million songs a year—and there's only 12 notes that are available."[699]

Despite such wins, cases alleging plagiarism of even short sections of a musical work will still be brought because at its core copyright is based on the concept that everything created should be owned by someone and protected from being stolen by others. However, fighting lawsuits over similarities between melodies runs counter to the universal practices of music creation. In all cultures, and throughout history, each generation of musicians has learned from the works of those who came before, and built on their ideas. It's how all art functions. As well as the many other problems noted in this chapter, it turns out that copyright is a poor fit for creativity itself.

CHAPTER 9

True Fans Are the Real Solution

Helping creators and culture thrive without Big Content

Copyright is manifestly not working for the vast majority of creators or their fans. Instead, as Michelle Wu,[700] director of Georgetown University Law Center, writes in her 2021 paper 'The Corruption of Copyright and Returning It to Its Original Purposes':

> "Across the board, every Industry Conglomerates action described in this paper harms all communities. The damage is not equally borne, though, as every instance of limiting access to information affects poorer communities more than they do wealthy ones and future generations more than current ones, increasing the nation's existing inequality divide. By building strategies on profit, and undermining dissemination and preservation, publishers have disrupted copyright's purpose and have done so in a way that has not just held the public interest in check but has actively harmed it."[701]

Techdirt's Mike Masnick puts it more succinctly: 'when you look at how industries around copyright have developed, they have often been very anti-creator.'[702]

If the situation in the West is bad, in developing economies it is even worse. Harsh copyright laws—often imposed by the United States and the European Union on behalf of their local companies, as a condition of signing one-sided trade deals—cause large and continuing outflows of money to pay for copyright material produced by Western companies, typically at Western rates. That leaves less disposable income for local artists, and a smaller creative sector in which local companies can operate and grow to a size where they can compete against existing Western players. It is an issue whose salience will only increase, for reasons explained by Katherine Maher,[703] former CEO and executive director of the Wikimedia Foundation:

> "We tend to think of the world as sort of being mapped and all the free knowledge as existing and all of the great works as being already accessible or already being produced. And the reality is, that's simply not true. The next century very much belongs to places and cultures and peoples that we have not yet fully heard from."[704]

Some of copyright's problems are easy to state and easy to fix—in principle, at least. For example, bringing back formalities for copyright would mean that most activities on the Internet would—at a stroke—no longer be covered pointlessly by copyright law. It would halt the growing mound of orphan works, but still leaves the problem of the millions that already exist. That could be addressed by allowing them to be reprinted and reused freely, until such time as copyright owners make themselves known, in which case they could discuss formal licensing arrangements. Similarly, it should be legal to make copies of films and games in order to preserve them.

Making copies of games will often require circumvention of digital rights management (DRM). In order to legalise that practice, the parts of the DMCA and the equivalent legislation around the world should be repealed. This would also allow people to make backups of material they own, for people to repair devices that contain software, and for security issues in IoT devices and elsewhere to be addressed routinely and in a timely fashion.

The asymmetry of takedown notices should be addressed by adding the threat of civil damages for false DMCA claims, perhaps coupled with attorneys' fees or some automatic multiplier of statutory damages. In addition, the disproportionate fines of the DMCA for single copyright infringements should be removed. All legal action against individuals, whatever its form, should cease, given it is punitive, inequitable and ineffectual.

On 20 September 2017, Felix Reda outlined the background to a study on the central question of whether online infringement is actually a problem or rather an obsession of the copyright industry:

> "In January 2014, the European Commission awarded the Dutch company Ecorys a contract[705] worth €360,000 to conduct a study on the question.
>
> The 300-page study was delivered to the Commission in May 2015, but was never published. Until today—I have managed to get access to a copy: Estimating displacement rates of copyrighted content in the EU.[706]
>
> The study's conclusion: With the exception of recently released blockbusters, there is no evidence to support the idea that online copyright infringement displaces

> sales. While this result is not unique, but consistent with previous studies, it begs the question:
>
> Why did the Commission, after having spent a significant amount of money on it, choose not to publish this study for almost two years?'"[707]

The answer is that there is an inherent bias in favour of the copyright industries in everything:[708] not only the laws that are passed, but also the consultations[709] and the studies leading up to them. When the facts do not match the policy of boosting copyright protection yet further—as with the EU study cited by Reda—it is ignored. No wonder that many people refuse to respect unfair copyright laws. Similarly, imposing new, harsher copyright laws as part of international trade agreements negotiated behind closed doors, with no input from the public, is another reason why people often choose to disobey them in their daily lives. Such policy laundering is another anti-democratic practice that should be stopped.

There is ample evidence that people turn to unauthorised sources for material because they cannot find official offerings that are fairly priced. This is borne out by what happened in Sweden, as *Techdirt* reported in 2015:

> "Sweden was home to the Pirate Bay and had sky high piracy rates. And then Spotify—a company also born in Sweden—launched at home. And piracy rates fell off a cliff. But only for music. Piracy for other products such as TV and movies remained high. Under pressure from the US, Sweden passed a strict anti-piracy law, IPRED. And, when it went into effect, there was a notable decline in piracy rates ... but, within months, those rates rebounded to where they had been before, as people quickly figured out new ways to do what they were do-

ing before. And then Netflix launched in Sweden. And piracy rates for TV and movies dropped."[710]

Nor is this development unique as is shown by a report published in 2015 by the digital think tank Copia Institute entitled 'The Carrot or the Stick',[711] which examined the situation in France, Sweden, the United Kingdom, South Korea, Japan and New Zealand. The report concluded that 'the data across several countries strongly supports the carrot approach of encouraging and enabling greater innovation, while finding little support for stricter laws (which may also create other unintended consequences).' In the software world, research even suggests that unauthorised copying can stimulate innovation by pushing companies to stay ahead of imitation products.[712]

There are some straightforward fixes for the increasing problems libraries face in the digital world. For example, publishers should not be allowed to charge more for ebooks than analogue books. In addition, ebooks must be provided on similar terms and treated as a perpetual purchase, rather than with a time-limited licence, and there should be no restrictions on how many times or how often an ebook can be lent out. To take advantage of ebook technology, text-to-speech options must always be available for visually impaired readers and others.

Similarly, in the academic world, the Ingelfinger rule preventing academics from submitting their work to more than one journal should be dropped. This would force publishers to compete by offering better terms to researchers. The requirement for academics to assign copyright should be forbidden and publishers should only be allowed to take the non-exclusive licence that is necessary to publish a paper. These two measures would drive down the article processing charges and allow researchers to share copies of their papers freely. Funding bodies should divert money from expensive gold open access solutions to diamond open access: this will help researchers in developing economies both read and write papers without the current barriers.

Text and data mining on any scale and by anyone should be permitted. This would include allowing academics to aggregate and mine all papers—including global projects like Google Books—and licensing in order to scan and index should not be required. Such a policy means the problem of locating the owners of orphan works and of negotiating with thousands of publishers would be avoided.

The EU Copyright Directive has one element that needs to be added—freedom of panorama—and several parts that need to go. Article 15, the snippet tax, was introduced because of lobbying by some large press publishers despite all the evidence against it, and should be removed. It is biased in favour of major publishers and will lead to more disinformation circulating. Sites keen to spread their lies will impose no conditions on the reuse of their material, which will therefore circulate widely as it is re-used by other outlets looking for free stories. Meanwhile, much of the best, most professional journalism will be locked away behind paywalls, read by only those who can afford to do so.[713]

An analysis of legislative changes conducted in 2021 by two academics Martin Husovec[714] and João Quintais,[715] working respectively at the London School of Economics and the University of Amsterdam, showed that Article 17 is similarly biased in favour of larger players:

> "[The] licensing provisions in Art. 17, unless implemented through collective licensing at the national level, result in a direct advantage to large right-holders. They

> will be proactively approached by OCSSPs [online-content sharing service providers] to grant authorisations, which will save them time and resources. Conversely, smaller right-holders, in particular user-creators—must monitor the market, review the use of their works by third parties, and approach each OCSSP separately. In addition, the enforcement mechanism embedded in Art. 17 disadvantages (often small) amateur creators who are more likely to rely on exceptions for content creation, rather than the type of commercial cross-licensing most often available to large right-holders."[716]

The authors suggest that this situation might be serious enough to violate the European Union's 'principle of equal treatment', which derives from Article 20 of the European Union Charter of Fundamental Rights: 'Everyone is equal before the law.'[717] As a consequence, Husovec and Quintais write, 'if national governments do not proactively address unequal treatment of small creators (for example, through collective licensing solutions), their national implementations might violate EU law.'[718]

There are so many problems with Article 17 at every level, it needs to be repealed. It is the most harmful piece of copyright legislation since the DMCA and EU Information Society Directive, and will have enormous negative effects on the digital world, not just in the European Union, but more widely if other countries adopt it as a model.

One of the consequences of Article 17 will be a continuing concentration of power in the hands of a few digital behemoths. This is already a serious problem in the copyright world. Alongside trillion-dollar companies such as Amazon, Apple, Google and Microsoft, there is increasing consolidation of power at the next level. Spotify is emerging as a potentially dominant player in the world of audio.[719] Also, music companies are buying up classic song catalogues for which the copyright will run for many years more, locking them into commercial exploitation. Furthermore, the Big Five publishers are shrinking to the Big Four.[720]

One approach to halting the slide towards oligopoly and worse is to use antitrust law. There is renewed interest[721] in this well-established approach[722] to diluting monopoly power, not least from the chair of the US Federal Trade Commission (FTC),[723] Lina Khan.[724] However, any battles are likely to be long ones because of the immense financial and lobbying resources such large companies have at their disposal. The danger is that if the antitrust investigations ever result in action—by breaking up companies into smaller parts[725] for example—they will be too late and when current oligopolists are already in decline.

However, support is growing[726] for a very different approach to competition policy for the digital era[727] suggested in 2019 by two leading thinkers in the area, Cory Doctorow and Mike Masnick. Instead of companies such as Facebook being broken up, they would be forced to allow competitors to interoperate with them in a friction-free fashion. Doing so would reduce the switching costs that make it hard to move from one service to another. Doctorow calls this approach 'adversarial interoperability',[728] while Masnick frames it as 'protocols, not platforms'.[729] The background to the concept is outlined in a report published in 2021 by the Digital Regulation Project at Yale's Tobin Center for Economic Policy entitled 'Equitable Interoperability: the "Super Tool" of Digital Platform Governance'.[730] Doctorow told *Walled Culture* the principles behind the idea:

> "By lowering the switching costs, we will make these companies so much weaker because people who don't

like them can leave. We'll also make them better, because they'll be worried that people who don't like them will leave. But as they get weaker, it'll make it easier for us to take on more muscular action, like breaking them up, like limiting their bad contractual terms, like limiting what can be in terms of service, like other forms of regulation that would make them more democratically accountable and less able to structure the market for our culture."[731]

As well as reining in oligopolies, much more must be done to empower creators—all of them, not just the tiny number of superstars who benefit handsomely from copyright's 'winner takes all'[732] dynamic—and to diminish creators' reliance on companies that derive profit from exploiting copyright material produced by others.[733] Measures to strengthen the position of artists in any negotiations might help but they would only tip the balance in favour of creators slightly. For example, a general right to renegotiate contracts after a set period—the so-called 'reversion right', advocated by Rebecca Giblin, ARC Future Fellow and Professor within the Melbourne Law School, in an interview with *Walled Culture*[734] —would certainly benefit creators. But what is needed is a more radical approach to funding creativity. Fortunately, just as the rise of the digital world has rendered the 18th-century analogue approach of copyright unworkable, so the Internet offers a way for artists to become more independent and increase the rewards for their creations.

Already, many thousands of people are making a living by creating and posting a wide variety of material online. These are the modern so-called 'influencers', who typically earn a cut of advertising that is placed alongside their material. Influencers who gain a large following on social media might also garner lucrative sponsorship deals. However, earning an income in this way places creators at the mercy of the major platforms such as YouTube, Instagram and TikTok. Creators have no control over the percentage of advertising revenue that they receive, and are subject to arbitrary decisions about what can and cannot be posted. Accounts can be shut down without apparent cause, and with few rights to challenge such decisions, as Giblin has pointed out:

> "Creators shouldn't have to choose between Big Content and Big Tech. Neither of them have their interests at heart. And similarly, society shouldn't have to rely on the crumbs that Big Content and Big Tech are willing to give us. We do have alternatives. And in order to access them and to do a better job, we need to cut into that corporate power. We need to form new alliances that bring people together united over these common interests, which are, of course, to make sure that our amazing creators are recognised and rewarded for their work, and that that work can be made available so that all of us can benefit from it."[735]

One way to cut out the intermediaries is to sell directly to fans. This approach has been adopted by online audio distribution platform Bandcamp.[736] Founded in 2008, Bandcamp says that fans had paid artists $929 million using the service by 2022, and $194 million in the year to 2022. One indication that such crowdfunding[737] sites are entering the mainstream is the acquisition of Bandcamp[738] by the major gaming company Epic Games in 2022. Bandcamp also shows that fans are prepared to pay for quality since they can—and do—opt to pay more than the average price for music:

> "[Leaving] 'let fans pay more if they want' checked is key: fans pay more than the minimum a whopping 40% of the time, driving up the average price paid by

> nearly 50% (in fact, every day, we see überfans paying
> $50, $100, $200 for albums priced far lower).”[739]

The fact that devoted fans are often willing to pay extra in order to support the work of creators whose work they love lies at the heart of another approach to funding that is becoming popular. It derives its power from the special bond that links creators with their most loyal fans, and the fact that the Internet allows them to connect, wherever either party may be located. It removes what Fight for the Future's campaigns and communications director Lia Holland has called the 'choke point that is created by these big moneyed interests between creators and their fans that want to support them.'[740]

One of the earliest and best expositions of the concept came from Kevin Kelly,[741] former Executive Editor at *Wired* magazine, in an essay he wrote in 2008. He has updated the idea in the light of more recent developments that make it even more compelling and easier to realise:

> "To be a successful creator you don't need millions. You don't need millions of dollars or millions of customers, millions of clients or millions of fans. To make a living as a craftsperson, photographer, musician, designer, author, animator, app maker, entrepreneur, or inventor you need only thousands of true fans.
>
> A true fan is defined as a fan that will buy anything you produce. These diehard fans will drive 200 miles to see you sing; they will buy the hardback and paperback and audible versions of your book; they will purchase your next figurine sight unseen; they will pay for the 'best-of' DVD version of your free youtube channel; they will come to your chef's table once a month. If you have roughly a thousand of true fans like this (also

known as super fans), you can make a living—if you are content to make a living but not a fortune."[742]

Kelly has pointed out that this is not exclusively about the special relationship a creator has with those true fans, although they remain vital. Alongside the true fans, there are the regular fans, who like a creator's work, and will buy it from time to time. They represent additional income over and above the core income from true fans, and are also potential converts to a closer relationship with the artist. He explained how the arrival of the Internet means that creators can do better than all the well-established intermediaries in the copyright world:

> "[The] benefits of modern retailing meant that most creators in the last century did not have direct contact with consumers. Often even the publishers, studios, labels and manufacturers did not have such crucial information as the name of their customers. For instance, despite being in business for hundreds of years no New York book publisher knew the names of their core and dedicated readers. For previous creators these intermediates (and there was often more than one) meant you need much larger audiences to have a success. With the advent of ubiquitous peer-to-peer communication and payment systems—also known as the web today—everyone has access to excellent tools that allow anyone to sell directly to anyone else in the world."[743]

A significant consequence of the ability to connect to anyone, anywhere in the world, is that creators can serve niche audiences, which is hard for conventional intermediaries and harder the bigger they become. As Kelly explained: 'You'll have your one-in-a-million true fans to yourself. And the tools for connecting keep getting better, including the recent innovations in social media. It has never been easier to gather 1,000 true fans around a creator, and never easier to keep them near.'[744]

If finding and keeping true fans is easier than ever before, so is generating and collecting an income. One of the major developments since Kelly's original essay was published in 2008 is the rise of crowdfunding—yet again, something that is only possible thanks to the uptake of the Internet. There are thousands of different crowdfunding platforms, with various kinds of models that allow creators to choose the one that suits them best, as Kelly said: 'Some platforms require "all or nothing" funding goals, others permit partial funding, some raise money for completed projects, some like Patreon, fund ongoing projects. Patreon supporters might fund a monthly magazine, or a video series, or an artist's salary.'[745]

A good example of how a well-known creator can use the crowdfunding platform Kickstarter[746] to support work is the writer and digital rights activist Cory Doctorow. In 2020, when Doctorow's publisher could not afford to pay for an audio version of his latest book, he asked his fans to fund it.[747] They not only pre-ordered 6,700 copies of the audiobook at $15 each, they also bought previous audiobooks in the series:

> "Between ebooks, audiobooks, and some special perks, I grossed $267k; about $130k of that went straight out again to my publishers, and about 30% of that will come right back to me as a royalty. I'm calling that a success."[748]

Not everyone commands the level of support that Doctorow has garnered. But more recently, Li Jin,[749] founder and managing partner at Atelier, an early-stage venture capital firm, suggested that the situation in what she called the 'passion economy' is even better than Kelly predicted:

> "As the Passion Economy grows, more people are monetizing what they love. The global adoption of social platforms like Facebook and YouTube, the mainstreaming of the influencer model, and the rise of new creator tools has shifted the threshold for success. I believe that creators need to amass only 100 True Fans— not 1,000—paying them $1,000 a year, not $100. Today, creators can effectively make more money off fewer fans."[750]

Before copyright existed, most creation was supported in this way, through funding by true fans, except that typically there was only one fan, a rich and powerful patron—perhaps a member of royalty, an aristocrat or senior cleric— who provided the money required to make a work of art. In return, they received both the work and the kudos of supporting the creative endeavour. It is striking that almost all of what are now acknowledged as some of the world's greatest masterpieces—in literature, music, art, sculpture and architecture—were produced thanks to this system of patronage rather than during a time when copyright existed for these fields. It is also how most academic research is supported. Here, the patrons are universities and other higher education establishments. They pay their professors and researchers, who then write books and papers, sometimes alongside other work, such as teaching. The money they earn from those books and papers is often too little to live on, but is in this case ancillary to the institutional funding.

The difference in the 21st century is that the Internet has democratised patronage: anyone who is online can make a donation, whether small or big. Contributors receive the benefit of the completed project, together with an acknowledgement for backing the idea. Minting a non-fungible token (NFT)[751]—a kind of unique digital barcode associated with other digital material, for example an image—as public recognition of support is one of the few situations where doing so makes sense. *Techdirt*'s Mike Masnick calls this 'digital hipsterism': owning one of these NFTs is 'effectively saying "I was here first, I supported this first and I have a way to display that".'[752]

That's in contrast with most uses of NFTs, which are usually based on the fallacious idea that they confer ownership of the underlying copyright of the associated material. Andrés Guadamuz,[753] reader in Intellectual Property Law at the University of Sussex, has written a series of blog posts[754] exploring the copyright issues raised by NFTs.

One of the first to succeed with the Internet-based patronage model was the interactive live-streaming service Twitch,[755] which is best known for its video game streaming. Launched in 2011, Twitch added a twist to the idea of encouraging fans to support creators, as journalist Cecilia D'Anastasio wrote on *Wired*:

> "The streamer was right there, and you were giving them money, and then they were responding to you giving them money, all in real time. A model emerged: Give $5 and get a shout-out. The sure acknowledgement tickled something in our lizard brains. Early streamers adopted text-to-speech software that, in computer-monotone, read out the messages fans attached to donations."[756]

Twitch's model proved such a success that in 2014 the company was purchased by Amazon for a reported $970 million. According to the site Business of Apps, in 2021 Twitch had nine million active channels, and 2.78 million users who watched streams for 22.8 billion hours. Twitch's revenue in 2021 was $2.6 billion.[757] D'Anastasio wrote:

> "Ten years after Twitch's debut, this is the creator economy. Twitch COO Sara Clemens says that while we're still in its infancy, Twitch was 'the original player.' With traditional media, there was 'a lack of recognition that fans want to connect directly with creators and have a relationship, and that can be monetized really effectively,' she says. 'If you have 1,000 fans willing to support you, that can be a really meaningful way to build a career.' Other industries are starting to catch up—witness the recent wave of writers monetizing their followings on Substack, or influencers soulfully peddling icky skinny teas."[758]

The scale of this fan-based patronage ecosystem is underappreciated. According to one research report, crowdfunding was valued at $17 billion in 2021. By 2028, the global crowdfunding market is projected to grow to $43 billion, with an average compound growth rate of 16.5% over the forecast period.[759] Not all of that will go to creators, but many billions certainly will, which will put it on a par with payments made by traditional intermediaries such as publishers, film studios and music labels. Crucially, nearly all the crowdfunding revenue flows to artists, not to businesses, and is under the direct control of the creators.

One of the most conspicuous differences of this kind of distributed, Internet-based patronage from current artist remuneration schemes, is that the former does not depend on copyright. Moreover, unlike the copyright world's obsession with stopping the sharing of material, the true-fans approach encourages such sharing, since it acts as free marketing that allows more true fans to be recruited to boost the creator's income. There is no danger that such fans will simply enjoy the results of other people's funding, because they are, by definition, true fans who know that creators must be paid in some way, or they will stop creating. It is in their own interests—as true fans—to keep sending money to their preferred artists. As Fight for the Future's director Evan Greer has said in a *Walled Culture* interview:

> "When you enter a digital world, that sense of copyright as an enforcer of false scarcity just exponentially grows, because you now have something that can be copied and shared infinite times, essentially without any cost. And so the only thing that's enforcing that false scarcity is copyright. And that is framed as a benefit to the person that created that song or photograph or image. But what we see over and over again is that [those] who benefit are the middlemen or corporations. Individual artists who are building a fan base often actually benefit from people sharing their songs or music and building a larger fan base."[760]

This book has described the growing problems that copyright is causing in the online world as a result of the inherent incompatibility of a law designed for analogue creativity and the digital world of the Internet. There are dozens of actions that could be taken to ameliorate some—but not all—of these problems. Given the likely impossibility of making even a fraction of those changes, which in any case would not address the underlying issue, maybe it is time to consider a simpler strategy. Might abolishing copyright altogether be a better and simpler way to solve the problems it has created?

Although such a move would cause massive upheavals for companies in the business of exploiting the creativity of others, it would not stop artists from earning as much as at present, they might even earn more, thanks to support from true fans and the application of other business models that already exist. Cultural institutions like libraries, museums and schools would not suffer in a world based on patronage, since it would be in the interest of creators to make copies of their works freely available to this group, both as a marketing tool to gain more true fans and thus more financial support, and also with an eye to securing a place in the artistic pantheon.

The world of fashion, where copyright protection is absent or minimal[761]—notably in the United States[762]—proves that copyright is not needed for creativity to flourish and for profits to flow on an immense scale. The value of the global fashion industry is $3 trillion,[763] greater than all the other creative industries combined. Even without intellectual monopolies, the fashion world is synonymous with rapid, incessant introduction of innovative ideas that drive its success.

Copyright is supposed to be about providing the public with the fruits of a creator's work, while at the same time rewarding that creativity fairly. It is not about sustaining huge corporations whose sole interest is in preserving their profit margins by lobbying for one-sided laws and exploiting hapless artists. Abolishing copyright would remove what is essentially a parasitic element from the system, while still encouraging artists to create, and rewarding them for doing so. Abolishing copyright may be bold, but it could be achieved, perhaps by paying appropriate compensation to ease the transition. Such compensation could be funded by the digital platforms that have the most to gain.

The choice the world faces is stark. Society can either continue to suffer the negative consequences of present and future punitive laws, designed solely to preserve an ancient intellectual monopoly that profits a few; or it can choose to maximise the potential of the digital sphere, for the general benefit of humankind. Copyright or the Internet—choose one.

Notes

1   https://web.archive.org/web/20220615182457/https://
    en.wikipedia.org/wiki/Statute_of_Anne
2   https://web.archive.org/web/20220615182511/https://
    en.wikipedia.org/wiki/Berne_Convention
3   https://web.archive.org/web/20220615182557/https://www.
    plagiarismtoday.com/2021/05/13/why-did-the-united-states-
    wait-103-years-to-sign-the-berne-convention/
4   https://web.archive.org/web/20220615182616/https://
    en.wikipedia.org/wiki/Moore%27s_law
5   https://web.archive.org/web/20220615182647/https://
    en.wikipedia.org/wiki/Digital_Audio_Tape
6   https://web.archive.org/web/20220615182709/https://
    en.wikipedia.org/wiki/Audio_Home_Recording_Act
7   https://web.archive.org/web/20220615182728/https://
    en.wikipedia.org/wiki/Information_superhighway
8   https://web.archive.org/web/20220615182751/https://
    en.wikipedia.org/wiki/National_Information_Infrastructure
9   https://web.archive.org/web/20220615182813/https://
    en.wikipedia.org/wiki/Bruce_Lehman
10 https://web.archive.org/web/20220614172420/https://
    repository.law.umich.edu/books/1/
11 https://web.archive.org/web/20220615183505/https://michigan.
    law.umich.edu/faculty-and-scholarship/our-faculty/jessica-litman
12 https://web.archive.org/web/20220701120031/https://
    en.wikipedia.org/wiki/United_States_Patent_and_Trademark_
    Office

13 https://web.archive.org/web/20220701123552/https://en.wikipedia.org/wiki/Random-access_memory

14 https://web.archive.org/web/20220615183532/https://en.wikipedia.org/wiki/First-sale_doctrine

15 https://web.archive.org/web/20220615183551/https://en.wikipedia.org/wiki/CompuServe

16 https://web.archive.org/web/20220615183612/https://en.wikipedia.org/wiki/AOL

17 https://web.archive.org/web/20220614172420/https://repository.law.umich.edu/books/1/

18 https://web.archive.org/web/20220614184956/https://en.wikipedia.org/wiki/Limitations_and_exceptions_to_copyright

19 https://web.archive.org/web/20220615183731/https://en.wikipedia.org/wiki/Digital_Future_Coalition

20 https://web.archive.org/web/20220615183751/https://en.wikipedia.org/wiki/Home_Recording_Rights_Coalition

21 https://web.archive.org/web/20220615183813/https://en.wikipedia.org/wiki/World_Intellectual_Property_Organization

22 https://web.archive.org/web/20220615183834/https://en.wikipedia.org/wiki/Policy_laundering

23 https://web.archive.org/web/20220614173121/https://en.wikipedia.org/wiki/WIPO_Copyright_Treaty

24 https://web.archive.org/web/20220615184513/https://en.wikipedia.org/wiki/Fair_use

25 https://web.archive.org/web/20220614172420/https://repository.law.umich.edu/books/1/

26 https://web.archive.org/web/20220615184534/https://en.wikipedia.org/wiki/Digital_Millennium_Copyright_Act

27 https://web.archive.org/web/20220614185543/https://en.wikipedia.org/wiki/Information_Society_Directive

28 https://web.archive.org/web/20220615184613/https://en.wikipedia.org/wiki/Dot-com_bubble

29 https://web.archive.org/web/20220701090414/https://en.wikipedia.org/wiki/Digital_rights_management

30 https://web.archive.org/web/20220705085628/https://en.wikipedia.org/wiki/Cory_Doctorow

31 https://web.archive.org/web/20220615184637/https://walledculture.org/interview-cory-doctorow-part-1-newspapers-big-tech-link-tax-drm-and-right-to-repair/

32 https://web.archive.org/web/20220621063129/https://en.wikipedia.org/wiki/Copyright_formalities

33 https://web.archive.org/web/20220621063142/https://
en.wikipedia.org/wiki/Public_domain

34 https://web.archive.org/web/20220621063226/https://
en.wikipedia.org/wiki/Orphan_work

35 https://web.archive.org/web/20220701061911/https://papers.
ssrn.com/sol3/papers.cfm?abstract_id=2049685

36 https://web.archive.org/web/20220701062629/https://
en.wikipedia.org/wiki/United_States_Copyright_Office

37 https://web.archive.org/web/20220621153223/https://www.
copyright.gov/orphan/orphan-report.pdf

38 https://web.archive.org/web/20220701061911/https://papers.
ssrn.com/sol3/papers.cfm?abstract_id=2049685

39 https://web.archive.org/web/20220621153305/https://
en.wikipedia.org/wiki/Public_domain

40 https://web.archive.org/web/20220705074438/https://fortune.
com/2020/11/28/digital-publishing-copyright-champion-lila-
bailey-internet-archive/

41 https://web.archive.org/web/20220621182436/https://www.
techdirt.com/2015/10/13/digital-orphans-massive-cultural-
black-hole-our-horizon/

42 https://web.archive.org/web/20220817075337/
https://eur-lex.europa.eu/legal-content/EN/TXT/
HTML/?uri=CELEX%3A32012L0028

43 https://web.archive.org/web/20220621153443/https://
en.wikipedia.org/wiki/Machine_learning

44 https://euipo.europa.eu/orphanworks/

45 https://web.archive.org/web/20220620162553/https://ec.europa.
eu/commission/presscorner/detail/en/MEMO_12_743

46 https://web.archive.org/web/20220620162614/https://assets.
publishing.service.gov.uk/government/uploads/system/uploads/
attachment_data/file/32564/response-2011-copyright.pdf

47 https://web.archive.org/web/20220621154455/https://www.gov.
uk/government/news/uk-opens-access-to-91-million-orphan-
works

48 https://web.archive.org/web/20220620162702/https://www.
hb.se/en/Shortcuts/Contact/Employee/MEMA/

49 https://web.archive.org/web/20220621154624/https://www.
ed.ac.uk/profile/professor-melissa-terras

50 https://web.archive.org/web/20220621154652/https://olh.
openlibhums.org/article/id/4573/

51 https://web.archive.org/web/20220620162815/https://
s3.amazonaws.com/s3.documentcloud.org/documents/2094366/
orphan-works2015.pdf

52 https://web.archive.org/web/20220621154752/https://
en.wikipedia.org/wiki/Michael_S._Hart

53 https://web.archive.org/web/20220620163648/http://www.
gutenbergnews.org/about/history-of-project-gutenberg/

54 https://web.archive.org/web/20220620163648/http://www.
gutenbergnews.org/about/history-of-project-gutenberg/

55 https://web.archive.org/web/20220620163725/https://pro.
europeana.eu/about-us/mission

56 https://web.archive.org/web/20220621071000/https://www.
europeana.eu/en

57 https://web.archive.org/web/20220621070928/https://pro.
europeana.eu/post/the-missing-decades-the-20th-century-black-
hole-in-europeana

58 https://web.archive.org/web/20160206043510/http://books.
google.com/googlebooks/about/history.html

59 https://web.archive.org/web/20220621071024/https://
en.wikipedia.org/wiki/Optical_character_recognition

60 https://web.archive.org/web/20220621071132/https://
en.wikipedia.org/wiki/Google_Books

61 https://web.archive.org/web/20220621071154/https://www.
authorsguild.org/who-we-are/

62 https://web.archive.org/web/20220621071953/https://www.
nytimes.com/2005/09/21/technology/writers-sue-google-
accusing-it-of-copyright-violation.html

63 https://web.archive.org/web/20220621072029/https://www.
cnet.com/tech/tech-industry/publishers-sue-google-over-book-
search-project/

64 https://web.archive.org/web/20220620164503/https://www.
theatlantic.com/technology/archive/2017/04/the-tragedy-of-
google-books/523320/

65 https://web.archive.org/web/20220620171524/https://www.
authorsguild.org/wp-content/uploads/2012/08/Amended-
Settlement-Agreement.pdf

66 https://web.archive.org/web/20220621072210/https://
facultydirectory.virginia.edu/faculty/sv2r

67 https://web.archive.org/web/20220620171618/https://
lawreview.law.ucdavis.edu/issues/40/3/copyright-creativity-
catalogs/DavisVol40No3_Vaidhyanathan.pdf

68 https://web.archive.org/web/20220620164503/https://www.
theatlantic.com/technology/archive/2017/04/the-tragedy-of-
google-books/523320/

69 https://web.archive.org/web/20131103165236/http://publishers.
org/press/85/

70 https://web.archive.org/web/20220621072300/https://www.eff.
org/cases/authors-guild-v-google-part-ii-fair-use-proceedings

71 https://web.archive.org/web/20220621072320/https://www.
hathitrust.org/authors_guild_lawsuit_information

72 https://web.archive.org/web/20220621072339/https://www.
hathitrust.org/press_10-13-2008

73 https://web.archive.org/web/20220620172106/https://
www.publishersweekly.com/pw/by-topic/digital/copyright/
article/48659-authors-guild-sues-libraries-over-scan-plan.html

74 https://web.archive.org/web/20220621073236/https://www.
nytimes.com/2011/09/13/business/media/authors-sue-to-remove-
books-from-digital-archive.html

75 https://web.archive.org/web/20220620172106/https://
www.publishersweekly.com/pw/by-topic/digital/copyright/
article/48659-authors-guild-sues-libraries-over-scan-plan.html

76 https://web.archive.org/web/20220621073355/https://
en.wikipedia.org/wiki/Transformative_use

77 https://web.archive.org/web/20220620173115/https://
www.publishersweekly.com/pw/by-topic/digital/copyright/
article/54321-in-hathitrust-ruling-judge-says-google-scanning-
is-fair-use.html

78 https://web.archive.org/web/20220620173140/https://www.
wipo.int/marrakesh_treaty/en/

79 https://web.archive.org/web/20220705085826/https://
en.wikipedia.org/wiki/James_Love_%28NGO_director%29

80 https://web.archive.org/web/20220620173240/https://www.
keionline.org/

81 https://web.archive.org/web/20220909084848/https://
walledculture.org/interview-james-love/

82 https://web.archive.org/web/20220701065841/https://
corporateeurope.org/en/power-lobbies/2017/03/marrakesh-
brussels-long-arm-eu-copyright-lobby

83 https://web.archive.org/web/20220621164103/https://www.
wired.com/2017/04/how-google-book-search-got-lost/

84 https://web.archive.org/web/20220620183320/https://www.
hathitrust.org/files/14MillionBooksand6MillionVisitors_1.pdf

85 https://web.archive.org/web/20220621164158/https://www.europeana.eu/en/about-us

86 https://web.archive.org/web/20220620183528/https://dp.la/

87 https://web.archive.org/web/20220621034828/https://archive.org/

88 https://web.archive.org/web/20220701073551/https://www.nytimes.com/2005/10/03/business/in-challenge-to-google-yahoo-will-scan-books.html

89 https://web.archive.org/web/20220701073629/https://openlibrary.org/

90 https://web.archive.org/web/20220621034828/https://archive.org/

91 https://web.archive.org/web/20220621074031/https://walledculture.org/interview-brewster-kahle-libraries-role-3-internet-battles-licensing-pains-the-national-emergency-library-and-the-internet-archives-controlled-digital-lending-efforts-vs-the-publishers-lawsuit/

92 https://web.archive.org/web/20220817072842/https://digitalcommons.du.edu/collaborativelibrarianship/vol12/iss2/8

93 https://web.archive.org/web/20220621074146/https://www.hathitrust.org/ETAS-Description

94 https://web.archive.org/web/20220621075018/https://en.wikipedia.org/wiki/Controlled_digital_lending

95 https://web.archive.org/web/20220621075101/https://controlleddigitallending.org/

96 https://web.archive.org/web/20220621075139/https://controlleddigitallending.org/faq

97 https://web.archive.org/web/20220621183602/http://openlibraries.online/

98 https://web.archive.org/web/20220701075026/https://www.wsj.com/articles/SB10001424052748703279704575335193054884632

99 https://web.archive.org/web/20220121095547/https://archive.org/details/TransformingourLibrariesintoDigitalLibraries102016

100 https://web.archive.org/web/20220701075207/https://docs.google.com/document/u/1/d/e/2PACX-1vQeYK7dKWH7Qqw9wLVnmEo1ZktykuULBq15j7L2gPCXSL3zem4WZO4JFyj-dS9yVK6BTnu7T1UAluOl/pub

101 https://web.archive.org/web/20220701075343/https://www.newyorker.com/books/page-turner/the-national-emergency-library-is-a-gift-to-readers-everywhere

102 https://web.archive.org/web/20220621164306/https://
www.authorsguild.org/industry-advocacy/internet-archives-
uncontrolled-digital-lending/

103 https://web.archive.org/web/20220621164330/https://
publishers.org/news/comment-from-aap-president-and-ceo-
maria-pallante-on-the-internet-archives-national-emergency-
library/

104 https://web.archive.org/web/20220621164359/https://www.
publishersweekly.com/pw/by-topic/industry-news/publisher-
news/article/83472-publishers-charge-the-internet-archive-with-
copyright-infringement.html

105 https://web.archive.org/web/20220620201839/https://www.
publishersweekly.com/binary-data/ARTICLE_ATTACHMENT/
file/000/004/4388-1.pdf

106 https://web.archive.org/web/20220620201859/https://blog.
archive.org/2020/06/10/temporary-national-emergency-library-
to-close-2-weeks-early-returning-to-traditional-controlled-
digital-lending/

107 https://web.archive.org/web/20220621165251/https://
walledculture.org/interview-brewster-kahle-libraries-role-3-
internet-battles-licensing-pains-the-national-emergency-library-
and-the-internet-archives-controlled-digital-lending-efforts-vs-
the-publishers-lawsuit/

108 https://web.archive.org/web/20220621164359/https://www.
publishersweekly.com/pw/by-topic/industry-news/publisher-
news/article/83472-publishers-charge-the-internet-archive-with-
copyright-infringement.html

109 https://web.archive.org/web/20220701075637/https://www.
techdirt.com/2020/06/04/major-publishers-sue-internet-
archives-digital-library-program-midst-pandemic/

110 https://web.archive.org/web/20220701075917/https://help.
archive.org/help/national-emergency-library-faqs/

111 https://web.archive.org/web/20220621165356/https://www.
publishersweekly.com/pw/by-topic/industry-news/trade-shows-
events/article/62877-ala-2014-raising-the-stakes.html

112 https://web.archive.org/web/20220620202027/https://www.
publishersweekly.com/pw/by-topic/industry-news/libraries/
article/77532-tor-scales-back-library-e-book-lending-as-part-of-
test.html

113 https://web.archive.org/web/20220621075324/https://www.
authorsguild.org/industry-advocacy/e-book-library-pricing-the-
game-changes-again/

114 https://web.archive.org/web/20220620202210/https://www.
publishersweekly.com/pw/by-topic/digital/content-and-e-books/
article/46333-librarian-unhappiness-over-new-harper-e-book-
lending-policy-grows.html

115 https://web.archive.org/web/20220620203003/https://www.
publishersweekly.com/pw/by-topic/industry-news/libraries/
article/80758-after-tor-experiment-macmillan-expands-
embargo-on-library-e-books.html

116 https://web.archive.org/web/20220621075545/https://www.ala.
org/news/press-releases/2019/07/ala-denounces-new-macmillan-
library-lending-model-urges-library-customers

117 https://web.archive.org/web/20220620203047/https://www.
publishersweekly.com/binary-data/ARTICLE_ATTACHMENT/
file/000/004/4353-1.pdf

118 https://web.archive.org/web/20220621165501/https://www.
newyorker.com/news/annals-of-communications/an-app-called-
libby-and-the-surprisingly-big-business-of-library-e-books

119 https://web.archive.org/web/20220621165531/https://company.
overdrive.com/2020/05/14/check-out-mays-trending-titles-on-
libby/

120 https://web.archive.org/web/20220621165603/https://
publishers.org/news/aap-october-2020-statshot-report-
publishing-industry-up-7-3-for-month-down-1-0-year-to-date/

121 https://web.archive.org/web/20220620203518/https://www.
authorsalliance.org/2021/12/10/update-aap-sues-maryland-over-
e-lending-law/

122 https://web.archive.org/web/20220620203541/https://www.
publishersweekly.com/pw/by-topic/industry-news/libraries/
article/85785-maryland-legislature-passes-law-supporting-
library-access-to-digital-content.html

123 https://web.archive.org/web/20220620203604/https://
publishers.org/wp-content/uploads/2021/12/AAP-v.-Maryland.
pdf

124 https://web.archive.org/web/20220621075905/https://
walledculture.org/guest-post-ebooksos-crisis-price-gouging-
publishers/

125 https://web.archive.org/web/20220621075943/https://
academicebookinvestigation.org/2020/09/27/campaign-update-
215-signatures-in-less-than-48-hrs/

126 https://web.archive.org/web/20220620204509/https://
academicebookinvestigation.org/

127 https://web.archive.org/web/20220621080755/https://
academicebookinvestigation.org/2021/11/25/outrage-as-
pearson-increase-ebook-prices-by-500-in-one-week/

128 https://web.archive.org/web/20220705090057/https://
en.wikipedia.org/wiki/Techdirt

129 https://web.archive.org/web/20220701080457/https://www.
techdirt.com/2009/05/15/one-more-reminder-that-you-dont-
own-the-books-on-your-kindle/

130 https://web.archive.org/web/20220701080025/https://archive.
nytimes.com/bits.blogs.nytimes.com/2009/02/27/amazon-backs-
off-text-to-speech-feature-in-kindle/

131 https://web.archive.org/web/20220621171126/https://
en.wikipedia.org/wiki/Memory_hole

132 https://web.archive.org/web/20220621081042/https://www.
nytimes.com/2009/07/18/technology/companies/18amazon.html

133 https://web.archive.org/web/20220621081149/https://
walledculture.org/interview-cory-doctorow-part-1-newspapers-
big-tech-link-tax-drm-and-right-to-repair/

134 https://web.archive.org/web/20220617112218/https://
en.wikipedia.org/wiki/TeX

135 https://web.archive.org/web/20220617122120/https://
en.wikipedia.org/wiki/Donald_Knuth

136 https://web.archive.org/web/20220615135309/https://
en.wikipedia.org/wiki/Paul_Ginsparg

137 https://web.archive.org/web/20220615152914/https://arxiv.org/
pdf/1108.2700v2.pdf

138 https://web.archive.org/web/20220620141741/https://arxiv.org/

139 https://web.archive.org/web/20220615152932/https://
en.wikipedia.org/wiki/Philosophical_Transactions_of_the_
Royal_Society

140 https://web.archive.org/web/20220620095426/https://
en.wikipedia.org/wiki/Peer_review

141 https://web.archive.org/web/20220617123729/https://
en.wikipedia.org/wiki/Curriculum_vitae

142 https://web.archive.org/web/20220617123741/https://
en.wikipedia.org/wiki/Ingelfinger_rule

143 https://web.archive.org/web/20150824014630/http://scielo.org/
local/File/book.pdf

144 https://web.archive.org/web/20220617125254/https://pubmed.
ncbi.nlm.nih.gov/

145 https://web.archive.org/web/20220615153123/https://www.
ncbi.nlm.nih.gov/Web/Newsltr/aug97.pdf

146 https://web.archive.org/web/20220617130129/https://
en.wikipedia.org/wiki/David_J._Lipman

147 https://web.archive.org/web/20220620100032/https://
en.wikipedia.org/wiki/Vitek_Tracz

148 https://web.archive.org/web/20220617130155/https://www.
infotoday.com/it/jan05/poynder.shtml

149 https://web.archive.org/web/20220617130213/https://www.
ncbi.nlm.nih.gov/genbank/

150 https://web.archive.org/web/20220617130234/https://www.
genome.gov/human-genome-project

151 https://web.archive.org/web/20220620100415/https://
en.wikipedia.org/wiki/Harold_E._Varmus

152 https://web.archive.org/web/20220620101511/https://
en.wikipedia.org/wiki/Patrick_O._Brown

153 https://web.archive.org/web/20220615153344/https://www.
ncbi.nlm.nih.gov/books/NBK190606/

154 https://web.archive.org/web/20220615153329/https://
collections.nlm.nih.gov/ext/document/101584926X356/
PDF/101584926X356.pdf

155 https://web.archive.org/web/20220615153329/https://
collections.nlm.nih.gov/ext/document/101584926X356/
PDF/101584926X356.pdf

156 https://web.archive.org/web/20220617130155/https://www.
infotoday.com/it/jan05/poynder.shtml

157 https://web.archive.org/web/20220620102157/https://
en.wikipedia.org/wiki/Michael_Eisen

158 https://web.archive.org/web/20220617130429/https://plos.org/

159 https://web.archive.org/web/20220617130413/https://plos.org/
open-letter/

160 https://web.archive.org/web/20220617130413/https://plos.org/
open-letter/

161 https://web.archive.org/web/20220620102423/https://www.
ncbi.nlm.nih.gov/pmc/articles/PMC212706/

162 https://web.archive.org/web/20220615153344/https://www.
ncbi.nlm.nih.gov/books/NBK190606/

163 https://web.archive.org/web/20220617131247/https://www.
budapestopenaccessinitiative.org/read/

164 https://web.archive.org/web/20220617131247/https://www.
budapestopenaccessinitiative.org/read/

165 https://web.archive.org/web/20220615081804/https://dash.
harvard.edu/bitstream/handle/1/4725199/Suber_bethesda.htm

166 https://web.archive.org/web/20220620135626/https://openaccess.mpg.de/Berlin-Declaration

167 https://web.archive.org/web/20220617135015/https://en.wikipedia.org/wiki/List_of_wealthiest_charitable_foundations

168 https://web.archive.org/web/20220701124017/https://en.wikipedia.org/wiki/Wellcome_Trust

169 https://web.archive.org/web/20220701124107/https://en.wikipedia.org/wiki/Research_Councils_UK

170 https://web.archive.org/web/20220701090553/https://en.wikipedia.org/wiki/Embargo_%28academic_publishing%29

171 https://web.archive.org/web/20220617135046/https://openaccesseks.mitpress.mit.edu/

172 https://web.archive.org/web/20220704130518/https://en.wikipedia.org/wiki/Peter_Suber

173 https://web.archive.org/web/20220615082705/https://dash.harvard.edu/bitstream/handle/1/4725004/suber_rcukcomment.htm;sequence=1

174 https://web.archive.org/web/20220617135122/https://www.nature.com/articles/445347a/

175 https://web.archive.org/web/20130808163543/www.hhmi.org/news/hhmi-announces-new-policy-publication-research-articles

176 https://web.archive.org/web/20130210022552/https://legacy.earlham.edu/~peters/fos/newsletter/03-02-08.htm

177 https://web.archive.org/web/20220617135142/https://www.govtrack.us/congress/bills/112/hr3699/summary

178 https://web.archive.org/web/20220617135225/https://www.nature.com/articles/481409a

179 https://web.archive.org/web/20171205173447/https://plus.google.com/+PeterSuber/posts/cspR3h4ZAv4

180 https://web.archive.org/web/20220617135246/https://en.wikipedia.org/wiki/Timothy_Gowers

181 https://web.archive.org/web/20220617142258/https://en.wikipedia.org/wiki/Elsevier

182 https://web.archive.org/web/20220617142316/https://gowers.wordpress.com/2012/01/21/elsevier-my-part-in-its-downfall/

183 https://web.archive.org/web/20220617142316/https://gowers.wordpress.com/2012/01/21/elsevier-my-part-in-its-downfall/

184 https://web.archive.org/web/20220617142358/http://thecostofknowledge.com/

185 https://web.archive.org/web/20220615160851/https://gowers.files.wordpress.com/2012/02/elsevierstatementfinal.pdf

186 https://web.archive.org/web/20220617142429/https://www.
theguardian.com/science/2012/apr/09/frustrated-blogpost-
boycott-scientific-journals

187 https://web.archive.org/web/20220127171755/https://www.
researchinfonet.org/finch/

188 https://web.archive.org/web/20131107075102/http://www.
researchinfonet.org/wp-content/uploads/2012/06/Finch-Group-
report-FINAL-VERSION.pdf

189 https://web.archive.org/web/20131107075102/http://www.
researchinfonet.org/wp-content/uploads/2012/06/Finch-Group-
report-FINAL-VERSION.pdf

190 https://web.archive.org/web/20220701090621/https://
en.wikipedia.org/wiki/Hybrid_open-access_journal

191 https://web.archive.org/web/20151228025805/http://www.
researchinfonet.org/wp-content/uploads/2015/09/Full-report-
FINAL-AS-PUBLISHED.pdf

192 https://web.archive.org/web/20140403223156/https://blog.
wellcome.ac.uk/2014/03/28/the-cost-of-open-access-publishing-
a-progress-report/

193 https://web.archive.org/web/20150508124215/https://blog.
wellcome.ac.uk/2015/03/03/the-reckoning-an-analysis-of-
wellcome-trust-open-access-spend-2013-14/

194 https://web.archive.org/web/20140411210045/http://www.
hefce.ac.uk/pubs/year/2014/201407/

195 https://web.archive.org/web/20220617142456/https://blogs.lse.
ac.uk/impactofsocialsciences/2014/04/01/hefce-open-access-ref-
gamechanger/

196 https://web.archive.org/web/20220617142522/https://oai.
events/etn-speaker/dr-danny-kingsley/

197 https://web.archive.org/web/20220617142555/https://
unlockingresearch-blog.lib.cam.ac.uk/?p=488

198 https://web.archive.org/web/20220617142614/http://bjoern.
brembs.net/2016/04/how-gold-open-access-may-make-things-
worse/

199 https://web.archive.org/web/20220617142645/https://blogs.lse.
ac.uk/impactofsocialsciences/2019/06/04/the-gold-rush-why-
open-access-will-boost-publisher-profits/

200 https://web.archive.org/web/20220615162019/https://council.
science/wp-content/uploads/2020/06/The-normalization-of-
preprints.pdf

201 https://web.archive.org/web/20220617143451/https://www. theguardian.com/books/2022/apr/11/the-big-idea-should-we- get-rid-of-the-scientific-paper

202 https://web.archive.org/web/20220617143517/https://www. ssrn.com/index.cfm/en/

203 https://web.archive.org/web/20220617143601/https:// en.wikipedia.org/wiki/Mendeley

204 https://web.archive.org/web/20220617143541/https://www. elsevier.com/about/press-releases/corporate/elsevier-acquires- the-social-science-research-network-ssrn,-the-leading-social- science-and-humanities-repository-and-online-community

205 https://web.archive.org/web/20220617143615/https://link. springer.com/article/10.1007/s00799-018-0234-1

206 https://web.archive.org/web/20220620113433/https:// scholarlykitchen.sspnet.org/2020/05/27/publishers-invest-in- preprints/

207 https://web.archive.org/web/20220617151308/https://zenodo. org/record/5526635

208 https://web.archive.org/web/20220617151335/https:// en.wikipedia.org/wiki/Article_processing_charge

209 https://web.archive.org/web/20220620113542/https:// symomega.wordpress.com/2012/08/09/green-gold-or-diamond- access/

210 https://web.archive.org/web/20220617155825/https:// symomega.wordpress.com/2012/07/09/academic-spam/

211 https://web.archive.org/web/20220615164332/https:// thatsmathematics.com/blog/archives/102

212 https://web.archive.org/web/20220617155902/https:// scholarlyoa.com/publishers/

213 https://web.archive.org/web/20220615145828/https://journals. plos.org/plosone/article?id=10.1371%2Fjournal.pone.0127502

214 https://web.archive.org/web/20220617160053/http://info- research.blogspot.com/2007/11/green-brass-and-platinum-three- routes.html

215 https://web.archive.org/web/20220615165419/https://www. southampton.ac.uk/~harnad/Hypermail/Amsci/6442.html

216 https://web.archive.org/web/20220615150111/https:// en.wikipedia.org/wiki/Stevan_Harnad

217 https://web.archive.org/web/20220615150203/http:// openscience.ens.fr/OPEN_ACCESS_MODELS/DIAMOND_ OPEN_ACCESS/2012_06_07_Mail_Marie_Farge_a_Jean- Pierre_Bourguignon_lui_proposant_le_modele_Diamant.pdf

218 https://web.archive.org/web/20220615150400/https://fuchsc.uti.at/

219 https://web.archive.org/web/20220620113901/https://www.city.ac.uk/about/people/academics/marisol-sandoval-gomez

220 https://web.archive.org/web/20220615150710/https://www.triple-c.at/index.php/tripleC/article/download/502/497

221 https://web.archive.org/web/20220701090859/https://en.wikipedia.org/wiki/Plan_S

222 https://web.archive.org/web/20220615150819/https://www.coalition-s.org/about/

223 https://web.archive.org/web/20220615150937/https://www.scienceeurope.org/our-resources/oa-diamond-journals-study/

224 https://web.archive.org/web/20220615150937/https://www.scienceeurope.org/our-resources/oa-diamond-journals-study/

225 https://web.archive.org/web/20220617171324/https://journals.plos.org/plosone/article?id=10.1371%2Fjournal.pone.0238372

226 https://web.archive.org/web/20220615150937/https://www.scienceeurope.org/our-resources/oa-diamond-journals-study/

227 https://web.archive.org/web/20220617171348/http://bjoern.brembs.net/2016/05/why-havent-we-already-canceled-all-subscriptions/

228 https://web.archive.org/web/20220617171407/https://www.rollingstone.com/culture/culture-news/the-brilliant-life-and-tragic-death-of-aaron-swartz-177191/

229 https://web.archive.org/web/20220617171543/https://archive.org/stream/GuerillaOpenAccessManifesto/Goamjuly2008_djvu.txt

230 https://web.archive.org/web/20220617171543/https://archive.org/stream/GuerillaOpenAccessManifesto/Goamjuly2008_djvu.txt

231 https://web.archive.org/web/20220617171728/https://en.wikipedia.org/wiki/JSTOR

232 https://web.archive.org/web/20220617171810/https://sci-hub.se/alexandra

233 https://web.archive.org/web/20220617171835/https://sci-hub.se/

234 https://web.archive.org/web/20220617172623/https://journals.plos.org/plosone/article?id=10.1371%2Fjournal.pone.0093949

235 https://web.archive.org/web/20220613001455/https://sci-hub.se/database

236 https://web.archive.org/web/20160501160246/http://www.
sciencemag.org/news/2016/04/whos-downloading-pirated-
papers-everyone

237 https://web.archive.org/web/20220617172704/https://www.
techdirt.com/2015/12/09/elsevier-granted-injunction-against-
research-paper-pirate-site-which-immediately-moves-to-new-
domain-to-dodge-it/

238 https://web.archive.org/web/20220617172723/https://
arstechnica.com/tech-policy/2016/05/piracy-site-for-academic-
journals-playing-game-of-domain-name-whac-a-mole/

239 https://web.archive.org/web/20220617172755/https://www.
nature.com/articles/nature.2017.22196

240 https://web.archive.org/web/20220617172812/https://www.
techdirt.com/2019/08/08/elsevier-says-infringing-to-link-to-sci-
hub-hypocrite-elsevier-links-to-sci-hub-all-time/

241 https://web.archive.org/web/20220617172830/https://
arstechnica.com/tech-policy/2016/04/a-spiritual-successor-to-
aaron-swartz-is-angering-publishers-all-over-again/

242 https://web.archive.org/web/20220617172851/https://cdn.
arstechnica.net/wp-content/uploads/2016/02/sci-hub.pdf

243 https://web.archive.org/web/20220617172912/https://www.
researchgate.net/

244 https://www.researchgate.net/press-newsroom/researchgate-
secures-wellcome-trust-goldman-sachs-investment-partners-
four-rivers-group

245 https://web.archive.org/web/20220617172912/https://www.
researchgate.net/

246 https://web.archive.org/web/20220617173751/https://systass.
org/texts/jon-tennant/

247 https://web.archive.org/web/20220617173809/http://
fossilsandshit.com/illegal-file-hosting-site-researchgate-acquires-
massive-financial-investment/

248 https://web.archive.org/web/20220617173835/https://www.
researchgate.net/ip-policy

249 https://web.archive.org/web/20220701125355/https://
en.wikipedia.org/wiki/International_Association_of_Scientific,_
Technical,_and_Medical_Publishers

250 https://web.archive.org/web/20220214195106/https://www.
elsevier.com/__data/assets/pdf_file/0010/509068/STM_letter_
ResearchGate.20170916.pdf

251 https://web.archive.org/web/20220617173906/http://www.
responsiblesharing.org/about-us/founding-statement/

252 https://web.archive.org/web/20220617173931/https://www.
science.org/content/article/publishers-take-researchgate-court-
alleging-massive-copyright-infringement

253 https://web.archive.org/web/20220617173951/http://www.
responsiblesharing.org/2022-02-02-statement-munich-regional-
court-ruling/

254 https://web.archive.org/web/20220616144512/https://
en.wikipedia.org/wiki/Secure_Digital_Music_Initiative

255 https://web.archive.org/web/20220616144529/https://
en.wikipedia.org/wiki/MP3

256 https://web.archive.org/web/20220616144545/https://
en.wikipedia.org/wiki/Rio_PMP300

257 https://web.archive.org/web/20220701125611/https://
en.wikipedia.org/wiki/Recording_Industry_Association_of_
America

258 https://web.archive.org/web/20220701090920/https://scholar.
google.com/scholar_case?case=16234294480765009725

259 https://web.archive.org/web/20220616150102/https://
en.wikipedia.org/wiki/Modem

260 https://web.archive.org/web/20220615185512/https://
en.wikipedia.org/wiki/MP3.com

261 https://web.archive.org/web/20220701125757/
https://en.wikipedia.org/wiki/Michael_
Robertson_%28businessman%29

262 https://web.archive.org/web/20220701125847/https://
en.wikipedia.org/wiki/Shawn_Fanning

263 https://web.archive.org/web/20220701125937/https://
en.wikipedia.org/wiki/Sean_Parker

264 https://web.archive.org/web/20220616150138/https://
en.wikipedia.org/wiki/Napster

265 https://web.archive.org/web/20220615185551/https://
en.wikipedia.org/wiki/Peer-to-peer

266 https://web.archive.org/web/20220616153814/https://
walledculture.org/interview-cory-doctorow-part-2-new-
publishing-models-for-creators-amazon-as-a-frenemy-and-the-
internet-archive-court-case/

267 https://web.archive.org/web/20220617092736/https://hls.
harvard.edu/faculty/directory/10519/Lessig

268 https://web.archive.org/web/20220616153851/https://lessig.org/
product/free-culture/

269 https://web.archive.org/web/20220616154652/https://
en.wikipedia.org/wiki/Madster

270   https://web.archive.org/web/20220616070008/https://
      en.wikipedia.org/wiki/AIM_%28software%29
271   https://web.archive.org/web/20220616155008/https://
      en.wikipedia.org/wiki/Gnutella
272   https://web.archive.org/web/20220616155027/https://
      en.wikipedia.org/wiki/Client_%28computing%29
273   https://web.archive.org/web/20220616155104/https://
      en.wikipedia.org/wiki/Rebel_Code
274   https://web.archive.org/web/20220616071105/https://
      en.wikipedia.org/wiki/Source_code
275   https://web.archive.org/web/20220616155211/https://
      en.wikipedia.org/wiki/BitTorrent
276   https://web.archive.org/web/20220616155234/https://www.eff.
      org/wp/riaa-v-people-five-years-later
277   https://web.archive.org/web/20031223084449/http:/www.post-
      gazette.com/columnists/20030914edroddy0914p1.asp
278   https://web.archive.org/web/20220616155234/https://www.eff.
      org/wp/riaa-v-people-five-years-later
279   https://web.archive.org/web/20220616155256/https://
      en.wikipedia.org/wiki/Kazaa
280   https://web.archive.org/web/20220616155317/https://www.eff.
      org/deeplinks/2008/09/capitol-v-thomas-judge-orders-new-trial-
      implores-c
281   https://web.archive.org/web/20220616160107/https://www.
      techdirt.com/2009/06/18/jammie-thomas-ordered-to-pay-1-92-
      million/
282   https://web.archive.org/web/20220616153814/https://
      walledculture.org/interview-cory-doctorow-part-2-new-
      publishing-models-for-creators-amazon-as-a-frenemy-and-the-
      internet-archive-court-case/
283   https://web.archive.org/web/20220616160148/https://law.
      unimelb.edu.au/about/staff/rebecca-giblin
284   https://web.archive.org/web/20220616160226/https://papers.
      ssrn.com/sol3/papers.cfm?abstract_id=2322516
285   https://web.archive.org/web/20220616160247/https://
      en.wikipedia.org/wiki/Internet_service_provider
286   https://web.archive.org/web/20220701130751/https://
      en.wikipedia.org/wiki/International_Federation_of_the_
      Phonographic_Industry
287   https://web.archive.org/web/20070203004312/https:/www.ifpi.
      org/content/library/digital-music-report-2007.pdf

288 https://web.archive.org/web/20220616073020/https://en.wikipedia.org/wiki/HADOPI_law

289 https://web.archive.org/web/20220616160435/https://www.nextinpact.com/

290 https://web.archive.org/web/20220616160415/https://walledculture.org/interview-marc-rees-a-la-francaise-de-lhadopi-par-la-copie-privee-jusquaux-algorithmes-de-larticle-17/

291 https://web.archive.org/web/20220616160226/https://papers.ssrn.com/sol3/papers.cfm?abstract_id=2322516

292 https://web.archive.org/web/20220616160458/https://www.techdirt.com/2013/06/17/first-french-file-sharer-sentenced-to-disconnection-under-hadopi-judgment-may-be-unenforceable/

293 https://web.archive.org/web/20220616160521/https://www.techdirt.com/2013/09/11/french-farce-hadopis-first-only-suspension-has-been-suspended/

294 https://web.archive.org/web/20220616160226/https://papers.ssrn.com/sol3/papers.cfm?abstract_id=2322516

295 https://web.archive.org/web/20220616160226/https://papers.ssrn.com/sol3/papers.cfm?abstract_id=2322516

296 https://web.archive.org/web/20220616160226/https://papers.ssrn.com/sol3/papers.cfm?abstract_id=2322516

297 https://web.archive.org/web/20220616163555/https://www.nextinpact.com/article/30433/109205-hadopi-82-millions-deuros-subventions-publiques-87000-euros-damendes

298 https://web.archive.org/web/20220615192453/https://en.wikipedia.org/wiki/Telecoms_Package

299 https://web.archive.org/web/20220615192453/https://en.wikipedia.org/wiki/Telecoms_Package

300 https://web.archive.org/web/20220507004149/https://en.wikipedia.org/wiki/Frank_William_La_Rue

301 https://web.archive.org/web/20220603094452/https://www2.ohchr.org/english/bodies/hrcouncil/docs/17session/A.HRC.17.27_en.pdf

302 https://web.archive.org/web/20220616163839/https://en.wikipedia.org/wiki/Stop_Online_Piracy_Act

303 https://web.archive.org/web/20220616163858/https://en.wikipedia.org/wiki/PROTECT_IP_Act

304 https://web.archive.org/web/20220615192636/https://en.wikipedia.org/wiki/Combating_Online_Infringement_and_Counterfeits_Act

305 https://web.archive.org/web/20220616163942/https://www.techdirt.com/

306 https://web.archive.org/web/20220616164011/https://www.
techdirt.com/2022/01/18/remembering-fight-against-sopa-10-
years-later-what-it-means-today/

307 https://web.archive.org/web/20220817064446/https://www.
nytimes.com/2012/01/20/technology/public-outcry-over-
antipiracy-bills-began-as-grass-roots-grumbling.html

308 https://web.archive.org/web/20220615193358/https://
theconnector.substack.com/p/jan-18-2012-the-day-when-tech-
changed

309 https://web.archive.org/web/20220615193427/https://www.
fightforthefuture.org/

310 https://web.archive.org/web/20220615193447/https://
en.wikipedia.org/wiki/Fight_for_the_Future

311 https://web.archive.org/web/20220705092831/https://
en.wikipedia.org/wiki/Evan_Greer

312 https://web.archive.org/web/20220616172705/https://
walledculture.org/interview-evan-greer-lia-holland-rethinking-
copyright-fighting-creative-monopolies-and-more/

313 https://web.archive.org/web/20220616172726/https://
en.wikipedia.org/wiki/Anti-Counterfeiting_Trade_Agreement

314 https://web.archive.org/web/20220616172745/https://brocku.
ca/social-sciences/political-science/people-in-the-department/
blayne-haggart/

315 https://web.archive.org/web/20220817064239/https://books.
google.be/books/about/Copyfight.html?id=2T-WAwAAQBAJ

316 https://web.archive.org/web/20220616172827/https://
en.wikipedia.org/wiki/WikiLeaks

317 https://web.archive.org/web/20220616172858/https://www.
laquadrature.net/en/2010/03/23/0118-version-of-acta-
consolidated-text-leaks/

318 https://web.archive.org/web/20100322191648/http:/keionline.
org/node/806

319 https://web.archive.org/web/20120120155721/http:/www.wcl.
american.edu/pijip/go/acta-communique

320 https://web.archive.org/web/20120120155721/http:/www.wcl.
american.edu/pijip/go/acta-communique

321 https://web.archive.org/web/20120425080452/http:/www.bbc.
co.uk/news/world-europe-16735219

322 https://web.archive.org/web/20220705075900/https://
en.wikipedia.org/wiki/Donald_Tusk

323 https://web.archive.org/web/20220616172922/https://www.
techdirt.com/2012/01/26/people-poland-come-out-to-protest-
acta-large-numbers-polish-govt-calls-it-blackmail/

324 https://web.archive.org/web/20220616173713/https://www.
techdirt.com/2012/02/16/eu-member-bulgaria-halts-acta-
minister-economy-offers-resignation/

325 https://web.archive.org/web/20220704132341/https://
en.wikipedia.org/wiki/David_Martin_%28Scottish_
politician%29

326 https://web.archive.org/web/20220616173734/https://www.
techdirt.com/2012/04/12/eu-rapporteur-deals-major-blow-to-
acta-recommends-rejection-european-parliament/

327 https://web.archive.org/web/20220616173734/https://www.
techdirt.com/2012/04/12/eu-rapporteur-deals-major-blow-to-
acta-recommends-rejection-european-parliament/

328 https://web.archive.org/web/20220616173819/https://www.
techdirt.com/2012/06/21/fifth-eu-committee-recommends-
rejection-acta-european-parliament/

329 https://web.archive.org/web/20220616173849/https://www.
techdirt.com/2012/07/04/european-parliament-declares-its-
independence-european-commission-with-massive-rejection-
acta-now-what/

330 https://web.archive.org/web/20220618055249/https://
en.wikipedia.org/wiki/Martin_Schulz

331 https://web.archive.org/web/20220616173849/https://www.
techdirt.com/2012/07/04/european-parliament-declares-its-
independence-european-commission-with-massive-rejection-
acta-now-what/

332 https://web.archive.org/web/20220616083734/https://
en.wikipedia.org/wiki/Online_Copyright_Infringement_
Liability_Limitation_Act

333 https://web.archive.org/web/20220616083747/https://
en.wikipedia.org/wiki/Title_17_of_the_United_States_Code

334 https://web.archive.org/web/20220616083800/https://www.eff.
org/about/staff/katharine-trendacosta

335 https://web.archive.org/web/20220616083815/https://
walledculture.org/interview-katharine-trendacosta-the-us-dmca-
upload-filters-sopa-pipa-fanfiction-platform-competition/

336 https://web.archive.org/web/20220616083832/https://papers.
ssrn.com/sol3/papers.cfm?abstract_id=2411915

337 https://web.archive.org/web/20220616083851/https://
transparencyreport.google.com/copyright/overview

338 https://web.archive.org/web/20220616083909/https://www.
lumendatabase.org/pages/about

339 https://web.archive.org/web/20220616083922/https://papers.
ssrn.com/sol3/papers.cfm?abstract_id=2755628

340 https://web.archive.org/web/20220616083922/https://papers.
ssrn.com/sol3/papers.cfm?abstract_id=2755628

341 https://web.archive.org/web/20220616083922/https://papers.
ssrn.com/sol3/papers.cfm?abstract_id=2755628

342 https://web.archive.org/web/20220616083922/https://papers.
ssrn.com/sol3/papers.cfm?abstract_id=2755628

343 https://web.archive.org/web/20220616083941/https://
torrentfreak.com/man-pleads-guilty-to-23m-youtube-content-id-
scam-220423/

344 https://web.archive.org/web/20220620115209/https://www.
slwip.com/people/jeffrey-cobia/

345 https://web.archive.org/web/20220616084752/https://
conservancy.umn.edu/handle/11299/155689

346 https://web.archive.org/web/20220616084814/https://www.
lumendatabase.org/blog_entries/copyright-as-the-tool-of-choice-
for-censorship-and-reputation-management

347 https://web.archive.org/web/20220616084833/https://www.
techdirt.com/2021/09/30/copyright-continues-to-be-abused-to-
censor-critics-entities-both-big-small/

348 https://web.archive.org/web/20220616084853/https://
en.wikipedia.org/wiki/Reputation_management

349 https://web.archive.org/web/20220616084907/https://
restofworld.org/2022/documents-reputation-laundering-firm-
eliminalia/

350 https://web.archive.org/web/20210508172129/https://storage.
courtlistener.com/recap/gov.uscourts.ned.84712/gov.uscourts.
ned.84712.1.0.pdf

351 https://web.archive.org/web/20220616090546/https://cyberlaw.
stanford.edu/blog/2017/01/dmca-counter-notice-does-it-work-
correct-erroneous-takedowns

352 https://web.archive.org/web/20220616084926/https://www.eff.
org/deeplinks/2019/08/youtubes-new-lawsuit-shows-just-how-
far-copyright-trolls-have-go-theyre-stopped

353 https://web.archive.org/web/20220616083922/https://papers.
ssrn.com/sol3/papers.cfm?abstract_id=2755628

354 https://web.archive.org/web/20220616091349/https://papers.
ssrn.com/sol3/papers.cfm?abstract_id=2464969

355 https://web.archive.org/web/20220616091407/https://
     en.wikipedia.org/wiki/DNS_blocking

356 https://web.archive.org/web/20220616091421/https://
     en.wikipedia.org/wiki/SABAM

357 https://web.archive.org/web/20220616091434/https://
     en.wikipedia.org/wiki/Deep_packet_inspection

358 https://web.archive.org/web/20220701131823/https://
     en.wikipedia.org/wiki/Court_of_Justice_of_the_European_
     Union

359 https://web.archive.org/web/20220603094009/https://
     curia.europa.eu/jcms/upload/docs/application/pdf/2011-11/
     cp110126en.pdf

360 https://web.archive.org/web/20220616093040/https://
     en.wikipedia.org/wiki/IP_address_blocking

361 https://web.archive.org/web/20220616093008/https://www.
     theguardian.com/technology/2011/jul/28/high-court-bt-
     filesharing-website-newzbin2

362 https://web.archive.org/web/20220817063842/https://
     en.wikipedia.org/wiki/Australian_Securities_&_Investments_
     Commission

363 https://web.archive.org/web/20220616093105/https://www.
     theage.com.au/technology/how-asics-attempt-to-block-one-
     website-took-down-250000-20130605-2np6v.html

364 https://web.archive.org/web/20220616093128/https://www.
     theage.com.au/technology/government-accused-of-sneaking-in-
     web-filter-20130517-2jq3p.html

365 https://web.archive.org/web/20220701132035/https://
     en.wikipedia.org/wiki/Autorit%C3%A0_per_le_Garanzie_
     nelle_Comunicazioni

366 https://web.archive.org/web/20220616093155/https://
     torrentfreak.com/off-us-blacklist-italy-begins-torrent-site-
     blackout-no-trials-needed-140510/

367 https://web.archive.org/web/20220616093944/https://
     torrentfreak.com/rapid-pirate-site-blocking-mechanism-
     introduced-by-portugal-150731/

368 https://web.archive.org/web/20220704132837/https://
     en.wikipedia.org/wiki/Information_Technology_and_
     Innovation_Foundation

369 https://web.archive.org/web/20220616093958/https://itif.org/
     publications/2018/06/12/normalization-website-blocking-
     around-world-fight-against-piracy-online/

370 https://web.archive.org/web/20220616094012/https://itif.org/
     publications/2022/01/26/decade-after-sopa-pipa-time-to-revisit-
     website-blocking/

371 https://web.archive.org/web/20220616094041/https://www.
     michaelgeist.ca/2018/02/case-bell-coalitions-website-blocking-
     plan-part-8-ineffectiveness-website-blocking/

372 https://web.archive.org/web/20220616094123/https://www.
     bailii.org/eu/cases/ECHR/2012/2074.html

373 https://web.archive.org/web/20220616094141/https://
     en.wikipedia.org/wiki/European_Court_of_Human_Rights

374 https://web.archive.org/web/20220616094155/https://
     en.wikipedia.org/wiki/Google_Sites

375 https://web.archive.org/web/20220610124514/https://www.
     echr.coe.int/Documents/Guide_Art_10_ENG.pdf

376 https://web.archive.org/web/20220616094208/https://
     ukhumanrightsblog.com/2013/01/16/turkish-block-on-google-
     site-breached-article-10-rights-rules-strasbourg/

377 https://web.archive.org/web/20220616094304/https://
     en.wikipedia.org/wiki/Megaupload

378 https://web.archive.org/web/20220616095048/https://
     en.wikipedia.org/wiki/Kim_Dotcom

379 https://web.archive.org/web/20220616095118/https://
     s3.documentcloud.org/documents/4172926/Press-2-
     Brelease171003.pdf

380 https://web.archive.org/web/20220616095048/https://
     en.wikipedia.org/wiki/Kim_Dotcom

381 https://web.archive.org/web/20220616095158/https://
     arstechnica.com/tech-policy/2012/03/megaupload-user-asks-for-
     his-perfectly-legal-videos-back/

382 https://web.archive.org/web/20220616095118/https://
     s3.documentcloud.org/documents/4172926/Press-2-
     Brelease171003.pdf

383 https://web.archive.org/web/20220618164456/https://www.
     politico.eu/article/battle-on-eu-copyright-law-re-opened-by-
     commission/

384 https://web.archive.org/web/20180623005034/http://ec.europa.
     eu/internal_market/consultations/2013/copyright-rules/docs/
     contributions/consultation-report_en.pdf

385 https://web.archive.org/web/20220618164539/https://felixreda.
     eu/copyright-evaluation-report-explained/

386 https://web.archive.org/web/20180623005034/http://ec.europa.eu/internal_market/consultations/2013/copyright-rules/docs/contributions/consultation-report_en.pdf

387 https://web.archive.org/web/20180623005034/http://ec.europa.eu/internal_market/consultations/2013/copyright-rules/docs/contributions/consultation-report_en.pdf

388 https://web.archive.org/web/20220618164615/https://ec.europa.eu/info/index_en

389 https://web.archive.org/web/20220618164658/https://www.consilium.europa.eu/en/european-council/

390 https://web.archive.org/web/20220618053202/https://www.europarl.europa.eu/portal/en

391 https://web.archive.org/web/20220701132359/https://en.wikipedia.org/wiki/Member_of_the_European_Parliament

392 https://web.archive.org/web/20220701132439/https://en.wikipedia.org/wiki/Felix_Reda

393 https://web.archive.org/web/20220701132519/https://en.wikipedia.org/wiki/Pirate_Party

394 https://web.archive.org/web/20220618164539/https://felixreda.eu/copyright-evaluation-report-explained/

395 https://web.archive.org/web/20220618164812/https://en.wikipedia.org/wiki/Copyright_status_of_works_by_the_federal_government_of_the_United_States

396 https://web.archive.org/web/20220701094105/https://www.twitch.tv/

397 https://web.archive.org/web/20220615193427/https://www.fightforthefuture.org/

398 https://web.archive.org/web/20220618174345/https://walledculture.org/interview-evan-greer-lia-holland-rethinking-copyright-fighting-creative-monopolies-and-more/

399 https://web.archive.org/web/20220618055808/https://en.wikipedia.org/wiki/Freedom_of_panorama

400 https://web.archive.org/web/20220618164539/https://felixreda.eu/copyright-evaluation-report-explained/

401 https://web.archive.org/web/20220618164539/https://felixreda.eu/copyright-evaluation-report-explained/

402 https://web.archive.org/web/20220701132934/https://en.wikipedia.org/wiki/Wikimedia_Foundation

403 https://web.archive.org/web/20220705082303/https://en.wikipedia.org/wiki/Katherine_Maher

404 https://web.archive.org/web/20220618175152/https://
walledculture.org/interview-katherine-maher-the-monkey-
selfie-public-domain-freedom-of-panorama-the-eu-copyright-
directive-remix-culture-the-20th-century-black-hole/
405 https://web.archive.org/web/20220701133101/https://
en.wikipedia.org/wiki/Text_mining
406 https://web.archive.org/web/20180623005034/http://ec.europa.
eu/internal_market/consultations/2013/copyright-rules/docs/
contributions/consultation-report_en.pdf
407 https://web.archive.org/web/20220618055943/https://felixreda.
eu/eu-copyright-reform/text-and-data-mining/
408 https://web.archive.org/web/20220618060002/https://
en.wikipedia.org/wiki/Therese_Comodini_Cachia
409 https://web.archive.org/web/20220618060400/https://
en.wikipedia.org/wiki/Axel_Voss
410 https://web.archive.org/web/20220618070203/
https://eur-lex.europa.eu/legal-content/EN/TXT/
HTML/?uri=CELEX%3A32019L0790&from=EN
411 https://web.archive.org/web/20220618070218/https://
en.wikipedia.org/wiki/CAPTCHA
412 https://web.archive.org/web/20220618070234/https://copybuzz.
com/copyright/ensuring-text-data-mining-future-europe/
413 https://web.archive.org/web/20220701133224/https://
en.wikipedia.org/wiki/Agence_France-Presse
414 https://web.archive.org/web/20220618175431/https://www.
techdirt.com/2005/03/20/afp-gets-confused-as-to-how-the-
internet-works/
415 https://web.archive.org/web/20220618175506/https://www.
techdirt.com/2006/09/18/how-dare-google-send-belgian-news-
sites-traffic-court-orders-them-to-stop/
416 https://web.archive.org/web/20220618180258/https://www.
techdirt.com/2011/07/18/newspapers-win-suit-against-google-
get-their-wish-to-be-delisted-then-complain/
417 https://web.archive.org/web/20220618180333/https://www.
techdirt.com/2011/05/09/belgian-appeals-court-says-google-
must-pay-up-linking-to-newspaper-websites/
418 https://web.archive.org/web/20220618180355/https://www.
techdirt.com/2011/07/19/belgian-newspapers-give-permission-
to-google-to-return-them-to-search-results/
419 https://web.archive.org/web/20220618072722/https://www.
corint-media.com/en/rebranding-vg-media-becomes-corint-
media/

420 https://web.archive.org/web/20220618180447/https://www.
techdirt.com/2014/06/20/german-publishers-demand-big-chunk-
googles-revenue-sending-them-traffic-even-as-they-try-to-rank-
higher-google/

421 https://web.archive.org/web/20220618180508/https://www.
techdirt.com/2014/10/23/german-publishers-grant-google-free-
license-google-never-needed-to-post-news-snippets/

422 https://web.archive.org/web/20220618180529/https://www.
techdirt.com/2014/12/11/google-pulls-out-nuclear-option-shuts-
down-google-news-spain-over-ridiculous-copyright-law/

423 https://web.archive.org/web/20220701133542/https://
en.wikipedia.org/wiki/Spanish_Newspaper_Publishers%27_
Association

424 https://web.archive.org/web/20220618180552/https://www.
techdirt.com/2014/12/12/surprise-spanish-newspapers-beg-
government-eu-to-stop-google-news-shutting-down/

425 https://web.archive.org/web/20220618180619/https://www.
techdirt.com/2015/07/29/study-spains-google-tax-news-shows-
how-much-damage-it-has-done/

426 https://web.archive.org/web/20220618070203/
https://eur-lex.europa.eu/legal-content/EN/TXT/
HTML/?uri=CELEX%3A32019L0790&from=EN

427 https://web.archive.org/web/20220618183701/https://doctorow.
medium.com/big-tech-isnt-stealing-news-publishers-content-
a97306884a6b

428 https://web.archive.org/web/20220618183724/https://
walledculture.org/why-the-snippet-tax-of-the-eu-copyright-
directive-is-pointless-and-doomed-to-fail/

429 https://web.archive.org/web/20220618183752/https://www.ben-
evans.com/benedictevans/2022/3/18/unbundling-advertising

430 https://web.archive.org/web/20220618070203/
https://eur-lex.europa.eu/legal-content/EN/TXT/
HTML/?uri=CELEX%3A32019L0790&from=EN

431 https://web.archive.org/web/20220618081604/https://digital-
strategy.ec.europa.eu/en/library/licences-europe-stakeholder-
dialogue

432 https://web.archive.org/web/20220618183853/https://www.
techdirt.com/2013/05/30/researcher-smes-civil-society-groups-
open-access-publishers-pull-out-licensing-obsessed-eu-talks-
text-data-mining/

433 https://web.archive.org/web/20220417074813/https://
torrentfreak.com/images/Engine_-_Empirical_Study.pdf

434 https://web.archive.org/web/20220417074813/https://
torrentfreak.com/images/Engine_-_Empirical_Study.pdf
435 https://web.archive.org/web/20220704133605/http://cyberlaw.
stanford.edu/about/people/annemarie-bridy
436 https://web.archive.org/web/20220618183937/https://papers.
ssrn.com/sol3/papers.cfm?abstract_id=3412249
437 https://web.archive.org/web/20220618183937/https://papers.
ssrn.com/sol3/papers.cfm?abstract_id=3412249
438 https://web.archive.org/web/20220705085426/https://www.eff.
org/about/staff/katharine-trendacosta
439 https://web.archive.org/web/20220618184059/https://
walledculture.org/interview-katharine-trendacosta-the-us-dmca-
upload-filters-sopa-pipa-fanfiction-platform-competition/
440 https://web.archive.org/web/20220618184121/https://www.
liberties.eu/en/stories/delete-article-thirteen-open-letter/13131
441 https://web.archive.org/web/20220618084121/https://felixreda.
eu/2018/02/voss-upload-filters/
442 https://web.archive.org/web/20220618084146/https://www.
europarl.europa.eu/committees/en/juri/about
443 https://web.archive.org/web/20220618084121/https://felixreda.
eu/2018/02/voss-upload-filters/
444 https://web.archive.org/web/20220618084248/https://felixreda.
eu/2018/01/censorship-machines/
445 https://web.archive.org/web/20220618084319/https://felixreda.
eu/eu-copyright-reform/censorship-machines/
446 https://web.archive.org/web/20220618084451/https://felixreda.
eu/2017/11/civil-liberties-censorship-machines/
447 https://web.archive.org/web/20220618084520/https://felixreda.
eu/2017/09/censorship-machines-concerns-ignored/
448 https://web.archive.org/web/20180209194223/https://
www.spd.de/fileadmin/Dokumente/Koalitionsvertrag/
Koalitionsvertrag_2018.pdf
449 https://web.archive.org/web/20220618084121/https://felixreda.
eu/2018/02/voss-upload-filters/
450 https://web.archive.org/web/20220618185222/https://blog.
youtube/news-and-events/youtube-at-15-my-personal-journey/
451 https://web.archive.org/web/20220618185238/https://www.
forbes.com/sites/insertcoin/2013/12/19/the-injustice-of-the-
youtube-content-id-crackdown-reveals-googles-dark-side/
452 https://web.archive.org/web/20220618084755/https://www.
blog.google/outreach-initiatives/public-policy/protecting-what-
we-love-about-internet-our-efforts-stop-online-piracy/

453 https://web.archive.org/web/20220618085655/https://felixreda.eu/2017/09/when-filters-fail/

454 https://web.archive.org/web/20220618085655/https://felixreda.eu/2017/09/when-filters-fail/

455 https://web.archive.org/web/20220620134016/https://en.wikipedia.org/wiki/Alec_Muffett

456 https://web.archive.org/web/20220618190133/https://threadreaderapp.com/thread/1015594170424193024.html

457 https://web.archive.org/web/20220618190155/https://www.techdirt.com/2019/01/23/there-was-heavy-tech-lobbying-article-13-company-hoping-to-sell-everyone-filters/

458 https://web.archive.org/web/20220618190216/https://www.bbc.com/news/technology-14322957

459 https://web.archive.org/web/20220618190255/https://eur-lex.europa.eu/legal-content/EN/TXT/HTML/?uri=CELEX%3A32000L0031&from=en

460 https://web.archive.org/web/20220603094009/https://curia.europa.eu/jcms/upload/docs/application/pdf/2011-11/cp110126en.pdf

461 https://web.archive.org/web/20220618190328/http://copyrightblog.kluweriplaw.com/2021/08/09/youtube-and-cyando-injunctions-against-intermediaries-and-general-monitoring-obligations-any-movement/

462 https://web.archive.org/web/20220701134156/https://en.wikipedia.org/wiki/General_Data_Protection_Regulation

463 https://web.archive.org/web/20220618190351/https://gdpr-info.eu/art-22-gdpr/

464 https://web.archive.org/web/20180713064910/https://www.theguardian.com/technology/2018/jun/20/eu-votes-for-copyright-law-that-would-make-internet-a-tool-for-control

465 https://web.archive.org/web/20220402115757/https://www.politico.eu/wp-content/uploads/2018/06/copyright-email-to-MEPs.docx

466 https://web.archive.org/web/20220402115757/https://www.politico.eu/wp-content/uploads/2018/06/copyright-email-to-MEPs.docx

467 https://web.archive.org/web/20220618203153/https://copybuzz.com/copyright/meps-email-says-article-13-will-not-filter-the-internet-juri-meps-tweet-says-it-will/

468 https://web.archive.org/web/20220701134919/https://en.wikipedia.org/wiki/Independent_Music_Companies_Association

469 https://web.archive.org/web/20180704010146/http://
impalamusic.org/content/copyright-say-no-scaremongering-and-
yes-creators-getting-paid

470 https://web.archive.org/web/20220701135001/https://
en.wikipedia.org/wiki/David_Kaye_%28academic%29

471 https://web.archive.org/web/20220428083157/https://www.
ohchr.org/sites/default/files/Documents/Issues/Opinion/
Legislation/OL-OTH-41-2018.pdf

472 https://web.archive.org/web/20220618203237/https://
en.wikipedia.org/wiki/Vint_Cerf

473 https://web.archive.org/web/20220618203338/https://
internethalloffame.org/vint-cerf

474 https://web.archive.org/web/20220618203358/https://
en.wikipedia.org/wiki/Tim_Berners-Lee

475 https://web.archive.org/web/20220618203414/https://www.
w3.org/People/Berners-Lee/

476 https://web.archive.org/web/20220618203428/https://
en.wikipedia.org/wiki/Jimmy_Wales

477 https://web.archive.org/web/20220620000819/https://twitter.
com/Jimmy_wales

478 https://web.archive.org/web/20180708003333/https://www.eff.
org/files/2018/06/13/article13letter.pdf

479 https://web.archive.org/web/20180708003333/https://www.eff.
org/files/2018/06/13/article13letter.pdf

480 https://web.archive.org/web/20220618213154/https://felixreda.
eu/2018/09/ep-endorses-upload-filters/

481 https://web.archive.org/web/20220618213222/https://www.
europarl.europa.eu/news/en/press-room/20180906IPR12103/
parliament-adopts-its-position-on-digital-copyright-rules

482 https://web.archive.org/web/20220618214015/https://www.
techdirt.com/2018/12/12/legacy-copyright-industries-lobbying-
hard-eu-copyright-directive-while-pretending-that-only-google-
is-lobbying/

483 https://web.archive.org/web/20220618214015/https://www.
techdirt.com/2018/12/12/legacy-copyright-industries-lobbying-
hard-eu-copyright-directive-while-pretending-that-only-google-
is-lobbying/

484 https://web.archive.org/web/20220618214041/https://
corporateeurope.org/en/2018/12/copyright-directive-how-
competing-big-business-lobbies-drowned-out-critical-voices

485 https://web.archive.org/web/20220618214059/https://
en.wikipedia.org/wiki/Catherine_Stihler

486 https://web.archive.org/web/20220618214120/https://en.wikipedia.org/wiki/Creative_Commons

487 https://web.archive.org/web/20220704134108/https://walledculture.org/interview-catherine-stihler-creative-commons-the-eu-copyright-directive-and-civil-societys-role/

488 https://web.archive.org/web/20220618214136/https://en.wikipedia.org/wiki/Formal_trilogue_meeting

489 https://web.archive.org/web/20220618214155/https://felixreda.eu/2018/11/eu-council-upload-filters/

490 https://web.archive.org/web/20190320092740/https://juliareda.eu/2019/01/copyright-hits_wall/

491 https://web.archive.org/web/20220618214225/https://www.techdirt.com/2019/03/25/new-report-germany-caved-to-france-copyright-deal-russian-gas/

492 https://web.archive.org/web/20190320092739/https://www.eff.org/deeplinks/2019/01/german-government-abandons-small-businesses-worst-parts-eu-copyright-directive

493 https://web.archive.org/web/20190321012132/https://www.change.org/p/european-parliament-stop-the-censorship-machinery-save-the-internet

494 https://web.archive.org/web/20190220103450/https://www.faz.net/aktuell/wirtschaft/diginomics/tausende-menschen-demonstrieren-gegen-urheberrechtsreform-16045816.html

495 https://web.archive.org/web/20190321104438/https://www.dw.com/en/thousands-in-berlin-protest-eus-online-copyright-plans/a-47753399

496 https://web.archive.org/web/20220620092750/https://twitter.com/AralePyon/status/1096714251153092609

497 https://web.archive.org/web/20220701135233/https://en.wikipedia.org/wiki/Sven_Schulze

498 https://web.archive.org/web/20220618224045/https://www.techdirt.com/2019/02/19/german-politician-thinks-gmail-constituent-messages-are-all-faked-google/

499 https://web.archive.org/web/20220618224104/https://edri.org/our-work/join-the-ultimate-action-week-against-article-13/

500 https://web.archive.org/web/20190216094123/https://medium.com/@EuropeanCommission/the-copyright-directive-how-the-mob-was-told-to-save-the-dragon-and-slay-the-knight-b35876008f16

501 https://web.archive.org/web/20220618224855/https://
europeancommission.medium.com/the-copyright-directive-
how-the-mob-was-told-to-save-the-dragon-and-slay-the-knight-
b35876008f16

502 https://web.archive.org/web/20220618224933/https://www.
techdirt.com/2019/03/01/why-is-eu-parliament-pushing-fake-
propaganda-hollywood/

503 https://web.archive.org/web/20220618225007/http://www.
fosspatents.com/2019/02/germanys-federal-data-protection.html

504 https://web.archive.org/web/20220704114049/https://www.
ohchr.org/en/news/2019/03/eu-must-align-copyright-reform-
international-human-rights-standards-says-expert

505 https://web.archive.org/web/20220704114049/https://www.
ohchr.org/en/news/2019/03/eu-must-align-copyright-reform-
international-human-rights-standards-says-expert

506 https://web.archive.org/web/20220618225049/https://
nextcloud.com/blog/130-eu-businesses-sign-open-letter-against-
copyright-directive-art-11-13/

507 https://www.google.com/maps/d/u/0/
viewer?mid=1tHaOiCgjION6hK0rrajIJyuHnG5FgBzH

508 https://web.archive.org/web/20220618225136/https://
netzpolitik.org/2019/weit-mehr-als-100-000-menschen-
demonstrieren-in-vielen-deutschen-staedten-fuer-ein-offenes-
netz/

509 https://web.archive.org/web/20220620134734/https://
de.wikipedia.org/wiki/Daniel_Caspary

510 https://web.archive.org/web/20220618225214/https://
www.bild.de/politik/ausland/politik-inland/upload-
filter-im-europarlament-abgeordneter-bekommt-
morddrohung-60746158.bild.html

511 https://web.archive.org/web/20220618225252/https://medium.
com/@emanuelkarlsten/german-mep-claims-copyright-
protesters-are-bought-here-are-the-twelve-people-hes-talking-
about-8f836be3056e

512 https://web.archive.org/web/20220618225331/https://edri.org/
about-us/who-we-are/

513 https://web.archive.org/web/20220618230135/https://edri.org/
our-work/join-us-in-strasbourg-to-saveyourinternet/

514 https://web.archive.org/web/20220618230156/https://
medium.com/@emanuelkarlsten/sweden-democrats-swedish-
social-democrats-defeat-motion-to-amend-articles-11-13-
731d3c0fbf30

515 https://web.archive.org/web/20220618230156/https://
medium.com/@emanuelkarlsten/sweden-democrats-swedish-
social-democrats-defeat-motion-to-amend-articles-11-13-
731d3c0fbf30

516 https://web.archive.org/web/20220618230225/https://www.
techdirt.com/2019/03/26/enough-meps-say-they-mistakenly-
voted-articles-11-13-that-vote-should-have-flipped-eu-
parliament-says-too-bad/

517 https://web.archive.org/web/20220618232000/https://www.
europarl.europa.eu/doceo/document/PV-8-2019-03-26-RCV_
EN.pdf

518 https://web.archive.org/web/20220619000203/https://
en.wikipedia.org/wiki/Directive_%28European_Union%29

519 https://web.archive.org/web/20220619000221/https://www.
techdirt.com/2019/06/18/polish-governments-legal-challenge-
to-eu-copyright-directives-article-13-17-remains-shrouded-
mystery-details-may-not-matter/

520 https://web.archive.org/web/20220620094934/https://twitter.
com/PremierRP_en/status/1131575949542199297

521 https://web.archive.org/web/20220701135436/https://
en.wikipedia.org/wiki/G%C3%BCnther_Oettinger

522 https://web.archive.org/web/20220619010007/https://www.
techdirt.com/2019/04/03/eu-commissioner-gunther-oettinger-
admits-sites-need-filters-to-comply-with-article-13/

523 https://web.archive.org/web/20220619010036/https://www.
techdirt.com/2019/03/28/after-insisting-that-eu-copyright-
directive-didnt-require-filters-france-immediately-starts-
promoting-filters/

524 https://web.archive.org/web/20220619010842/https://felixreda.
eu/2019/12/french_uploadfilter_law/

525 https://web.archive.org/web/20220619010842/https://felixreda.
eu/2019/12/french_uploadfilter_law/

526 https://web.archive.org/web/20220619010842/https://felixreda.
eu/2019/12/french_uploadfilter_law/

527 https://web.archive.org/web/20220619010842/https://felixreda.
eu/2019/12/french_uploadfilter_law/

528 https://web.archive.org/web/20220619010942/https://
walledculture.org/unleashing-the-power-of-online-sharing-for-
all-the-birth-and-rise-of-creative-commons/

529 https://web.archive.org/web/20220619012521/https://www.
techdirt.com/2020/09/30/germany-drops-idea-pre-flagging-
legal-uploads-which-could-have-stopped-eu-copyright-filters-
blocking-memes-parodies-quotes/

530 https://web.archive.org/web/20220619012547/https://www.
communia-association.org/2021/05/20/german-article-17-
implementation-law-sets-the-standard-for-protecting-user-
rights-against-overblocking/

531 https://web.archive.org/web/20220817075947/
https://eur-lex.europa.eu/legal-content/DE/TXT/
HTML/?uri=CELEX%3A32019L0790

532 https://web.archive.org/web/20220619012633/https://
torrentfreak.com/upload-filters-23-eu-member-states-face-legal-
action-over-copyright-law-delays-210727/

533 https://web.archive.org/web/20220619012648/https://www.
techdirt.com/2021/06/07/european-commission-betrays-
internet-users-cravenly-introducing-huge-loophole-copyright-
companies-upload-filter-guidance/

534 https://web.archive.org/web/20220619012708/http://
copyrightblog.kluweriplaw.com/2020/11/11/cjeu-hearing-in-the-
polish-challenge-to-article-17-not-even-the-supporters-of-the-
provision-agree-on-how-it-should-work/

535 https://web.archive.org/web/20220521202300/https://
curia.europa.eu/jcms/upload/docs/application/pdf/2022-04/
cp220065en.pdf

536 https://web.archive.org/web/20220521202300/https://
curia.europa.eu/jcms/upload/docs/application/pdf/2022-04/
cp220065en.pdf

537 https://web.archive.org/web/20220521202300/https://
curia.europa.eu/jcms/upload/docs/application/pdf/2022-04/
cp220065en.pdf

538 https://web.archive.org/web/20220619013517/https://
walledculture.org/interview-marc-rees-a-la-francaise-de-lhadopi-
par-la-copie-privee-jusquaux-algorithmes-de-larticle-17/

539 https://web.archive.org/web/20220521202300/https://
curia.europa.eu/jcms/upload/docs/application/pdf/2022-04/
cp220065en.pdf

540 https://web.archive.org/web/20220701135921/https://
en.wikipedia.org/wiki/Advocate_general_%28European_
Union%29

541 https://web.archive.org/web/20220705083329/https://curia.
europa.eu/jcms/jcms/rc4_170789/en/

542 https://web.archive.org/web/20220619013536/https://
curia.europa.eu/jcms/upload/docs/application/pdf/2021-07/
cp210138en.pdf

543 https://web.archive.org/web/20220521202300/https://
curia.europa.eu/jcms/upload/docs/application/pdf/2022-04/
cp220065en.pdf

544 https://www.notion.so/DSM-Directive-Implementation-Tracker-
361cfae48e814440b353b32692bba879

545 https://web.archive.org/web/20220619013615/https://ipkitten.
blogspot.com/2021/08/towards-national-transpositions-of-dsm.
html

546 https://web.archive.org/web/20220617071526/https://www.
techdirt.com/2021/02/26/best-summary-australias-news-link-
tax-bargaining-code/

547 https://web.archive.org/web/20220617071548/https://www.
cigionline.org/articles/bad-news-ottawas-proposed-online-news-
act-misses-the-mark/

548 https://web.archive.org/web/20220526132018/https://www.
tillis.senate.gov/services/files/435EB2FD-145A-4AD6-BF01-
855C0A78CEFC

549 https://web.archive.org/web/20220701140259/https://
en.wikipedia.org/wiki/Eric_Goldman

550 https://web.archive.org/web/20220616135345/https://blog.
ericgoldman.org/archives/2022/03/wouldnt-it-be-great-if-
internet-services-had-to-license-technologies-selected-by-
hollywood-comments-on-the-very-dumb-smart-copyright-act.
htm

551 https://web.archive.org/web/20220616135345/https://blog.
ericgoldman.org/archives/2022/03/wouldnt-it-be-great-if-
internet-services-had-to-license-technologies-selected-by-
hollywood-comments-on-the-very-dumb-smart-copyright-act.
htm

552 https://web.archive.org/web/20220617075408/https://www.
techdirt.com/2015/07/29/study-spains-google-tax-news-shows-
how-much-damage-it-has-done/

553 https://web.archive.org/web/20220617075436/https://
walledculture.org/interview-cory-doctorow-part-1-newspapers-
big-tech-link-tax-drm-and-right-to-repair/

554 https://web.archive.org/web/20220617075502/https://www.
smh.com.au/business/companies/the-big-tech-companies-are-
hard-to-deal-with-senator-bragg-20210602-p57xfw.html

555 https://web.archive.org/web/20220701140827/https://
en.wikipedia.org/wiki/News_Media_Alliance

556 https://web.archive.org/web/20170711223412/https://www.
newsmediaalliance.org/release-digital-duopoly/

557 https://web.archive.org/web/20220617075524/https://www.
techdirt.com/2021/07/01/denmarks-media-companies-form-
copyright-collective-to-force-google-facebook-to-pay-more-
sending-them-traffic/

558 https://web.archive.org/web/20220620130419/https://
mathewingram.com/work/index.php/2017/07/10/newspaper-
groups-hope-for-antitrust-exemption-is-a-hail-mary-pass/

559 https://web.archive.org/web/20220701141146/https://www.
congress.gov/bill/117th-congress/senate-bill/673

560 https://web.archive.org/web/20220617084132/https://
s3.documentcloud.org/documents/20949935/jcpa-letter-to-
congress.pdf

561 https://web.archive.org/web/20220617084149/https://
publicknowledge.org/

562 https://web.archive.org/web/20220617084132/https://
s3.documentcloud.org/documents/20949935/jcpa-letter-to-
congress.pdf

563 https://web.archive.org/web/20220705065218/https://www.
copyright.gov/policy/publishersprotections/

564 https://web.archive.org/web/20130112213232/http://www.ipo.
gov.uk/ipreview-finalreport.pdf

565 https://web.archive.org/web/20220701141304/https://
en.wikipedia.org/wiki/Ian_Hargreaves

566 https://web.archive.org/web/20130112213232/http://www.ipo.
gov.uk/ipreview-finalreport.pdf

567 https://web.archive.org/web/20220617084203/https://
en.wikipedia.org/wiki/Copyright_Hub

568 https://web.archive.org/web/20220617084222/https://advanced-
television.com/2015/07/31/uk-copyright-hub-launches/

569 https://web.archive.org/web/20220617084247/https://www.
copyrightdoneright.org/

570 https://web.archive.org/web/20190616012328/http://www.
copyrighthub.org/digital-rights-holder-statement-published

571 https://web.archive.org/web/20220617084308/https://www.
ardito-project.eu/about-us

572 https://web.archive.org/web/20210921051650/http://cepic.org/
app/uploads/2017/02/Rights-Data-Integration.pdf

573 https://web.archive.org/web/20220617084358/http://www.linkedcontentcoalition.org/index.php/news-press/press-room

574 https://web.archive.org/web/20220617084418/https://www.copyrightdoneright.org/want-to-get-involved/

575 https://web.archive.org/web/20220617084450/https://www.copyrightdoneright.org/check-out-our-wonderful-supporters/

576 https://web.archive.org/web/20220617085236/https://www.copyrightdoneright.org/how-it-works/

577 https://web.archive.org/web/20220617085254/https://www.wipo.int/edocs/pubdocs/en/copyright/855/wipo_pub_855.pdf

578 https://web.archive.org/web/20220701141536/https://en.wikipedia.org/wiki/Collective_rights_management

579 https://web.archive.org/web/20220617085320/https://papers.ssrn.com/sol3/papers.cfm?abstract_id=2149036

580 https://web.archive.org/web/20220617085320/https://papers.ssrn.com/sol3/papers.cfm?abstract_id=2149036

581 https://web.archive.org/web/20220617085341/https://en.wikipedia.org/wiki/GEMA_%28German_organization%29

582 https://web.archive.org/web/20220617085412/https://www.techdirt.com/2016/11/01/youtube-finally-buries-hatchet-with-gema-meaning-people-germany-can-watch-videos-again/

583 https://web.archive.org/web/20220817082824/https://eur-lex.europa.eu/legal-content/EN/TXT/HTML/?uri=CELEX%3A32014L0026

584 https://web.archive.org/web/20220617085448/https://ec.europa.eu/commission/presscorner/api/files/document/print/en/memo_14_79/MEMO_14_79_EN.pdf

585 https://web.archive.org/web/20220617085542/http://infojustice.org/archives/39886

586 https://web.archive.org/web/20220617085542/http://infojustice.org/archives/39886

587 https://web.archive.org/web/20220617085448/https://ec.europa.eu/commission/presscorner/api/files/document/print/en/memo_14_79/MEMO_14_79_EN.pdf

588 https://web.archive.org/web/20220617085612/https://walledculture.org/interview-cory-doctorow-part-1-newspapers-big-tech-link-tax-drm-and-right-to-repair/

589 https://web.archive.org/web/20220617092632/https://walledculture.org/interview-katharine-trendacosta-the-us-dmca-upload-filters-sopa-pipa-fanfiction-platform-competition/

590 https://web.archive.org/web/20220521202300/https://
curia.europa.eu/jcms/upload/docs/application/pdf/2022-04/
cp220065en.pdf

591 https://web.archive.org/web/20220617092715/https://papers.
ssrn.com/sol3/papers.cfm?abstract_id=2628827

592 https://web.archive.org/web/20220617092715/https://papers.
ssrn.com/sol3/papers.cfm?abstract_id=2628827

593 https://web.archive.org/web/20220617092736/https://hls.
harvard.edu/faculty/directory/10519/Lessig

594 https://web.archive.org/web/20220617092802/https://lessig.org/
product/code

595 https://web.archive.org/web/20220617092632/https://
walledculture.org/interview-katharine-trendacosta-the-us-dmca-
upload-filters-sopa-pipa-fanfiction-platform-competition/

596 https://web.archive.org/web/20220617092830/https://abc.
xyz/investor/static/pdf/2021Q3_alphabet_earnings_release.
pdf?cache=f1ba3f6

597 https://web.archive.org/web/20220617094352/https://www.
hollywoodreporter.com/business/business-news/youtube-netflix-
revenue-content-licensing-1235013502/

598 https://web.archive.org/web/20220617094419/https://www.
musicbusinessworldwide.com/youtube-just-generated-5bn-from-
ads-in-a-quarter-and-youtube-music-has-over-30m-subscribers/

599 https://web.archive.org/web/20220617094457/https://www.
musicbusinessworldwide.com/youtubes-ads-business-is-now-
bigger-than-the-entire-global-record-business2/

600 https://web.archive.org/web/20220701141838/https://
en.wikipedia.org/wiki/Universal_Music_Group

601 https://web.archive.org/web/20220617095249/https://
qz.com/2062550/universal-music-groups-ipo-shows-the-
potential-of-streaming/

602 https://web.archive.org/web/20220705070707/https://
en.wikipedia.org/wiki/Initial_public_offering

603 https://web.archive.org/web/20220531053439/https://www.
vivendi.com/wp-content/uploads/2021/09/Universal-Music-
Group-Prospectus-14-September-2021.pdf

604 https://web.archive.org/web/20220617095449/https://
walledculture.org/interview-evan-greer-lia-holland-rethinking-
copyright-fighting-creative-monopolies-and-more/

605 https://web.archive.org/web/20220617095509/https://www.musicbusinessworldwide.com/universal-buys-bob-dylan-publishing-rights-acquiring-catalog-worth-hundreds-of-millions-of-dollars/

606 https://web.archive.org/web/20220617095530/https://www.musicbusinessworldwide.com/neil-diamond-sells-complete-song-catalog-and-all-master-recordings-to-universal/

607 https://web.archive.org/web/20220617095555/https://www.wsj.com/articles/tencent-in-talks-to-buy-stake-in-universal-music-group-11565078272

608 https://web.archive.org/web/20220617095627/https://www.musicbusinessworldwide.com/major-record-companies-are-losing-market-share-on-spotify-but-spotify-is-gaining-market-share-in-warners-own-revenues/

609 https://web.archive.org/web/20220617095653/https://www.forbes.com/sites/stevenbertoni/2021/11/29/spotify-has-plans-to-move-beyond-music-and-become-the-instagram-and-tiktokofaudio/

610 https://web.archive.org/web/20220617095449/https://walledculture.org/interview-evan-greer-lia-holland-rethinking-copyright-fighting-creative-monopolies-and-more/

611 https://web.archive.org/web/20220701142134/https://en.wikipedia.org/wiki/Penguin_Random_House

612 https://web.archive.org/web/20201109153839/https://en.wikipedia.org/wiki/Simon_%26_Schuster

613 https://web.archive.org/web/20220701142307/https://en.wikipedia.org/wiki/Hachette_Book_Group

614 https://web.archive.org/web/20220629234053/https://en.wikipedia.org/wiki/HarperCollins

615 https://web.archive.org/web/20220630003959/https://en.wikipedia.org/wiki/Macmillan_Publishers

616 https://web.archive.org/web/20220617095734/https://www.justice.gov/opa/pr/justice-department-sues-block-penguin-random-house-s-acquisition-rival-publisher-simon

617 https://web.archive.org/web/20220617100520/https://www.hollywoodreporter.com/business/digital/activision-blizzard-microsoft-ea-disney-sony-buy-1235081056/

618 https://web.archive.org/web/20220617100557/https://www.theverge.com/22910846/sony-bungie-acquisition-playstation-destiny-halo

619 https://web.archive.org/web/20220617100858/https://www.mordorintelligence.com/industry-reports/global-gaming-market

620 https://web.archive.org/web/20220617100924/https://www.globenewswire.com/news-release/2020/12/18/2147663/0/en/Global-Publishing-Industry-Almanac-2020.html

621 https://web.archive.org/web/20220516043610/https://www.forbes.com/sites/rosaescandon/2020/03/12/the-film-industry-made-a-record-breaking-100-billion-last-year/

622 https://www.toptal.com/finance/market-research-analysts/state-of-music-industry

623 https://web.archive.org/web/20220617101104/https://www.niskanencenter.org/author/brink-lindsey/

624 https://web.archive.org/web/20220617101209/https://www.niskanencenter.org/author/steles/

625 https://web.archive.org/web/20220617101040/https://capturedeconomy.com/

626 https://web.archive.org/web/20220617101233/https://en.wikipedia.org/wiki/Rent-seeking

627 https://web.archive.org/web/20220617104335/https://www.communia-association.org/2021/05/31/the-public-domain-belongs-to-all-and-is-often-defended-by-no-one-we-want-to-change-that/

628 https://web.archive.org/web/20220617101040/https://capturedeconomy.com/

629 https://web.archive.org/web/20220408054820/https://scholarlycommons.law.northwestern.edu/cgi/viewcontent.cgi?article=6939&context=jclc

630 https://web.archive.org/web/20220617104420/https://www.copyright.gov/about/

631 https://web.archive.org/web/20220617104443/https://www.techdirt.com/2022/01/06/top-disney-lawyer-to-become-top-copyright-office-lawyer-because-who-cares-about-public-interest/

632 https://web.archive.org/web/20220617104505/https://publicknowledge.org/policy/captured-systemic-bias-at-the-u-s-copyright-office/

633 https://web.archive.org/web/20220619010942/https://walledculture.org/unleashing-the-power-of-online-sharing-for-all-the-birth-and-rise-of-creative-commons/

634 https://web.archive.org/web/20220616121321/https://walledculture.org/interview-lawrence-lessig-internet-architecture-remix-culture-creative-commons-nfts-aaron-swartz-and-the-internet-archive/

635 https://web.archive.org/web/20220616121340/https://doctorow.medium.com/a-bug-in-early-creative-commons-licenses-has-enabled-a-new-breed-of-superpredator-5f6360713299

636 https://web.archive.org/web/20220616121359/https://en.wikipedia.org/wiki/Copyright_troll

637 https://web.archive.org/web/20220616121340/https://doctorow.medium.com/a-bug-in-early-creative-commons-licenses-has-enabled-a-new-breed-of-superpredator-5f6360713299

638 https://web.archive.org/web/20220616121412/https://en.wikipedia.org/wiki/Protection_of_Broadcasts_and_Broadcasting_Organizations_Treaty

639 https://web.archive.org/web/20220616121437/https://www.keionline.org/31905

640 https://web.archive.org/web/20220616121455/https://www.eff.org/deeplinks/2013/04/only-thing-broadcasting-treaty-good-crushing-innovation

641 https://web.archive.org/web/20220616121517/https://www.deere.com/en/index.html

642 https://web.archive.org/web/20220616121544/https://copyright.gov/1201/2015/comments-032715/class%2021/John_Deere_Class21_1201_2014.pdf

643 https://web.archive.org/web/20220616121604/https://www.wired.com/2015/04/dmca-ownership-john-deere/

644 https://web.archive.org/web/20220616122417/https://en.wikipedia.org/wiki/Internet_of_things

645 https://web.archive.org/web/20220704120923/https://en.wikipedia.org/wiki/Bruce_Schneier

646 https://web.archive.org/web/20220616122437/https://www.theatlantic.com/technology/archive/2015/12/internet-of-things-philips-hue-lightbulbs/421884/

647 https://web.archive.org/web/20220616122459/https://walledculture.org/interview-cory-doctorow-part-1-newspapers-big-tech-link-tax-drm-and-right-to-repair/

648 https://web.archive.org/web/20220616122519/https://filmschoolrejects.com/fetishizing-celluloid-is-bad-for-film-preservation/

649 https://web.archive.org/web/20220616122545/https://nofilmschool.com/missing-movies

650 https://web.archive.org/web/20220616121321/https://walledculture.org/interview-lawrence-lessig-internet-architecture-remix-culture-creative-commons-nfts-aaron-swartz-and-the-internet-archive/

651 https://web.archive.org/web/20220616122617/https://www.
theguardian.com/film/2021/oct/07/film-lost-netflix-the-
afterlight-london-film-fesitval-digital-media

652 https://web.archive.org/web/20220616122643/https://
fullstackeconomics.com/why-streaming-content-keeps-
vanishing-and-how-to-stop-it/

653 https://web.archive.org/web/20220616122643/https://
fullstackeconomics.com/why-streaming-content-keeps-
vanishing-and-how-to-stop-it/

654 https://web.archive.org/web/20220616122710/https://
en.wikipedia.org/wiki/Cloud_storage

655 https://web.archive.org/web/20220616122732/https://www.
theesa.com/

656 https://web.archive.org/web/20220616123532/https://www.
washingtonpost.com/video-games/2022/01/12/video-game-
preservation-emulation/

657 https://web.archive.org/web/20220616123630/https://
en.wikipedia.org/wiki/P-value

658 https://web.archive.org/web/20220616123645/https://papers.
ssrn.com/sol3/papers.cfm?abstract_id=2337682

659 https://web.archive.org/web/20220616123710/https://www.
copiefrance.fr/en/resources/faq

660 https://web.archive.org/web/20220616123731/https://
en.wikipedia.org/wiki/Private_copying_levy

661 https://web.archive.org/web/20220415115756/https://www.
copiefrance.fr/images/documents/tarifs_FR_2021_07_-_D22.pdf

662 https://web.archive.org/web/20220616125310/https://www.
nextinpact.com/article/30201/108870-la-redevance-copie-
privee-vache-a-lait-industries-culturelles

663 https://web.archive.org/web/20220616125328/https://
torrentfreak.com/goodbye-hadopi-france-will-launch-new-
arcom-anti-piracy-agency-in-2022-211029/

664 https://web.archive.org/web/20220616125347/https://www.
newsroom.co.nz/nz-agrees-to-mickey-mouse-copyright-law

665 https://web.archive.org/web/20220620151618/https://www.
tohatoha.org.nz/

666 https://web.archive.org/web/20220616125406/https://www.
newsroom.co.nz/profile/MichaelWolfe/posts

667 https://web.archive.org/web/20220616132424/https://
walledculture.org/canada-is-about-to-repeat-new-zealands-folly-
by-extending-copyright-term-so-bring-back-registration/

668 https://web.archive.org/web/20220616132442/https://
walledculture.org/interview-rebecca-giblin-reversion-rights-out-
of-print-books-and-how-to-fix-copyright/

669 https://web.archive.org/web/20220616132502/https://www.
authorsguild.org/industry-advocacy/authors-guild-survey-
shows-drastic-42-percent-decline-in-authors-earnings-in-last-
decade/

670 https://web.archive.org/web/20220616132502/https://www.
authorsguild.org/industry-advocacy/authors-guild-survey-
shows-drastic-42-percent-decline-in-authors-earnings-in-last-
decade/

671 https://web.archive.org/web/20220627194208/https://
en.wikipedia.org/wiki/Digital,_Culture,_Media_and_Sport_
Committee

672 https://web.archive.org/web/20220616132526/https://
publications.parliament.uk/pa/cm5802/cmselect/
cmcumeds/50/50.pdf

673 https://web.archive.org/web/20220616132526/https://
publications.parliament.uk/pa/cm5802/cmselect/
cmcumeds/50/50.pdf

674 https://web.archive.org/web/20220620151757/https://
alexsayfcummings.com/

675 https://web.archive.org/web/20220616132556/https://
walledculture.org/interview-alex-sayf-cummings-music-piracy-
alternative-remuneration-models-blurred-lines-sopa-and-out-of-
control-copyright-terms-and-penalties/

676 https://web.archive.org/web/20220616132625/https://
scholarship.law.tamu.edu/facscholar/1393/

677 https://web.archive.org/web/20220704135346/https://law.tamu.
edu/faculty-staff/find-people/faculty-profiles/glynn-s-lunney-jr

678 https://web.archive.org/web/20220616132625/https://
scholarship.law.tamu.edu/facscholar/1393/

679 https://web.archive.org/web/20220616132644/https://
en.wikipedia.org/wiki/Twitch_%28service%29

680 https://web.archive.org/web/20220616132700/https://www.wsj.
com/articles/twitch-streamer-earnings-increase-for-top-gamers-
data-from-hack-shows-11633802185

681 https://web.archive.org/web/20220616132728/https://www.
axios.com/2021/01/25/podcast-business-booming-few-making-
money

682 https://web.archive.org/web/20220616132625/https://
scholarship.law.tamu.edu/facscholar/1393/

683 https://web.archive.org/web/20220616132748/https://walledculture.org/interview-evan-greer-lia-holland-rethinking-copyright-fighting-creative-monopolies-and-more/
684 https://web.archive.org/web/20220705093110/https://www.fightforthefuture.org/about/team
685 https://web.archive.org/web/20220704135617/https://www.swlaw.edu/faculty/full-time/kevin-j-greene
686 https://web.archive.org/web/20220401040854/https://www.dri.org/docs/default-source/webdocs/other/2021/may/ip-greene.pdf?sfvrsn=2
687 https://web.archive.org/web/20220616133558/https://en.wikipedia.org/wiki/Andy_Warhol
688 https://web.archive.org/web/20220616133620/https://news.artnet.com/art-world/us-supreme-court-agrees-take-copyright-case-warhol-2091075
689 https://web.archive.org/web/20220705084319/https://en.wikipedia.org/wiki/Dua_Lipa
690 https://web.archive.org/web/20220616133638/https://copyrightlately.com/dua-lipa-faces-another-copyright-infringement-lawsuit-over-levitating/
691 https://web.archive.org/web/20220705084413/https://en.wikipedia.org/wiki/Taylor_Swift
692 https://web.archive.org/web/20220616133709/https://copyrightlately.com/taylor-swift-copyright-lawsuits/
693 https://web.archive.org/web/20220705084514/https://en.wikipedia.org/wiki/Katy_Perry
694 https://web.archive.org/web/20220705084624/https://en.wikipedia.org/wiki/Dark_Horse_%28Katy_Perry_song%29
695 https://web.archive.org/web/20220705084656/https://en.wikipedia.org/wiki/Flame_%28rapper%29
696 https://web.archive.org/web/20220616133757/https://www.billboard.com/business/legal/katy-perry-wins-dark-horse-copyright-appeal-1235042827/
697 https://web.archive.org/web/20220705084826/https://en.wikipedia.org/wiki/Ed_Sheeran
698 https://web.archive.org/web/20220616133945/https://www.musicbusinessworldwide.com/ed-sheeran-wins-copyright-lawsuit-in-the-uk/
699 https://web.archive.org/web/20220616134122/https://twitter.com/edsheeran/status/1511631955238047751

700   https://web.archive.org/web/20220616100535/
        https://gufaculty360.georgetown.edu/s/
        contact/00336000014RgZwAAK/michelle-wu
701   https://web.archive.org/web/20220616100554/https://papers.
        ssrn.com/sol3/papers.cfm?abstract_id=3892269
702   https://web.archive.org/web/20220830085146/https://
        walledculture.org/interview-mike-masnick/
703   https://web.archive.org/web/20220616100703/https://
        en.wikipedia.org/wiki/Katherine_Maher
704   https://web.archive.org/web/20220616100645/https://
        walledculture.org/interview-katherine-maher-the-monkey-
        selfie-public-domain-freedom-of-panorama-the-eu-copyright-
        directive-remix-culture-the-20th-century-black-hole/
705   https://web.archive.org/web/20170920144902/http://ted.
        europa.eu/TED/notice/udl?uri=TED:NOTICE:276982-
        2013:TEXT:EN:HTML&tabId=1
706   https://web.archive.org/web/20220301145136/https://felixreda.
        eu/wp-content/uploads/2017/09/displacement_study.pdf
707   https://web.archive.org/web/20220616100726/https://felixreda.
        eu/2017/09/secret-copyright-infringement-study/
708   https://web.archive.org/web/20220616100817/http://www.ip-
        watch.org/2012/02/27/%E2%80%98balanced%E2%80%99-
        copyright-not-a-magic-solving-word/
709   https://web.archive.org/web/20220616100837/https://copybuzz.
        com/copyright/eu-consultations-inherently-biased-members-
        public/
710   https://web.archive.org/web/20220616100946/https://www.
        techdirt.com/2015/10/08/right-way-to-stop-piracy/
711   https://web.archive.org/web/20220616101743/https://copia.is/
        library/the-carrot-or-the-stick/
712   https://web.archive.org/web/20220616101802/https://papers.
        ssrn.com/sol3/papers.cfm?abstract_id=3912074
713   https://web.archive.org/web/20220616101823/https://www.
        currentaffairs.org/2020/08/the-truth-is-paywalled-but-the-lies-
        are-free/
714   https://web.archive.org/web/20220620152453/https://www.lse.
        ac.uk/law/people/academic-staff/martin-husovec
715   https://web.archive.org/web/20220620152908/https://www.ivir.
        nl/employee/quintais/
716   https://web.archive.org/web/20220616101840/https://papers.
        ssrn.com/sol3/papers.cfm?abstract_id=3835930

717 https://web.archive.org/web/20220616101907/https://fra.
     europa.eu/en/eu-charter/article/20-equality-law
718 https://web.archive.org/web/20220616101840/https://papers.
     ssrn.com/sol3/papers.cfm?abstract_id=3835930
719 https://web.archive.org/web/20220616101927/https://
     walledculture.org/a-few-companies-dominate-the-music-market-
     meet-the-rising-giant-that-could-beat-them-all-spotify/
720 https://web.archive.org/web/20220616101947/https://
     walledculture.org/giant-penguin-attack-why-the-us-courts-
     should-block-a-publishing-mega-merger/
721 https://web.archive.org/web/20220607192525/https://judiciary.
     house.gov/uploadedfiles/competition_in_digital_markets.pdf
722 https://web.archive.org/web/20220616102041/https://www.
     klobuchar.senate.gov/public/index.cfm/2021/2/senator-
     klobuchar-introduces-sweeping-bill-to-promote-competition-
     and-improve-antitrust-enforcement
723 https://web.archive.org/web/20220616102110/https://www.ftc.
     gov/about-ftc/commissioners-staff/lina-m-khan
724 https://web.archive.org/web/20220426063859/https://www.
     yalelawjournal.org/pdf/e.710.Khan.805_zuvfyyeh.pdf
725 https://web.archive.org/web/20220616102945/https://www.
     wired.com/story/opinion-big-music-needs-to-be-broken-up-to-
     save-the-industry/
726 https://web.archive.org/web/20220607130113/https://papers.
     ssrn.com/sol3/papers.cfm?abstract_id=3639142
727 https://web.archive.org/web/20220519123413/http://ec.europa.
     eu/competition/publications/reports/kd0419345enn.pdf
728 https://web.archive.org/web/20220616103111/https://www.eff.
     org/deeplinks/2019/10/adversarial-interoperability
729 https://web.archive.org/web/20220616103132/https://
     knightcolumbia.org/content/protocols-not-platforms-a-
     technological-approach-to-free-speech
730 https://web.archive.org/web/20220329191619/https://
     tobin.yale.edu/sites/default/files/Digital%20Regulation%20
     Project%20Papers/Digital%20Regulation%20Project%20
     -%20Equitable%20Interoperability%20-%20Discussion%20
     Paper%20No%204.pdf
731 https://web.archive.org/web/20220616103205/https://
     walledculture.org/interview-cory-doctorow-part-2-new-
     publishing-models-for-creators-amazon-as-a-frenemy-and-the-
     internet-archive-court-case/

732   https://web.archive.org/web/20220817084624/https://
scholarship.law.tamu.edu/facscholar/1393/

733   https://web.archive.org/web/20220830085146/https://
walledculture.org/interview-mike-masnick/

734   https://web.archive.org/web/20220616103248/https://
walledculture.org/interview-rebecca-giblin-reversion-rights-out-
of-print-books-and-how-to-fix-copyright/

735   https://web.archive.org/web/20220616103248/https://
walledculture.org/interview-rebecca-giblin-reversion-rights-out-
of-print-books-and-how-to-fix-copyright/

736   https://web.archive.org/web/20220616110320/https://
bandcamp.com/

737   https://web.archive.org/web/20220616113457/https://
en.wikipedia.org/wiki/Crowdfunding

738   https://web.archive.org/web/20220616110335/https://blog.
bandcamp.com/2022/03/02/bandcamp-is-joining-epic/

739   https://web.archive.org/web/20220616111850/https://get.
bandcamp.help/hc/en-us/articles/360007802534-What-pricing-
performs-best-

740   https://web.archive.org/web/20220616111909/https://
walledculture.org/interview-evan-greer-lia-holland-rethinking-
copyright-fighting-creative-monopolies-and-more/

741   https://web.archive.org/web/20220616111928/https://kk.org/
biography

742   https://web.archive.org/web/20220616111942/https://kk.org/
thetechnium/1000-true-fans/

743   https://web.archive.org/web/20220616111942/https://kk.org/
thetechnium/1000-true-fans/

744   https://web.archive.org/web/20220616111942/https://kk.org/
thetechnium/1000-true-fans/

745   https://web.archive.org/web/20220616111942/https://kk.org/
thetechnium/1000-true-fans/

746   https://web.archive.org/web/20220616113521/https://www.
kickstarter.com/

747   https://web.archive.org/web/20220616113541/https://locusmag.
com/2021/03/cory-doctorow-free-markets/

748   https://web.archive.org/web/20220616113541/https://locusmag.
com/2021/03/cory-doctorow-free-markets/

749   https://web.archive.org/web/20220701143901/https://www.
atelierventures.co/team

750   https://web.archive.org/web/20220616114328/https://future.
com/1000-true-fans-try-100/

751 https://web.archive.org/web/20220616114347/https://
walledculture.org/nfts-are-mostly-useless-or-worse-but-heres-
one-important-way-they-could-help-creators/

752 https://web.archive.org/web/20220830085146/https://
walledculture.org/interview-mike-masnick/

753 https://web.archive.org/web/20220616114406/https://
walledculture.org/interview-dr-andres-guadamuz-the-eu-
copyright-directive-text-data-mining-web3-the-metaverse-nfts/

754 https://web.archive.org/web/20220616114427/https://www.
technollama.co.uk/can-copyright-teach-us-anything-about-nfts

755 https://web.archive.org/web/20220616114502/https://www.
twitch.tv/

756 https://web.archive.org/web/20220616114519/https://www.
wired.com/story/twitch-turns-10-creator-economy/

757 https://web.archive.org/web/20220713072402/https://www.
businessofapps.com/data/twitch-statistics/

758 https://web.archive.org/web/20220616114519/https://www.
wired.com/story/twitch-turns-10-creator-economy

759 https://web.archive.org/web/20220713071951/https://www.
vantagemarketresearch.com/industry-report/crowdfunding-
market-1484

760 https://web.archive.org/web/20220616111909/https://
walledculture.org/interview-evan-greer-lia-holland-rethinking-
copyright-fighting-creative-monopolies-and-more/

761 https://web.archive.org/web/20220616115428/https://www.
wipo.int/edocs/mdocs/mdocs/en/wipo_ipr_ge_15/wipo_ipr_
ge_15_t2.pdf

762 https://web.archive.org/web/20220616115440/https://
en.wikipedia.org/wiki/Fashion_design_copyright_in_the_
United_States

763 https://web.archive.org/web/20220616115454/https://
fashionunited.com/global-fashion-industry-statistics/

Index

Note: Unless otherwise indicated, companies and organizations are based out of the US.

Acknowledgments

As the hundreds of endnotes attest, this book builds on the work and ideas of many people. In particular, throughout the text there are quotations taken from interviews conducted for the *Walled Culture* blog about copyright[1] by Gwen Franck and Karlin Lillington: my thanks to them for their work. It also draws on my own writings in other forums, notably *Walled Culture*,[2] the *Copybuzz*[3] blog, and the indispensable *Techdirt*,[4] still the best place to stay abreast of the latest developments in copyright and much else.

In terms of the present text, I am grateful to many invaluable suggestions at all stages of its production from Caroline De Cock and Herman Rucic. Thanks are also due to Carol King for editing the text with her customary speed and professionalism, and to Fred von Lohmann for his important comments on key aspects of the book.

---

1 https://web.archive.org/web/20220620155227/https://walledculture.org/

2 https://web.archive.org/web/20220620155401/https://walledculture.org/author/glyn-moody/

3 https://web.archive.org/web/20220620155432/https://copybuzz.com/author/gmoody/

4 https://web.archive.org/web/20220620155506/https://www.techdirt.com/user/glynmoody/

Needless to say, regardless of all this invaluable help, the book's errors remain mine alone. However, I am a journalist, not a lawyer (IANAL), and nothing in this book should be taken as legal advice or as necessarily the correct summary of what are complex and often contested areas of law. If you need advice about copyright, or want to understand fully the legislation, get a lawyer, and a good one.

Finally, my thanks to the Kahle/Austin Foundation and the Internet Archive's Brewster Kahle for supporting both the *Walled Culture* blog and this book, and to my family for supporting me.

Glyn Moody

About the Author

lyn Moody studied mathematics at Trinity College, Cambridge, where he was Senior Wrangler in 1977. Cambridge University awarded him a PhD in Quantum Mechanics in 1981.

After university, he entered journalism, and was one of the first to explore the emerging field of microcomputers. In 1994, he started writing the weekly Getting Wired column about the business use of the Internet, which ran in the UK magazine *Computer Weekly* for nine years. During this time, his work appeared in a variety of other titles, including *The Economist*, *Financial Times*, *The Guardian*, and *The Telegraph*.

In 1997, *Wired* magazine published his in-depth feature about Linux and Linus Torvalds, the first mainstream article to describe the then-new world of free software. Moody's full-length book on the topic, *Rebel Code: Linux and the Open Source Revolution*, appeared in 2001. His book *Digital Code of Life: How Bioinformatics is Revolutionizing*

Science, Medicine, and Business, about the new field of bio-informatics, was published in 2004.

In addition, Moody has written nearly 2,000 posts for *Techdirt*, and over 400 articles for *Ars Technica*. More recently, his writing has focussed on digital rights and privacy. Numerous posts about copyright, another area of particular interest, have appeared on the *Copybuzz* and *Walled Culture* blogs.

Glyn Moody has given keynotes and speeches at conferences around the world, and appeared many times as a commentator on television. He lives in London.

Made in the USA
Monee, IL
07 July 2026

56550027R00184